I0755799

Saving Lives

The Stories of Corpsmen,
Medics, Dustoff Pilots, Nurses, and
Doctors who Served During the Vietnam War

Major Bruce H. "Doc" Norton USMC (Ret)
&
Dr. Harry J. Kantrovich, CNOCM, USN (Ret)

Saving Lives

The Stories of Corpsmen, Medics, Dustoff Pilots, Nurses, and Doctors who Served During the Vietnam War

Major Bruce H. "Doc" Norton USMC (Ret)
&
Dr. Harry J. Kantrovich, CNOCM, USN (Ret)

Academica Press
Washington

Library of Congress Cataloging-in-Publication Data
Names: Norton, Bruce H. (editor) | Kantrovich, Harry J. (editor)
Title: Saving lives : the stories of corpsmen, medics, dustoff pilots, nurses, and doctors who served during the vietnam war | Norton, Bruce H., Kantrovich, Harry J.
Description: Washington : Academica Press, 2026. | Includes references.
Identifiers: LCCN 2026935565 | ISBN 9781680536096 (hardcover) | 9781680536102 (paperback) | 9781680536119 (e-book)

Saving Lives is a very special tribute to the "life savers" during the Vietnam War: the medics, corpsmen, nurses, doctors, and dustoff pilots who not only rescued but tried desperately to treat the estimated 200,000 soldiers, sailors, Marines, and civilians who were sick or wounded during that war.

The stories contained in these pages are "in their own words," and it was our distinct honor to interview these incredible men and women these many years later. Their stories of bravery, sacrifice, and dedication will never be forgotten.

- *Major Bruce H. "Doc" Norton, USMC (Ret)*

Contents

Patients

Introduction

Approximately 20 military physicians died during the Vietnam War. Additionally, military nurses and medical personnel such as medics and corpsmen also suffered casualties, with about 20 military nurses and roughly 1,300 medics and 690 corpsmen killed during the conflict.

Physicians:

About 20 military physicians died in Vietnam due to accidents, illness, or hostile fire.

Nurses:

The Vietnam Veterans Memorial Wall lists the names of ten U.S. Army and Air Force nurses who died during the war.

Combat Medics and Corpsmen:

Approximately 1,300 Army medics and 690 Navy corpsmen were killed in action, and an estimated 1,100 medics overall died during the war.

Medics and Corpsmen: An Overview

Medics and corpsmen on the battlefields of Vietnam served mainly in the treatment and evacuation of wounded or injured troops. They resuscitated, stopped bleeding, managed pain, and did whatever else was necessary to keep troops alive until they could be evacuated.

Thanks to the widespread use of helicopters for medical evacuations (known as "dust-off" missions), the wounded often waited mere minutes for transport to the nearest medical centers. A soldier, sailor, or Marine in Vietnam had a 98% chance of survival if he was evacuated within the first hour of being injured — the best odds in the history of American warfare up to that time. It was the medic or corpsman who held death at bay during that crucial period.

Unlike their predecessors in previous wars, medics and corpsmen in Vietnam fought alongside their fellow soldiers and Marines — many carried rifles, sidearms, and even hand grenades along with their medical kits. When a soldier or Marine was injured on the battlefield, it was the training, composure, and medical kit of the corpsman or medic that often meant the difference between life and death. There are countless stories of medics and corpsmen risking their own lives to save wounded troops, and at least

20 of them earned the Congressional Medal of Honor – our nation's highest award for extraordinary courage under fire.

Even when they were not under fire, medics and corpsmen were essential to the health and wellness of their units. In fact, they spent most of their time preventing and treating day-to-day health issues such as dehydration, malaria, dysentery, and "immersion foot." They also treated South Vietnamese villagers, overlooking the possibility that some of them might be enemy combatants or sympathizers.

Fleet Marine Force Corpsmen: An Overview

Navy Corpsmen (MOS 8404), served alongside Fleet Marine Forces (FMF Marines) in Vietnam as the primary medical personnel, acting as both combatants and healers who were responsible for treating battlefield injuries and evacuating the wounded. Known as "docs" to the Marines, they were highly respected and faced an extremely dangerous role, often being the first on the scene to provide immediate care to save lives. They also treated local civilians and handled non-combat medical needs to their Marines.

Role and duties

- **Combat and healing:**

Corpsmen were trained as combatants and carried weapons alongside their fellow Marines. When a Marine was wounded, the corpsman would immediately shift to provide immediate medical aid.

- **First response:**

They provided immediate, life-saving care on the battlefield, including resuscitation, stoppage of bleeding, and managing pain until the wounded could be evacuated.

- **Evacuation:**

They were responsible for arranging the medical evacuation of the wounded, often via helicopters known as "Dustoffs."

- **Preventative care:**

They handled day-to-day medical needs, which included treating common ailments and injuries such as trench foot and leech bites.

- **Civilian medical aid:**

In addition to treating Marines, corpsmen often provided medical attention to Vietnamese civilians through Civic Action Programs (CAPs).

Dangers and risks

- **High casualty rate:**

The role of a corpsman was extremely dangerous, with a high casualty rate. More than 645 Navy corpsmen were killed in action in Vietnam, and over 3,300 were wounded.

- **Targeted for their role:**

Due to their focus on providing aid, corpsmen were often targeted by the enemy.

- **Medal of Honor recipients:**

Despite the risks, 20 medics and corpsmen were awarded the Medal of Honor for their extraordinary bravery during the war.

Respect from Marines

- **"Doc":**

The common affectionate nickname for corpsmen.

- **Deep trust:**

Marines developed deep respect and trust for their corpsmen, recognizing their dedication and bravery in the line of duty.

HM-3 Bruce H. "Doc" Norton, FMF Corpsman 3rd Force Recon Company/1st Force Recon Company 1969-1970

A scream in the middle of the night...

HM-3 Bruce H. "Doc" Norton, Hill 510 – June 1970

Not every injury or wound inflicted during the Vietnam War came from bullets, bombs, or shrapnel. Here is one case in point.

In June 1970, Marines from 1st Force Reconnaissance Company were patrolling in the Thuong Duc River Valley, located about 30 miles west of the port city of Danang. In order for these reconnaissance teams to communicate with their rear area operations office, a radio relay site had to be established and manned around the clock, allowing for a continuous flow of information to and from the half dozen six-man reconnaissance teams operating out in the bush. As a Force Recon Company Corpsman, I was, on this occasion, a member of that radio-relay team.

In April 1970, Hill 510 had been selected as the best location to establish a 292 radio relay site, which would allow the teams to transmit their radio traffic to the relay site, and have those reports immediately sent to the company rear area, located about 28 miles away in Danang. The power and range of this massive radio would facilitate this important requirement of passing on timely intelligence to higher headquarters.

A dozen Marines and one Navy corpsman, (me), were inserted by helicopter onto Hill 510, and after several days of very hard work a defendable position was improved upon, along with a small landing zone (LZ) that could accommodate a single CH-46 helicopter, or several "Huey" helicopters, able to land and resupply us at the radio relay site with requested replacements, water, chow, batteries, and ammunition. Those of us who were on top of Hill 510 would remain there for two weeks, before being relieved by another dozen fresh faces from 1st Force Reconnaissance Company.

The benefit of Hill 510 was that it provided a 360 degree view of the Thuong Duc River Valley and the surrounding mountains. Two rivers were joined at the base of Hill 510, and it was common to see individuals physically crossing the rivers or using small boats to navigate the waterways. Of course, the North Vietnamese forces knew we were there, and during the next several weeks their light probing attempts were becoming a routine event.

By June, Hill 510 had become a busy place with Marines constantly working to improve their defensive positions. A communication bunker had been built with logs and countless sandbags, which protected the massive 292 radio. A very tall and sturdy antenna was part of the radio position and of course this antenna could be seen for miles around by anyone watching the activity on top of the hill. A 60-millimeter mortar tube and several crates of illumination rounds had magically appeared, and two M-60 machine guns also bolstered our small defensive position, covering the landing zone. Every Marine had his M-16 rifle, and numerous .45 pistols added to our weaponry.

Hill 510 - Thuong Duc River Valley – June 1970

On this particular night there was no moonlight provided by Mother Nature. Once darkness came, the "smoking lamp" had been put out, and all movement was restricted. Without any movement allowed by those of us on top of Hill 510, we became acutely aware of the many sounds around us. The occasional buzzing of flying things and sounds of frogs and other insects was magnified and pinpointed by those of us who remained awake and on watch.

It was around 10 o'clock, on this particular night, when the "clacking of sticks" began. The North Vietnamese, who were no strangers to the use of "psychological warfare," applied their skills that night and with an unknown number of NVA positioned around Hill 510, they began to clap bamboo sticks together. An individual soldier would hit his sticks together two or three times and then go silent. Then 3 or 4 minutes later another NVA soldier, positioned some distance away, would do the same. Minutes later, a third individual would do the same; two or three sharp hits and then complete silence.

The object of this "exercise" was to draw our fire giving away our individual positions. It didn't work. Our fire discipline was extremely good, and no one fell for the NVA trick, but the psychological effect was telling. Everyone on Hill 510 had to deal with their individual imaginations. Where there only three NVA soldiers trying to draw out our positions, or were there one hundred and three of them waiting to assault our position and overrun us? Every man had to wrestle with the thought of what was going to happen next. It required the mental inner strength of every Marine, and one Corpsman, to remain calm and not move, for any reason. After several minutes, the clacking of the bamboo sticks suddenly stopped.

The senior leadership, out on Hill 510, with a dozen Marines there, was from two Marine Staff Sergeants: Staff Sergeant Martin and Staff Sergeant Byars, both experienced veterans of the Vietnam war. Before darkness fell we were instructed by them "not to move about the area for any reason" and to be on 50% alert throughout the night. We always slept in two's and it was not unusual for one Marine, or his partner, to be awake throughout the night.

Sometime, after midnight, the absolute quiet of the night was shattered by the horrific scream of a single Marine. My immediate response was to wonder if this was another "trick" on behalf of the NVA or was this scream coming from one of the Marines just a few yards away. When the scream was repeated, I grabbed my Unit-1 medical bag, my .45 Colt pistol, and moved in the direction of the scream.

There, inside a shallow bunker, dug out from the earth and reinforced with logs and sandbags, was Lance Corporal Ulysess Dixon, a tall, Black Marine, lying on his back and clutching his inner left thigh, and in obvious great pain. He said, "Something stung me, or bit me, and it hurts like a motherfucker." Dixon, dressed in a pair of green shorts, a T-shirt, and wearing his boots, had been asleep, and wrapped up in his camouflaged poncho liner. His "fox hole buddy," Corporal Bilbo, was holding a flashlight under a poncho to assist me in looking at the area of Dixon's thigh that was causing him so much pain. With the help of the flashlight, I could see a very large blue and yellow welt, about the size of a silver dollar, on Dixon's leg. He was doing everything possible to keep for crying out, but the pain was obviously excruciating.

There was very little aid that I could render to this young Marine, not knowing what had managed to bite him. Was this a snake bite, or some poisonous insect? Two small puncture wounds were visible, but no snake or insect was seen nor found near Dixon. The best medical aid that I was able to provide was in the form of Benadryl tablets that would help to relieve the pain and make Dixon "sleepy," a known side effect from Benadryl. I watched

Lance Corporal Dixon for almost an hour before the pain subsided and he decided to move out of this bunker to sleep on the ground.

In the morning, I walked over to see how the Lance Corporal was doing. The huge welt was still visible, but the pain had subsided considerably. Those of us who knew Dixon were at a loss for what could have caused his misery. But, only a few minutes later, while two Marines were repositioning the sandbags on top of Dizon's bunker, the suspected culprit was revealed.

Jumping back and away from the sandbags, two Marines exposed a huge mahogany colored centipede coiled up and motionless. It was at least a foot long and as wide around as man's wrist. The decision was made to capture this critter and get in back to the medical battalion in Danang, where it could be shown to all hands, alerting them to one of the lesser dangers that existed in Vietnam.

A thick glove, worn to remove hot machine gun barrels, was used to pin the centipede down, before it was placed in a C-ration box. The sound of its many legs could be heard from a distance as it tried to claw its way out of the cardboard box. Secured with electrical tape around the box, the centipede was on the next helicopter ride out and on its way to the 1st Medical Battalion, in Danang, for examination inside a large jar of alcohol.

Without any encouragement, every Marine on Hill 510 made a concerted effort to examine anything and everything in and around their respective fighting holes, hoping never to encounter any relatives from the centipede. A painful lesson learned, and taught to us all, by Lance Corporal Ulysess Dixon, USMC.

One giant centipede

1st Force Recon Patrol Roster - June 1970

CONFIDENTIAL MUFORM

13. PATROL MEMBERS:

2ND LT	BAKER	0110537
1ST LT	STAMM	0108199
1ST LT	TAYLOR	0106172
SSGT	MARTIN	1539314
SSGT	BYARS	1930576
CPL	GACNA	2437434
CPL	HERZBERG	2517781
LCPL	BRACEWELL	2476430
LCPL	DIXSON	2572402
LCPL	BEEDLE	2563602
LCPL	EMBREE	2546068
CPL	MEHKEWA	2427621
CPL	BILBO	2561460
HM3	NORTON	B447690
PFC	RAMSDELL	2616141
HM1	PALMER	34797096
CPL	SMITH	2396761
CPL	BEAN	2569150
LCPL	ABRAHAMS	2431786
LCPL	AIRAGHI	2589748
PVT	REZA	2582230
LCPL	FALCO	2570498

PATROL LEADER

DEBRIEFER

REVIEWED BY CAPT. G. A. HOULE

Lance Corporal Ulysses Dixon, USMC
1st Force Reconnaissance Company – 1970 RVN

Ulysses Dixson's Life's Story

Ulysses "Butch" Dixon, age 71, passed away peacefully in his home on October 19, 2020. He was born on December 7, 1948, in Jackson, Mississippi to the late Eddie and Ezella Mannie Dixon. Butch graduated from East Chicago Washington High School in East Chicago, Indiana. He went on to attend Pikeville College where he played basketball and met his wife. After college, Butch served in 1st Force Reconnaissance Company in Vietnam before returning home to work for the City of Kalamazoo Police Department for 26 years, eventually becoming the Department's first black Captain. Butch's first love was his family and he was always there for friends and family. He especially adored his granddaughter. In addition to being an exceptional handyman, Butch enjoyed the outdoors and was an avid fisherman.

Butch was united in marriage to Gaynell Dixon (July 21, 1969), who preceded him in death in 2014. He was also preceded in death by his parents, Eddie and Ezella, and his siblings, Doristeen Campbell, Leroy Dixon, Douglas Dixon, Bobby Dixon, and Carl Dixon. He is survived by his children, Derrick Dixon and Kelli Dixon, and granddaughter, Maci Charleston. Butch also leaves, to cherish his memory, many sister-in-loves, nieces, nephews, cousins, and friends. Cremation has taken place and plans for a post-pandemic memorial/celebration of life are being considered.

HM-3 James D. "Doc" Raab, FMF Corpsman

"Putting A Face to a Name"

James D. Raab is remembered at the New Jersey Vietnam Veterans' Memorial and Vietnam Era Educational Center.

"Corpsman Up!"

I am proud to say that I served with your son, now CDR James Raab, USN, at Fort Dix, NJ. The building that serves as the current Naval Operational Control Center (NOSC) was named in your honor, with your name permanently placed to the front. There is a Navy Anchor in front of the building with a plaque citing your sacrifice.

Serving with the Marines, as a Navy Corpsman, is no easy feat. For that bone chilling call of "Corpman Up," is an time honored call of faith. No Corpsman, never mind the Marine, wants that call … and no Corpsman hesitates when called. It is literally and figuratively, our calling. It is truly God's work. Before a Marine calls for God, or his mother or father in dire time of need, he or she calls the Corpsman. Too often the Corpsman is the last person a Marine sees and feels before meeting God. The Corpsman goes where no man goes… to the Marines aid. Other Marines lay down a field of fire to cover the Marine and the Corpman. "Doc" is what they call us. "Doc" is who they know us as. "Doc" is one of them, but he's not … he is "Doc," there is no other. "Doc" is the next thing to the Marine's rifle or another Marine. "Doc" is the only Sailor the Marines like. The only acceptable Squid. As so often in the annals of Marine Corps lore, "Doc" will lay down his life for "his" Marines. "Doc" will go through withering fire to that call of "Corpsman Up!!" It is not a request; it is THE calling. Your call came; undoubtedly not the first time you went to the call. Who knows even how many times you went before. But this time it was YOUR CALL. Your Final Call.

Your son has made you proud, rest easy knowing your full measure was not in vain.

"Doc" Rory Murphy LCDR, USN.

Silver Star Citation

*RAAB, JAMES D. (KIA)

Synopsis:

The President of the United States takes pride in presenting the Silver Star Medal (Posthumously) to James D. Raab (B-411174), Hospital Corpsman Third Class, U.S. Navy, for conspicuous gallantry and intrepidity in action against a hostile force in the Republic of Vietnam. Hospital Corpsman Third Class Raab distinguished himself by intrepid actions on 12 June 1968 while serving as a Corpsman attached to First Battalion, Twenty-Sixth Marines, Third Marine Division. His unquestionable valor in close combat is in keeping with the highest traditions of the military service and reflects great credit upon himself and the United States Naval Service.

Home Town: Beachwood, New Jersey

Bronze Star Citation:

James Donald Raab

Date of birth: January 12, 1943

Date of death: June 12, 1968

Home of record: Beachwood New Jersey

Status: KIA

AWARDS AND CITATIONS:

Bronze Star; Awarded for actions during the Vietnam War:

The President of the United States of America takes pride in presenting the Bronze Star Medal with Combat

"V" (Posthumously) to Hospital Corpsman Third Class James Donald Raab (NSN: B-411174), United States Navy, for heroic achievement in connection with operations against the enemy in the Republic of Vietnam while serving as a Corpsman with Company C, First Battalion, Twenty-Sixth Marines, Third Marine Division. On 12 June 1968, while conducting a search and destroy mission near DaNang, Petty Officer Raab's platoon was entering a graveyard when it suddenly came under intense hostile automatic weapons fire from three directions. Observing a Marine wounded during the initial moments of the fire fight, he unhesitatingly left his position of relative safety and maneuvered across the hazardous area toward the injured man. While attempting to aid his injured comrade, Petty Officer Raab was mortally wounded by enemy fire from a concealed enemy sniper. Petty Officer Raab's courage, bold initiative and selfless devotion to duty inspired all who observed him and were in keeping with the highest traditions of the Marine Corps and of the United States Naval Service. He gallantly gave his life in the service of his country. (The Combat Distinguishing Device is authorized.)

Action Date: June 12, 1968

Service: Navy
Rank: Hospital Corpsman Third Class
Company: Corpsman (Attached), Company C
Battalion: 1st Battalion

Regiment: 26th Marines
Division: Third Marine Division

Tributes for Doc Raab

A Good guy

I went through basic training with Jim. He was a great guy, intelligent, gentle, and caring. I'd heard somewhere while I was still serving that he'd been killed. But I didn't know for sure until I was able to verify it now. I liked Jim.

Thank you

Thank you for your ultimate gift -- your love and life live on through your family. When I look at your picture I now see my niece, your grandchild, Alex 'eyes in your eyes....' It is Veterans Day today. I thought of those now serving and all those that have gone before. God bless.

DOC RAAB - Doc Raab was the platoon Corpsman for 1st PLT of Charlie Co., 1st BN, 26th Marine Regiment. On June 12,1968 Charlie Co. was assaulting a tree line south of Da Nang in an area known as Dodge City. A Marine of 1st PLT was hit by machinegun fire and the call "Corpsman up!" went out. Doc ran forward to the fallen Marine and was also hit by machinegun fire. He died moments later. I miss him still- semper fi, Doc.

Posted by: HMCM John Bruneel, U.S.N. Retired

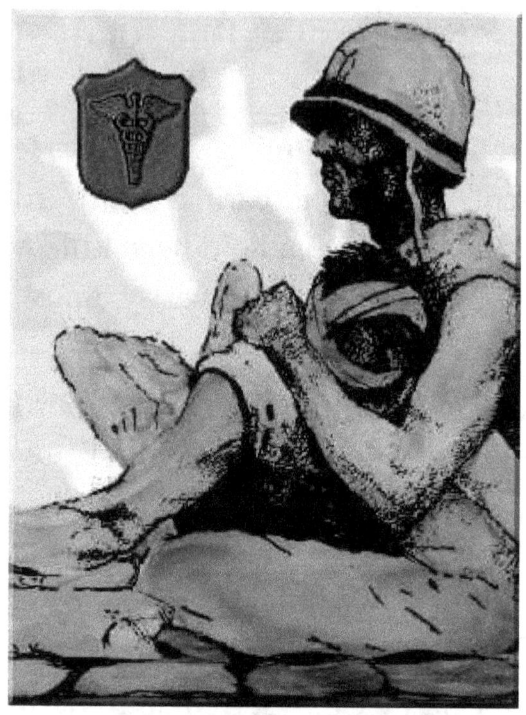

I'm the One Called "Doc…"
I shall not walk in your footsteps,
but I will walk by your side.
I shall not walk in your image,
I've earned my own title of pride.
We've answered the call together,
on sea and foreign land.
When the cry for help was given,
I've been there right at hand.
Whether I am on the ocean
or in the jungle wearing greens,
Giving aid to my fellow man,
be it Sailors or Marines.

So the next time you see a Corpsman
and you think of calling him "squid,"
Think of the job he's doing
as those before him did.
And if you ever have to go out there
and your life is on the block,
Look at the one right next to you…
I'm the one called "Doc."

Harry D. Penny, Jr. HMC(AC) USN

HM-3 John "Doc" Robinson, FMF Corpsman

My prelude to Vietnam began the Summer of 1967 with combat training and Field Medical Service School, at Camp Lejeune, North Carolina, for a month in the heat of the summer, which really prepared us for Vietnam. From Camp Lejeune, I was sent to San Diego, then Tokyo for a couple of days, and then off to Okinawa, all were commercial flights. From there it was a C-130, a small Air Force plane that was very uncomfortable, sitting on nylon webbed seats for the seven or eight-hour flight to Da Nang, Vietnam. I landed in Da Nang on July 1, 1967, and spent a day there getting all my paperwork straightened out. They told me I was going to Delta Company with the 1st Marines and the 1st Marine Battalion.

The next day, I was driven by jeep to a little town called Hoi An where I reported to the First Platoon, in a place they called "the Mud Flats." Someone pointed to a dead Marine on the ground, covered with a tarp, and told me I was replacing that Corpsman who was killed in a battle. I knew that when someone was wounded they were usually out in the open and Corpsmen were called on to rescue him and tend to his wounds until a medevac chopper arrived. So, from that very first moment, seeing that dead Corpsman, I knew I'd be fighting for my life.

The next day, on my first patrol, I wasn't sure what to expect. I saddled up with the sergeant, who became a dear friend, and with the radioman, and the lieutenant -- we formed the "headquarters group." Since a Corpsman goes out with every patrol, there was never a patrol that I didn't go out on. On patrol, we would depart with trepidation, hoping for the best -- usually expecting you're going to get shot at and hoping that you can get your enemy before he gets you. In many of the battles I was in, if it wasn't for close air support I wouldn't be here talking. We were often severely outnumbered or caught in a treacherous ambush that we wouldn't have survived if we couldn't have called in air strikes to get us out of the situation.

We did something that I thought was quite foolish, almost on a daily basis. It was called search-and-destroy, but I thought of it as a march through the jungle, search-and-get-destroyed; because we'd often walk into an ambush, booby trap, or whatever. Search-and-destroy didn't seem to accomplish very much, except getting a lot of guys wounded. That was my take on it. It would root out the enemy, I guess, or give away his location, but at the expense of a lot of young guys being either wounded or killed.

A few days after I got there, we were pinned down by sniper fire. I tried to fire my weapon in the direction of the sniper. Usually, the sergeant or lieutenant would give me orders to fire or not fire, but I became just like one of the foot soldiers. Our radioman's name was Kincaid. He was from Cincinnati; Ohio and we became good friends. He was a handsome guy with a dark beard that the Vietnamese found fascinating. The little children used to come up and rub his heavy whiskers. We were under intense sniper fire in the middle of an open field, and he yelled to me, "Doc,

I think I'm hit!" I was behind a little berm, and he was maybe twenty or thirty yards away from me. I said, "Well, crawl over here." We were in tall grass, maybe up to our knees, which was covering us. He said, "I can't move, and I feel something trickling down my neck. I said, "All right, I'll be right there." So, I made my way to him, pulled his radio off of his back and gave it to one of the other young guys. I saw three wounds, two in his back and one behind his ear. He was bleeding pretty heavily, and I applied direct pressure on all the wounds. I got the bleeding to subside and bandaged him up. The lieutenant or one of the other guys called in a medevac chopper. He asked, :Am I going to be okay? I said, "Yes, you'll definitely be okay." I got a letter from him afterward. He said, "You told me I was going to be perfect, but I've got a couple of neurological problems," but he thanked me for saving his life. That was one of my first patrols when Kincaid got wounded.

Another guy, Brady, had the back of his arm blown off. I called a chopper in for him. I got a minor wound on my bicep while taking him out to the chopper. Every day seemed like it was life or death. It was exciting and, yet, it was frightening at the same time.

We went on daily patrols and were frequently under sniper fire, incurring casualties and fighting for our lives. After some time we were transferred to Dong Ha, which was further north than Danang. Our mission in Dong Ha was to clear an area around Quang Tri, so they could build an airstrip. We went on many missions and operations and became a battle-hardened outfit that was called on to assist other units that were in trouble. We flew all over Vietnam, from the mountains to the plains to the ocean, rescuing other outfits and, of course, incurring casualties ourselves. In one operation, we were on amphibious tanks and landing craft. We invaded a small island that was just infiltrated with Vietcong, and our mission was to clear the island of the VC. We swept across that little island and in a week either killed or captured every Vietcong there. We sustained heavy casualties. I don’t remember what the operation was called, but it was intense fighting. Ninety percent of the time, our outfit was in the jungle fighting. I fought hard. I helped a lot of wounded guys along the way and came very close, a number of times, to being wounded or killed. It is just the luck of the draw that I’m here.

We spent a month at Con Tien, on the DMZ, over Thanksgiving and Christmas, taking rocket fire from the North Vietnamese on a daily basis. If we had to carry somebody by stretcher back to a base or to a chopper landing area, we’d make our own stretchers with bamboo and a piece of canvas. The mosquitos were intense, but we had insect repellant that kept most of them off of our skin. Sometimes, we’d march all day and all night and then fight a battle. We would catch a few winks here and there, protect the guy next to you while he slept, and he’d protect you while you slept. We were sleep deprived. We were hungry. We were fighting for our lives, most of the time in such intense heat we couldn't believe it. We perspired profusely and sometimes guys ran out of water and were dying for a drink. There were other dangers that lurked as well: accidental discharges from somebody cleaning his weapon, insect bites, leeches, snakes. The living conditions aside from fighting in combat were deplorable. During the monsoons, we'd be up to our knees in mud. We could go for weeks having wet feet, and having fungus, or what they called trench foot. We couldn't get dry. We'd go from intense heat and being so saturated with sweat, the least little breeze would feel like we were freezing. I remember most of the time just sleeping under the stars or out in the rain. We'd take a poncho and build a makeshift tent to try to keep dry. Unless you've lived it, it can be difficult to comprehend.

If a Marine was wounded, with what I carried in the field, I could control the bleeding and give him morphine for his pain. I did other things too. I had foot lotion for guys that had foot fungus. I had a scalpel and medical equipment so if guys had boils or serious infections, I could lance them. I had antibiotic ointments to prevent wound infections. With the perspiration and the heat, conditions were so ripe for infection, the least little cut could get infected. It was a constant struggle finding clean water. Most of the time, if someone was injured, I would stop the bleeding, wrap up the wound, and try to get the guy on a helicopter as quickly as possible.

My lowest point is recorded in a letter I wrote to my mother; "Mom, we were in a battle yesterday. Out of forty of us, thirty-five guys were wounded or killed and there are only five of us, five experienced guys left. I'm at a point now where I'm teaching the sergeant and the lieutenant how to read a map and how to call in artillery and how to call in medevac choppers. It's amazing how fast you learn when it's life or death. It was on-the-job training, and we learned very quickly. In Vietnam, you became experienced within a week.

Carmine Novembre was a guy I was supposed to call when I got home. He was from Passaic, New Jersey, When we were fighting together near Hue City in January 1968. He said, "Call me. I'm going to be home in March." When I called, I got his young wife on the phone and it turned out that Carmine didn't make it home. That's one of the few times I cried.

I had one dear friend die in my arms. We were stationed at Portsmouth together and we went to Vietnam together. He went to Alpha Company, and I went to Delta Company. He was on a patrol outside of Con Thien, near the DMZ. He was shot through both legs by a fifty-caliber machine-gun round while trying to save another Marine. When they told me there was a wounded Corpsman in the middle of the field, I just ran, picked him up, threw him over my shoulder, and brought him back. I tried to save him. He had put a tourniquet around his own legs, but he was unconscious when I got to him and he had lost so much blood that it was futile to try to save him. He took his last breath in my arms, on November 26, 1967. I wrote to his dad, Mike Thirkettle - he was from Southern California. His dad wrote me a beautiful letter back. I'd love to be able to find that letter. He was a state senator at the time and quoted Abraham Lincoln and Aristotle and it was just beautifully written. He said that I was one of the only people who ever told him the circumstances of his son's death and he thanked me greatly for it.

Combat definitely changed my personality. Once carefree and happy-go-lucky when I got home I became a lot more serious. I thought quite a bit about the guys that did not make it home and just tried to dedicate myself to being a good person and doing the best I could possibly do in my life; being a good family guy and a hardworking guy, making the most of my time, this extra time, I was granted. I didn't talk about it for a long time because, unless you were there, it is difficult to describe and maybe even harder to believe that a human can sustain himself or survive under those conditions. I came back to antiwar sentiment, and I just thought to myself, "There is a lot more to me than being a Vietnam veteran." I was proud of my service, I was proud that I had served, I was proud I was awarded the Bronze Star, but I didn't want to be classified solely as a Vietnam veteran.

There are two things that stand out from my time in Vietnam. The foremost thing I can't forget is my best friend dying in my arms. That was devastating. Secondly, the day I left Vietnam, as we were taking off, I was looking down at the country of Vietnam, the godforsaken place that it was. I opened my Stars and Stripes newspaper and I saw that my other dear friend, Ralph David Hale III, who graduated from Great Lakes Naval Hospital with me, was killed in Vietnam. Those two memories are so vivid for me. It's like they just happened. They have never left me.

I can remember being the hottest I've ever been and the coldest I've ever been. I saw more mosquitos than I've ever seen in my lifetime. I saw insects that I had never seen before, plus snakes, leeches, `and got dysentery from drinking awful tasting water.

There were life-and-death situations, yet I had friends who were going through the same thing with me, people that I respected and whom I became best friends with, that I would give my life up for, and who made it all tolerable. Every night, you laid down and you looked up at the stars and the moon and you'd think that's the same stars and the moon your mother's looking at halfway around the world, or your brothers and sisters are looking at, and you just looked forward to the day that you'd be home.

[John Robinson was born on September 26, 1945. He grew up in Spring Lake Heights, New Jersey and graduated from Manasquan High School in 1964. He served as a Navy Hospital Corpsman with the Delta Company, 1st Battalion, 1st Marine Regiment, in Vietnam from 1967 to 1968, and was awarded the Bronze Star Medal for his service. After the war, Mr. Robinson attended Cook College at Rutgers University, earning his degree in 1971. In 1972, he became the president of Mueller Supply Inc.]

Mr. & Mrs. Robinson
General Robert Nelle, USMC & "Doc" Robinson

HM-2 Robert J. "Doc" Topmiller, FMF Corpsman

by Michael Archer

Robert J. "Bob" Topmiller was born in Cincinnati, Ohio, on October 18, 1948. Bob's early life was difficult; his parents divorced when he was six, and his mother died when he was in high school. Despite that, Bob was an excellent student and a competitive athlete at Archbishop Moeller High School, establishing a city high school record in the 100-yard dash that stood for twenty years.

After graduation, Bob announced his intention to join the Marine Corps. His worried aunts pressed Bob's father not to allow him to go to Vietnam as a Marine. His father refused permission for his underage son to enlist in the Corps but agreed to sign him into the Navy, believing it was safer.

Bob began basic training in July 1966 at Great Lakes Naval Station near Chicago. Later he would learn that Navy Corpsmen served with Marines in combat. Now envisioning himself rushing to the aid of wounded men under enemy fire, Bob was struck by the irony of his family's insistence that he join the Navy to stay safe.

After boot camp, Bob trained at Hospital Corps School. Except for a short stint at the Field Medical Training School, with the Marines at Camp Lejeune, North Carolina, he remained at Great Lakes until the inevitable journey to the War. In late 1967, he received orders to South Vietnam, with a stopover on Okinawa for additional combat training. There, instructors replicated harsh Marine Corps boot camp methods, with verbal abuse, vigorous physical conditioning, and live fire exercises intended to toughen the Corpsmen up and increase their chances of survival in battle.

Doc, as he became known in the military, arrived at Khe Sanh Combat Base in mid-January 1968 and soon realized he was part of a significant buildup in preparation for an attack by thousands of NVA soldiers massing in the nearby mountains. He was appalled to find the 26th Marine Regimental Aid Station (RAS), where he was assigned to work, nothing more than a cramped, cinderblock bunker, half above ground, covered by a flimsy, plywood roof that barely provided protection against the weather let alone incoming artillery fire.

Just nine days later, his concern was justified when North Vietnamese incoming shells began hitting the base. The small bunker quickly filled with wounded men, and suddenly the base ammunition dump, a hundred yards away, erupted with a thundering explosion, with shock waves collapsing the roof of the RAS.

The blast rattled Bob, and when he regaining his senses, Doc dug himself out from under the dirt and shattered lumber. He was stunned by the bedlam around him as doctors and medical staff struggled to move the many wounded from the crumbling structure to a nearby bunker. Doc said the place quickly became "a gruesome chamber of horrors filled with moaning wounded men and packed like sardines," as enemy shells exploded around them and tear gas from the burning ammo dump filled the place.

That evening, in the glow of the still burning ammunition, Doc worked his way around the area, filling a body bag with parts from several Marines who had been blown to pieces. During the effort, he was wounded by shrapnel but was able to continue.

Over time, the constant incoming artillery fire created unique problems for the medical personnel. Concussion injuries from the force of nearby explosions were frequent. Also, Corpsmen were trained primarily to treat in-and-out bullet wounds, but most of the injuries during the siege of Khe Sanh were from jagged shrapnel and almost always became grossly infected. Psychological casualties from the stress of combat soared, and exotic diseases, including rat-borne rabies and plague, had to be dealt with. Almost everyone became ill upon arriving at the base, mostly developing diarrhea, and vomiting due to the high bacteria levels. Inadequate clean water supplies contributed to dehydration, which increased susceptibility to these and other health problems.

One of the first wounded men Doc treated after arriving at Khe Sanh was Rick Noyes, an acquaintance from high school. A reconnaissance Marine, Rick, was injured by shrapnel while on patrol seeking information on the NVA build-up around the base. Topmiller later treated Rick for a second injury after his bunker took a direct hit from an enemy rocket. Noyes suffered multiple shrapnel wounds and a ruptured eardrum, but four others in the bunker were killed. Doc patched him up and sent him back on duty, but because of the unsanitary conditions, Rick's wounds soon became infected, and he returned to the aid station for treatment.

A few days later, Noyes was standing nearby when some Marines, frustrated by the rats in their trench line, decided to burn them all with gasoline. After pouring the fuel into the trench and igniting it, a Marine slipped into the flames and was burned over nearly his entire body. Rick helped carry the man to the aid station, but Doc knew immediately that the injured man would not survive (the next day he died on a medevac flight to the Philippines). Doc immediately recognized that Rick was delirious with fever from a severe, life-threatening infection. Doc helped carry his friend to a helicopter, and though Rick was reluctant to leave his comrades behind, later credited Doc's professionalism with saving his life.

One day late in the siege, incoming artillery fire caught several Marines in the open. Doc was quickly notified, grabbed his medical kit, and went to the site. The first man he came across had lost both legs. As Doc looked around, he saw others sprawled on the ground with a variety of severe wounds. He told me, "I realized that I had to abandon the man with his legs gone to go to the guys who had a better chance of surviving." The man soon died, and Doc was subsequently hit by shrapnel while tending to the others. He argued that the wound was insignificant, and that he should not be put in for an award, but the senior chief at the RAS insisted it be recorded. Doc ended his account of that terrible day by saying: "The look on that legless Marine's face, when he realized I was about to leave him has haunted me ever since."

In the summer of 1968, Doc completed his tour of duty in Vietnam and returned to the Great Lakes Naval Hospital, where he met fellow Corpsman Theresa "Terri" Nicks. Though she had not gone to Vietnam, Terri was not spared the horrors, caring for some of the War' most severely mangled, burned, grossly infected, and mentally unhinged survivors of combat shipped to the Great Lakes for advanced treatment. Once discharged in 1969, Doc and Terri were married. The intensity of the nightmares that Doc experienced after Khe Sanh increased over time. "There were symptoms of post-traumatic stress disorder," Terri later recalled, "but we didn't know about it at that time."

On the advice of his VA counselor, Doc pursued academics and excelled, earning both a bachelor's and a master's degree in four years. As part of his doctoral research at the University of Kentucky, he studied under Dr. George Herring, the foremost Vietnam War scholar in the country, and made his first return to Vietnam. He promised Terri he would not visit Khe Sanh, but once in the country, he felt compelled to "settle the unfinished business of war." He knew of other veterans who had returned to former battle scenes and escaped their demons and wondered if this visit would end his nightmares - or potentially make them more terrifying.

Doc soon realized that he would not find redemption in merely reacquainting himself with a piece of geography because Khe Sanh, the "place," was not the problem. Doc had seen too many shattered lives, ruined minds, and wrecked families from the war, both in the U.S. and Vietnam, and was seeking answers to more profound, more personal questions. After repudiating Catholicism when he arrived in Vietnam, he came to admire the Buddhist nuns and monks he met during his research and travels throughout Vietnam, some of them aging religious-rights activists still under house arrest by the government; Doc embraced their teachings and soon considered himself a Buddhist.

He now understood that, as much as American veterans and their families had suffered in that war, the South Vietnamese had suffered more, forfeiting their freedom, and living under a political party "that hated them for fighting alongside the Americans and punished them repeatedly for it." He had wasted years of rage, hatred, and resentment on people who did not hate him in return. As he came to know more and more citizens and soldiers of the former nation of South Vietnam, he found that most appreciated what Americans tried to do during the war. "Even if our attempt seemed misguided and caused an unacceptable level of destruction to the cultural fabric of South Vietnam," Doc said, 'they realize that had we won, they might have avoided years of communist terror and not have borne the brunt of communist reprisals."

Topmiller received his doctorate in 1998 and accepted a teaching position at Eastern Kentucky University. His academic colleagues soon came to know him as strong and outspoken in his opinions yet possessing a fine sense of humor and outstanding dedication to his profession. He quickly earned a reputation among his students as an enthusiastic and inspiring teacher, fearless in the pursuit of truth.

Doc made his fourteenth visit to Vietnam in July 2008—it would be his last. He dreaded returning to the United States and the issues that weighed so heavily upon him when in the US: the military quagmires in Afghanistan and Iraq, the shoddy treatment of American veterans, and the seeming indifference of the American people.

Doc and Terri attend the annual Khe Sanh Veterans Association reunion two weeks after his 2008 visit. The first night there, he had a chance to meet with Rick Noyes, the wounded Marine mentioned earlier who .he'd saved in Vietnam. This awakened painful memories within. Terri later described how Doc had gone back to their hotel room and sobbed for nearly an hour.

Doc often said that part of the guilt he felt from his Vietnam experiences was because he had not been vocal enough in his opposition to the war after returning home. He was now remedying that with a vengeance. His ardor to educate the public on what the wars in Iraq and Afghanistan would mean in human suffering and national treasure, for generations after, became an obsession. He began to author a book. "It will be critical but not spiteful," Doc said. "I want the VA to be the best it can be." But by early August 2008, Doc told Terri the book was bringing up too many difficult emotions, and he doubted his ability to finish it.

By late August, Doc seemed content once again. He had accepted a position at the University of Kentucky to teach a history of U.S. diplomacy and foreign relations and was preparing another class on the Vietnam War. On August 19, he called me to discuss a joint book signing we had scheduled in Reno for Veterans Day. Doc had just purchased round-trip plane fare and spoke about how much he looked forward to it. He told me how thrilled he was by his new position in Kentucky, that he had just put together a syllabus, and had moved into an office on campus. It was, he said, his "dream job."

By this time, Doc had stopped seeking treatment and was taking two strong prescription medications for anxiety and insomnia. His first day of class was scheduled for Monday, August 25. He left home that morning in what Terri later described as "great spirits." But he never made it to campus. Two days later, in Georgetown, Kentucky, police found Doc's body in a motel room. He had died from a self-inflicted gunshot wound to the head from a pistol he'd purchased at a gun store the day before. He left no note.

His family was devastated. Terri, whom Doc had recognized in the Preface of his book *Red Clay on My Boots* as having "fought the battle of Khe Sanh by my side for almost forty years," would now have another battle to fight, surmounting her anguish and a myriad of conflicting emotions, to stay strong for her children and grandchildren. Her dignity and genuine compassion for the feelings of others during this darkest period in her life marked Terri as one of the most courageous women I have known, still the Corpsman "helper-healer" she was when she first met Doc at Great Lakes Naval Hospital over four decades before.

Doc's friends and colleagues were in shock, experiencing the hollowness of personal loss and despair at the utter waste of such a passionate individual and brilliant mind. His suicide seemed inexplicable. A note arrived from *Wandering Souls* author Wayne Karlin, who observed that we Marines always saw their Corpsmen as the strongest, the ones we could turn to. He said Doc remained a scholar and a healer in his passion for communicating the complex humanity of the Vietnamese. "There is some kind of sickening shift in the heart," Wayne wrote, 'when you realize how each wound our Corpsmen touched, physical or not, became their own. It's disheartening to realize that the War still has that power to reach over the stretch of forty years and snatch such a good person back." His Vietnamese friends had come to view Doc as a "living Buddha" for his compassion and generosity and took the news of his death with shock and deep sorrow. Doc Topmiller's dedication to those injured physically and emotionally by the war manifested itself daily across a broad spectrum, both in the United States and Vietnam.

Those Marines and Sailors who served alongside him during the war in Vietnam saw him as a fearless and highly principled individual. They recognized it was the cruelest of ironies that the most inspired, introspective, and caring among us were selected as Corpsmen. Navy Corpsmen and Army medics who survived combat suffered painful memories all their lives, blaming their "incompetence" for deaths they could not have prevented, and this painful truth reminds me of a verse by A.E. Houseman: "The saviors come not home tonight. Themselves they could not save."

Robert Topmiller was born Oct. 18, 1948, in Cincinnati, Ohio to Norbert Topmiller and Rita Meyer Topmiller. He attended St. Peter and Paul Elementary and graduated Moeller High School in 1966. He joined the Navy serving as a Navy Corpsmen with the US Marines in Vietnam. He was proud of his service and was an advocate to all veterans. He married Terri Nicks on Nov. 1, 1969, in Weiser, Idaho. They had four children, Chris Topmiller (Brianne), Kevin Topmiller (Jaime), Robert Topmiller (Emily), and Jamie Sadler (Keith); and four grandchildren, Brooke and Scott Topmiller and Ross and Aidan Sadler. After being in business for over 20 years, Bob returned to school receiving his Ph.D. in history. He taught history to military personnel in South Korea and at EKU until his retirement in May 2008. He was a teacher who truly cared about his students. He will be missed by his family and his many friends.

HM-2 Richard "Doc" Pustka, FMF Corpsman

Our war, the Vietnam War, was not fought for mom, the flag, or apple pie. It was about protecting your buddy; the guy on your left, on your right, and the six o'clock of the guy in front of you. I was proud to serve with the Marine Corps. I was born on March 7, 1946, in Japan. I came from a military family, and we eventually moved to Salina, Kansas, where I graduated from high school in 1964, and then attended Kansas States Teacher's College. While I was in school the Vietnam War was on television every night, and we were all very familiar with what was happening in Vietnam. Following school, in 1966, I enlisted in the United States Navy.

I had no idea that I would end up as a Corpsman. When I attend basic training, I was tested to see where I might serve best, and I had mentioned that I had worked as an orderly, in a hospital, when I was a teenager. The Marine Corps needed Corpsmen very badly, and the next thing I knew, that following basic training at the Naval Training Center, in San Diego, California, I was being sent to the Balboa Naval Hospital, also in San Diego, to learn how to become a Hospital Corpsman.

Following my training at Balboa Naval Hospiatl, which lasted about six months, I was sent "up the road" to Camp Pendleton, California, where I attended Field Medical Service School, where we were trained to function within a Marine Rifle Company, and given the MOS (Military Occupational Specialty) of 8404. We were referred to as "Bush Techicians." At Field Medical Service School, we fired rifles, threw hand grenades, practiced first aid procedures, and learned what would be expected of us as Corpsmen operating within a Marine Corps infantry unit.

Following my training at Camp Pendleton, I returned home to Kansas, and married my high school sweetheart, Mary Ann. We enjoyed 30 days leave before leaving for Vietnam. I landed in Danang, and was assigned to the 1st Marine Regiment, where we patrolled around that area looking for the Viet Cong. The North Vietnamese Army had not entered the war when I first got to Vietnam, in 1967, and we spent countless days patrolling in the jungle on search and destroy missions, trying to avoid VC ambushes and booby traps, before the regiment moved north to Phu Bai. All of that changed in 1968.

In January 1968, the people of Vietnam celebrated Tet, the beginning of the Lunar New Year. On 31 January 1968, the North Vietnamese Army attacked all of South Vietnam, hitting every major base and city. That morning the Sergeant Major woke us up and said that we were needed at Hue City. He said that the MACV (Military Assistance Command Vietnam), command post was under attack, but we would be back at Phu Bai by noontime. He said it "was no big deal." I was tasked with going with a Marine rifle company, Alpha Company, 1stBattalion, 1st Marine Regiment, to help set up a triage center.

When we got to Hue City it was complete chaos. There were at least 40 wounded soldiers laying around waiting to be treated. They thought we had come to rescue them. The company I was with consisted of about 160 of us, but there were 10,000 NVA, in and around Hue. Because Hue was the cultural center of Vietnam and recognized as the Summer Palace of the Imperial City, it was a big propaganda victory for the North Vietnamese Army to take the city. What happened next was 28 days of heavy house-to-house fighting in the city.

Our initial radio contact to the regimental commander, who was back at Phu Bai, told him that we were "out manned and out gunned." During the fighting for Hue we had 215 Marines and Corpsmen killed and 1500 wounded.

In Hue, it was uniformed NVA that we were fighting, not the Viet Cong. It was a culture shock to us and very scary.

I was awarded the Silver Star and the Purple Heart for things that happened in Hue, and we endured twenty four days on non-stop fighting with the NVA. We had come from patrolling in the dense jungle and into combat in an urban environment. I had a MULE, a small 4-wheel drive vehicle, and I was using it to carry wounded Marines back to where we had set up a triage unit at the MACV Compound, that was manned by Dr. James Beck, our regimental doctor.

We would off-load the wounded and he would start treating them for the various wounds they had received. I was driving around on my MULE when I came across a Marine with a bad chest wound. I began treating him, when heard a very audible "click" sound and turned around to see a uniformed NVA soldier with an RPG-7 on his shoulder. That RPG-7 was a reusable, anti-tank, grenade launcher, and he was aiming it directly at me and my wounded Marine. I threw myself on top of the Marine and that PRG round exploded against a brick wall very close to us. The NVA soldier started to reload his grenade launcher and I went for my .45. I always had thought that I was a pretty good shot, and I began shooting at him, and had nearly emptied my pistol when I got him with the sixth round. When I was standing over him, I looked down at myself and thought that I had pissed my pants. What had happened was my boots had filled up with my blood from multiple shrapnel wounds to my back and legs. I was able to carry that wounded Marine back to the MACV compound. There, Dr. Beck removed the biggest pieces of shrapnel that he could find from my back and legs and then he patched me up. I never left.

A M-274 Light Weapons carrier called a MULE

"I have walked beside heroes," is an old adage, and it is true in my case, but I wasn't one of them. The Marines and Corpsmen who were at the battle for Hue City earned three or four Medals of Honor, several more Navy Crosses, and many more Silver Star Medals for their extraordinary heroism. Hue was a turning point in the history of our Country and for thc Marine Corps. Then came the debate, not on how we win the war, but how do we get out of it?

After we took back the city of Hue from the North Vietnamese, our mission changed and we were sent to relieve the 26th Marines at Khe Sanh. They lived underground. When I got there I inherited an underground nest that I could sleep in. We took incoming rounds all of the time and that is what forced us to live in a subterranean environment.

While I was at Khe Sanh, the time came for me to take R&R (Rest and Relaxation), and I had made plans to meet Mary Ann in Hawaii. A Huey helicopter was designated to take me out of Khe San and down to Danang, where I would fly from and on to Hawaii. Shortly after leaving Khe Sanh, I watched as the door gunner removed his helmet from his head and sat on it. He motioned for me to do the same. We were taking ground fire and holes began to appear throughout our helicopter. We were hit badly and the pilot managed to crash into a river but several of us managed to survive. I got out of the wrecked Huey and got over to the copilot, but he was dead. I moved to the front of the helicopter and found the pilot had also been killed. I had managed to take a SAR (Search and Rescue) radio from the copilot and within ten minutes a Golly Green Giant appeared and picked up the survivors and the dead.

HH-E3 Golly Green Giant Helicopter

I was able to get to Danang and made it to my flight to Hawaii to see Mary Ann. Our weeklong R&R was nothing short of wonderful. I went back to Vietnam, rejoined my unit at Khe Sanh, and we finally moved out of Khe Sanh and resumed patrolling on search and destroy missions around the port city of Danang.

I returned to the States in 1968, and ended up at Miramar Air Station, just north of San Diego, where we conducted search missions along the California coast line. I received my discharge papers and received a generous three month "early out" from active duty, so that I could return to school.

My service to my Country was an important personal obligation, but the real honor for me was being assigned to a Marine Corps regiment while I was in Vietnam. I don't consider myself to be a sailor: I am a Fleet Marine Force

Corpsman, a title that I was privileged to have earned. The Marines with whom I served accepted me into their brotherhood, which is the greatest honor I have ever had. Today, with a loving wife, two beautiful daughters, three granddaughters, three Great-great grandchildren, and I am blessed with a wonderful family.

HM-3 Frank P. "Doc" Simione, Jr., U. S. Navy

Awestruck in '69, or Combat to Critical Care

Frank P. "Doc" Simione, Jr. (Far right)

I was expecting it, but when it arrived it was still a shock. College had been an exception, because of my military deferment, but having just graduated and with no lottery yet, I had to make a tough decision about my military obligation. After watching scenes from Vietnam on the television news, I wanted no part of combat. The fear of getting injured or killed was not the primary reason - it was the question of how I would respond in a firefight: I was not a fighter. So, I enlisted in the U.S. Navy. Because of my interest in medicine I became a Hospital Corpsman, despite advice against doing that, the majority of corpsmen ended up serving as medics with the Marines, most often in combat. I was one of the lucky ones.

My specialty school was located at the Philadelphia Naval Hospital, and when I arrived there in April 1969, I had six months to wait for the school to start. Tom, one of my classmates in Corps School, arrived at the same time. We had both been advised by someone in the school, or possibly someone at the Great Lakes Naval Hospital, to avoid the orthopedic wards. Midway through school we were assigned to work on a ward for a day or two, and I spent my time on an orthopedic ward. It was calm with one amputee whose dressing change I was only able to observe; orthopedics didn't seem so bad. Despite the warning to avoid orthopedics, the senior nursing supervisor at the Philadelphia Naval Hospital told us that we could choose between orthopedics or orthopedics, Ward 2A or 3A. I saw a slight smirk on her face when she told us that; she knew about the reputation of orthopedics.

I'm not sure how the assignments were made, but I got Ward 2A and Tom got Ward 3A.

Dressed in my summer whites, I approached Ward 2A on my first day trying to anticipate what I was going to find. What I encountered Philadelphia Naval Hospital was not even in my wildest imagination. The beds on the left side of the ward had been moved to the center and two corpsmen were swabbing the floor. Actually as I entered the ward they were jousting with the mop handles. Two young nurses were wiping down the beds, and the senior one yelled at the corpsmen to "knock it off." One of them laughingly responded with a wise crack, calling her by her first name. Wow! This was not at all what I had expected.

The two smiling corpsmen welcomed me to the ward, and one started to hand me his mop and jokingly said, "get to work." They both laughed, and then continued their swabbing. They only remained on the ward for a few more days and I learned that they had been in Vietnam; one flew Medevac missions, and both had been wounded. The ward did not have a full complement of patients, and most of them were ambulatory. The daily activities were routine, medications, and vital signs and a few dressing changes. There were no amputees and most of the patients either had broken bones or infections near the bone from shrapnel or bullet wounds. Other than a few older veterans with their particular issues, one had a stroke while on the ward, but most of the medical conditions were not serious.

The majority of the patients were constantly upbeat, smiling and joking. On one occasion I was called to the bed of an animated Tony, a Marine of Italian descent, by other patients standing around his bed. His friends asked me to explain to Tony that muscle is meat. “That can’t be, said Tony.” I replied that muscle is definitely meat. “You mean the same meat that we eat?” “Yes, Tony, we eat the muscles of animals.” Tony exclaimed, “I’m never eating meat again.” His friends nearly fell over laughing at him.

One patient, who was pleasant and responsive, had a concern about the additional surgery the doctors wanted to perform on his leg. He was afraid of the anesthesia, and thought that he might not wake up after the surgery. We finally convinced him that he would be ok, and after the surgery he returned to the ward smiling and laughing at his unfounded concern.

Only one patient on the ward was depressed and demanded a regular injection of Talwin, a medication for his pain. He had a gunshot wound on his right lower leg, and some of the other patients speculated that it might have been self-inflicted. I asked another patient, a recon Marine, to try to talk to him, however, after one session he told me that, “He is hopeless.” On one occasion when the depressed patient was anxiously clamoring for his pain medication, the doctor reviewed his chart with the nurse and me and wrote on it, “placebo.” The nurse prepared the syringe, and I gave him his injection. He immediately relaxed and fell asleep.

A Marine that we called Ski got my attention because of the contraption on his leg. While he was riding in a truck that hit a mine his lower left leg was severed completely, and he now had a Stader splint attached. The splint consisted of rods placed into each of the two pieces of the separated tibia at right angles to the bone. A cross bar running parallel to the bone was attached to each rod and was fitted with adjustment screws allowing the doctors to keep the severed ends of the bones aligned. It provided sturdy support for the broken bone even when the leg was moved. Otto Stader, a veterinarian, invented the splint for use in animals in the 1930s, and it was adopted by the U.S. Navy for stabilizing fractures on ships pitching and rolling on rough seas.

Although Ski was unable to walk he could get out of bed and into a wheelchair on his own, making him quite mobile on the ward and throughout the hospital. He was a gregarious, friendly individual who enjoyed visiting other patients and the staff. Ski was an immigrant from Brazil, and received his U.S. citizenship while in the hospital. He remained on Ward 2A until the ward was changed to a "hands only" ward. Later he came by to see me in tears, telling me that the senior surgeon wanted to cut off his leg; the Stader splint was not working. I explained that if the surgeon, one of the best orthopedic surgeons in the Navy, recommended cutting off his leg, it was probably best for him.

We had a few patients in traction, the best practice at the time, for broken femurs. One was a Marine who had been injured in a car accident; he had a broken femur and a ruptured bladder. After the bladder was repaired he was transferred to Ward 2A and placed into traction. Two incidents occurred with that patient, demonstrating the importance of attention to detail and communication. One of the incidents demonstrated that where the military command structure sometimes supersedes good medical practice. The patient was on limited liquid intake because of his bladder injury, and one afternoon as I was walking on the ward to start my PM shift, I noticed that his IV bottle was empty. When I reported it to the nurse she panicked. A new bottle had just been put in place by the day Corpsman and apparently when he started the drip, the line was blocked by pressure from the patient's arm. When the patient moved his arm, and the entire bottle drained too quickly. The day Corpsman and I were both candidates for senior Corpsman on Ward 2A, and that incident got me the job.

On another occasion, one of the nursing supervisors was making medical rounds and ordered me to change the traction on this same patient. I explained that the surgeon had set the traction, but she, a commander, gave me a direct order to change it under threat; a clear case of where military hierarchy got in the way of good medical care. I saw little of that during most of my time as a Corpsman. When the surgeon later made his rounds he asked me angrily, "Who changed the traction on this patient?" "I did, Sir," I replied. He asked why, and I explained that I was ordered to change it by the nursing supervisor. He told me to change it back and then angrily left the ward; I never saw that nursing supervisor again. Night duty on Ward 2a was always quiet with most patients sleeping, and the rule was lights-out at 11:00PM. On one occasion, three of the patients were playing cards in the utility room well past lights-out. I asked them twice to finish their game and get into bed, and the third time I demanded that they move. Their response was to throw the cards on the floor, knock over a few chairs and cuss me out intensely. They complied, and afterwards I questioned my right to force them to end their game; they had seen combat in Vietnam, and I had not. If a nursing supervisor found them playing cards after lights-out, I would have been reprimanded. I regretted later that I didn't take that chance and let them continue their game.

On occasion we were asked to assist with the transport of newly arriving patients. The patients entered the hospital on the ground floor; all were on gurneys. Some were alert and looking around, others were either sleeping or unconscious. From the appearance of the bandages it was likely that they had not been changed during their transport from Vietnam. These were casualties fresh from combat, carrying the evident scars of battle with them. The gurneys were labeled with patient information and the ward number where they were to be taken. Our job was to transport the gurneys through the hospital and turn the patient over to the ward staff.

Tom, my friend from Corps School, and I rented an apartment a few blocks from the hospital. He never talked about what he saw on Ward 3A, and I didn't ask. I constantly wondered what that experience was like. Tom did not express emotion, and I suspect that if he had been a combat Corpsman, he would have been a good one. When Joey Heatherton and her husband Lance Renzel visited the wards, another Corpsman on Ward 2A and I followed them to Ward 3A; she was beautiful, and we wanted to see more of her. However, when I walked onto the ward I was immediately distracted by the activity of the medical staff and the nature of the patients. It was literally an orthopedic intensive care unit.

Occasionally thinking about what I saw on Ward 3A, I became concerned that I might eventually be required to work there. Then the inevitable happened: my worst fear became reality; I was assigned to work for several 15 hour weekend shifts on Ward 3A. My first experience was performing dressing changes on amputees, initially accompanied by a doctor. On one occasion the doctor and I were joined by an Army medic, a weekend warrior. The doctor performed the debriding of the patient's stump while I held the surgical pack. The medic was standing between us observing. Suddenly, the medic slumped to the floor. When the doctor looked over at me I nodded to the floor and he said, "Leave him be, someone else will get him." After finishing our work, the medic was gone, and I never saw another weekend warrior on the wards again.

Another patient was a sailor who lost his lower left leg to an errant anchor chain on a ship. The end of his stump was jagged and obviously in need of more surgery. Debriding and redressing were performed by the doctor, but then he asked me to apply the bandage. I had never bandaged a stump, and he remained with me, guiding me in the proper application of a bandage on a stump. The difficulty was that the stump offered no anchor point for the bandage, but I completed it successfully. I was now allowed to perform debriding, dressing changes and bandaging on my own.

One of my patients was a muscular Marine who had lost both legs below the knee. His wounds were well healed except for a few areas that needed some minor debriding resulting in slight bleeding. Sitting on the end of the bed with his thighs extended, he talked to me while I worked. He told me that he was married, but was getting a divorce. I responded that I was sorry to hear that, and he explained that his wife could not live with a man in his condition. "How does she feel about that?" I asked, and he went into a tirade. Looking at me with a hard glare, he said, "It doesn't matter; she doesn't get a choice." I couldn't respond, but later thought about his decision. The war had changed his life, and although I wondered why he felt as he did, I couldn't rationalize his thinking. Only someone in the same condition could completely understand his decision.

Another patient, heavily sedated, was strapped into a Stryker Frame so that he could be periodically rotated, alleviating pressure on either side of his body. The Stryker Frame, originally called a turning frame, was invented by Homer Stryker, An orthopedic surgeon, in 1941. The frame was all metal with two ladder-like structures, open between the rung-like cross pieces, attached to two large metal hoops and all mounted on a support that sits on the floor. The patient is strapped between the two ladder-like structures such that most of the body is supported by straps covered in bedding, and could be rotated to allow access to both sides of the body without having to physically turn the patient. It is useful for burn patients and completely immobile patients that are prone to developing bedsores: patients are turned approximately every two hours.

This patient did not respond coherently to any of the staff. His wounds were extensive, and he was hooked up to multiple IV bottles. At one point the doctors demonstrated how to rotate the Stryker frame and I felt sorry for the patient as I watched the process from a distance. He was lying prone on the bed with just a sheet covering him. As I watched the demonstration my mind wandered to the battlefields in Vietnam contemplating how he might have received these wounds. It was obvious that his wounds were created by shrapnel of some type, not via gunshot or large explosion as all his limbs appeared to be intact. It was not clear to me why he was on the orthopedic ward.

One evening, his fiancée arrived to visit him and was escorted onto the ward by a few friends and some of the medical staff. She stopped just short of his bed and when he was pointed out to her she put her hand to her mouth and her face took on an expression of horror. He was lying in a prone position with a sheet

covering his mangled naked body. Standing silently for a few minutes staring at him she suddenly screamed loudly and ran from the ward. I don't know if she ever returned, and I never learned the disposition of the patient as he was relocated to a medical ward because his internal injuries were more severe than his orthopedic ones.

During a particularly delicate dressing change on a severely damaged thigh I was assisting a doctor and nurse, along with another Corpsman. I was standing to the left of the patient and holding the surgical pack and handing instruments to the doctor who stood next to me on my left. The nurse, standing to the left of the doctor, was assisting him by spreading open the wound and dabbing up blood as the doctor probed the wound. The Corpsman standing on the opposite side of the bed from me was monitoring vital signs.

Suddenly, as the doctor was probing, blood spurted from an artery in the patient's leg squirting over the front of the nurse's surgical gown and partially on her face. The doctor exclaimed "damn," and the nurse showing no fluster placed a clamp in the hand of the doctor within seconds. Applying pressure to the wound with dressing material the doctor began probing for the artery and several more jets of blood spewed from the wound before he was able to clamp it off.

My only participation was to provide clean dressing material to the doctor as he frantically tried to stop the bleeding. At one point I glanced up at the second Corpsman. He was staring at the wound with wide open eyes, and his face was white. Suddenly he put his hand to his mouth and ran for the utility room; I heard him throwing up. I did not see that Corpsman on the ward again, and I suspect he was given administrative duties or less traumatic medical duties on another ward. His response was rare: during my tenure on the wards, I do not remember observing the same response in any other Corpsman.

On another occasion I was asked to assist one of the doctors and a nurse with a severely injured patient. The doctor, with the nurse's assistance, was going to debride the left stump of the patient, located just at the hip joint. When I saw the patient, a young black Marine, he was nude, except for a surgical drape over his pubic area. What a sight! Both legs were missing at the hip, and his left arm was missing below the elbow. He was sutured starting just below his chin and continuing to his pubic area, the suture line disappearing from sight under the surgical drape.

My job was to monitor vital signs during the procedure. The blood pressure cuff was attached to his uninjured right arm, and I monitored his pulse at his right wrist. His breathing was monitored by observing his chest and face, and the first time I looked at him he was staring at me intently. I thought that he might be unconscious, but his eyes were wide open, and he was blinking on occasion. I tried to avoid looking at his eyes, which never moved in any direction, but his haunting stare kept drawing me back. His mouth was closed and he never moved to try to speak, but I could sense that he was mentally asking me to please help him. I was in awe the entire time and never said one word to him, simply assuring the doctor that his vitals were ok.

When we finished and I removed the blood pressure cuff, two other corpsmen then took over, covering him and otherwise ensuring his comfort. But as we changed places and I started to walk away, I glanced back, and he was still staring at me. The next time I worked on Ward 3A this patient was gone. I never learned his name, and my assumption was that he was transferred to a medical ward because of his internal injuries. Later I thought, maybe he didn't make it, and for several months that thought continued to haunt me. The problem with the advanced military medical care is that sometimes soldiers' lives are saved, who in past wars would have been killed in action. I tried to reassure myself that if he did not make it, it was probably the best for him.

On one weekend I was assigned to work the officer's ward where I encountered two interesting patients. The officers had their own individual rooms, some shared with another patient, but the one I was assigned to had his own private accommodation. He was a young Navy officer who communicated solely by repeating the words, "the weather business" over and over. With no physical or medical issues, his only problem was his mental condition. My job was simply to assist him. While I had to arrange his clothes for him, he could dress himself, and likewise Typical Ward (like 2A) after presenting his meals to him he could eat on his own.

Otherwise he simply sat in a chair or on the edge of the bed repeating "the weather business." Walking along with another Corpsman in the hallway outside the officers' rooms, he suddenly stopped me and pointed to a wheelchair parked in the hall ahead of us. The occupant, whose legs were missing, was talking to another patient. The Corpsman asked me if I knew who he was, and when I responded that I did not, he informed me that it was Chesty Puller's son. I knew who Chesty Puller was but did not even know that he had a son. I only learned more about Lewis Puller from his autobiography, *Fortunate Son*, published in 1991. One of the doctors in Vietnam who treated Puller after his legs were vaporized by a booby trap, wrote to him later noting that the decision to keep him alive was a difficult one. After a successful marriage and fathering two children, as well as a career as a lawyer and politician Puller eventually committed suicide. Is there a limit to the effort of care that should be provided based on the nature of the wounds? Medical personnel cannot make that judgment; each patient is treated with an all-out effort to save their life.

I've often thought about the corpsmen who worked with these injured Marines. One of them, who I met outside of ward duty was married with a pregnant wife. He told me that he had received orders to Vietnam. I was aghast at the thought of him leaving his pregnant wife to go into combat. However, he was upbeat and told me that she would be moving to live with her parents while he was gone. The senior Corpsman on Ward 3A, who I only knew as Stan, was a big guy with lots of energy. No matter what the situation he was always positive and had a good rapport with the patients. I learned later that Stan had also received orders to Vietnam, and I wondered how someone who spent time working on those severely injured Marines could then experience combat as a medic.

Needless to say, I left the wards awestruck and was a bit shaken by the experience. After finishing my specialty school, I was retained in the clinic as an instructor and supervisor. I often thought about the patients I left behind on the wards: some of them most likely did not survive, and what about those that did, like Lew Puller? One day I was told that someone was in the hall outside the clinic who wanted to see me. When I went out I was greeted by Ski. I had to look up, as he was taller than me; I had never seen him standing before. He stopped by to show me his new leg, and he grinned broadly as he pulled up his pants leg revealing his prosthesis. On another occasion a wheelchair nearly knocked me over as I was walking to the clinic. It stopped in front of me, and the occupant was facing me said “Hi doc, how are you?” I was dumbfounded. He had no legs, and his left arm was missing below the elbow. It was the patient from Ward 3A that I suspected might not have survived. After telling him that I was fine, he assured me he was fine too but he had to go. He was late for physical therapy. Maybe the effort to save lives is well worth it in any case.

U. S. Army Medics: An Overview

U. S. Army medics in Vietnam were highly valued soldiers who often ran toward danger to treat the wounded, a role that included both combat and day-to-day medical care. They provided critical care for battle injuries, managed illnesses such as malaria and dysentery, and served as a vital source of morale for their units. Medics in this war were distinguished from those in previous conflicts by their combat roles, often carrying weapons and facing the same dangers as the infantry they supported.

Role and responsibilities

- **Combat care**: Medics were often the first responders on the battlefield, providing immediate medical treatment to stabilize wounded soldiers and prepare them for evacuation. This frequently involved going through active firefights to reach casualties.
- **Medical kits**: Their medical kits were essential, containing items such as bandages, tourniquets, morphine, and supplies for IVs and treating chest wounds.

- **Preventative care**: Beyond combat injuries, medics spent significant time on daily health issues such as dehydration, malaria, and other tropical diseases, as well as treating sick villagers.
- **Morale and brotherhood**: Medics were also crucial for unit morale, and the bonds they formed with the soldiers they served were often very strong.

Dangers and sacrifices

- **Combat risks**: Medics faced immense danger, with their life expectancy during firefights sometimes cited as extremely low. They often operated without the benefit of body armor or bulletproof helmets.
- **Casualties**: Tragically, over 1,100 medics were killed in action during the War. Many more were wounded.
- **Awards**: Their bravery earned many of them national recognition, with at least 20 earning the Medal of Honor, the nation's highest award for military valor.

Training and equipment

- **Basic training**: Combat medics received about ten weeks of medical training, which focused on triaging wounds, administering first aid, and treating shock.
- **Combat gear**: Unlike medics in previous wars, Vietnam medics typically carried standard-issue

weapons, such as an M16 rifle, a .45 caliber pistol, and grenades, along with their medical equipment.

Combat and daily duties

- **Frontline treatment:** Medics were often the first responders to injuries in combat, treating wounds and stabilizing patients for medevac, frequently risking their own lives to do so.
- **Weaponry:** In contrast to previous wars, Vietnam medics were armed with M16A1 rifles, and sometimes a .45 caliber pistol and grenades, to protect themselves and their unit.
- **General health:** A significant portion of their work involved preventing and treating common health problems such as dehydration, malaria, and dysentery.
- **Treating civilians:** They also provided medical care to South Vietnamese villagers, regardless of potential risks.

Medical equipment and training

- **Basic medical training:** Medics received about 10 weeks of medical training, which included lessons on administering shots, bandaging, carrying the injured, applying tourniquets, and using morphine.
- **Advanced life support:** They were also trained in treating shock, administering IVs, and basic anatomy.

- **Medical kits:** A typical medical kit contained bandages, abdominal dressings, flexible plastic coverings for sucking chest wounds, IV clamps, and morphine.
- **Challenges:** Resources were not always readily available, and medics often had to work with limited supplies, as noted by one medic who had to treat with only a flashlight and burning matches, this Facebook post.

Dangers and sacrifices

- **High casualty rate:** Over 1,100 medics were killed in action during the war, and many more were wounded, underscoring the extreme dangers they faced.

My Vietnam Trip

by Lynden E Belin, U. S. Amy Medic

It was the middle of August 1966 and our training at the Medical Field Service School in Fort Sam Houston, Texas was almost over. Everyone was wondering what the next assignments would be. We were eating lunch in the mess hall when one of my friends told me that I was being assigned to Vietnam. Vietnam however was not high on our preference list, but everyone knew it was a strong possibility. I was not sure if my friend was giving me a bad time or if it was true, so after eating, I went to the company headquarters to check the poster board. As I stood in the hot San Antonio sun my eyes traced the names until I found mine, assigned to Vietnam.

My buddy Gary Likes had convinced me to have my name placed at the top of the draft board so we could train together since he was being drafted, and I had received my first letter from the board. I noticed that he was assigned to Korea. Lucky guy. Gary would go directly to South Korea, but I would get a thirty day leave. I had driven my car from Oregon for the Advanced Infantry Training (AIT) and with the leave I was granted, I could get my car home.

On March 23, 1966, Gary and I were drafted into the US army. After we were physically checked at the draft center, we were sitting at a long table with men on both sides. A man entered the room and told anyone who wanted to be a Marine to raise their hand. No one raised their hand, so he started picking men from the nearest end of the table. He stopped two men before me. What a relief. I am not a good swimmer so I may not have survived their training.

A week later Gary and I rode a Greyhound bus full of recruits from the San Francisco airport to the Fort Ord induction center. As soon as the bus door opened at Fort Ord the drill instructors (DI) were screaming at us. One poor recruit's suitcase flew open spilling everything on the ground. This gave the DIs a perfect target to start their indoctrination. A week later Gary, I and another drafted recruit flew from the Monterey Bay airport to Fort Sam Houston in San Antonio, Texas. The day of the flight we received a group of vaccinations including flu shots. Each of us came down with all the flu symptoms when we got to the Monterey Bay Airport. The next morning as I emerged from the airplane into the sweltering hot San Antonio sun, I was feeling well.

Basic training started April 4 at Fort Sam Houston. Since we were conscientious objectors, basic training was 6 weeks long, with no rifle training. Of course, the DIs gave us a hard time during training, and I was surprised on the day of graduation, when they brought us beer, soda pop, and snacks to celebrate with us. After basic training we had a thirty day leave before Advanced Individual Training (AIT) started. The ten weeks of Medic training started June 13 and ended August 19. AIT training covered essential skills for a field medic and for a hospital orderly. We learned how to observe a person's vital signs and how to watch for someone going into shock including how to treat them. CPR training was included. Training included the critical steps of how to treat a sucking chest wound. Application of bandages, splints and tourniquets was also learned. We studied giving IVs and shots. Gary never forgot how I double clutched when practicing shots on him. In other words, I poked him but didn't penetrate his skin, so I had to poke him again. For those of us headed for hospital duty, we also studied how to make hospital beds and use bed pans.

During medic training Kenny Walker ran around with Gary and me. Kenny received another thirty day leave as did everyone going to Vietnam. I agreed to take him to Denver to meet his wife at a store parking lot. A wire had come loose from my car's overdrive, so I crawled under my car to reattach it while we waited for Kenny's wife to arrive. Kenny's wife arrived while I was crawling out from under my car. She admonished me to drive carefully and be safe since my family wanted to see me. The irony of it is that Kenny returned from Vietnam in a body bag. I often felt sorry for his wife even though I only met her that one time.

When leave was over, I was at Travis Air Base for a couple of days. The last night before we were to fly to Vietnam, they locked us in a warehouse with cots because they were concerned that we would go Absent Without Leave (AWOL). If I had planned to go AWOL, I would not have shown up at Travis. The next afternoon we flew westward following the sun low on the horizon until we dropped into Hawaii. Again, they were afraid we would go AWOL, so we sat on the commercial airplane with the door open while we looked out the windows at palm trees in the airport lights. The stewardesses were very friendly and came and talked with us as we waited to continue the flight. I am sure that was because they knew where we were going.

Hot humid air engulfed us as we rode from Tan Son Nhut Air Base to the Long Binh holding company in the Saigon area. The dawn was starting to reveal coconut palms and banana trees amongst the din of the small motorcycles, lambretta taxies and 1940 vintage Ford sedans with diesel engine transplants. There was no sign of combat except for vehicle traffic but I was still apprehensive as all of Vietnam was a combat zone. It was September 22, and my tour of Vietnam had begun.

In a few days I was back at Tan Son Nhut Air Base sitting on a deuce and a half (2 ½ ton) truck with other troops headed up Highway 1 to the Cu Chi base camp twenty five kilometers northwest of Saigon. They issued everyone M16 rifles, except for me since I was a conscientious objector. All the ammunition was in wooden boxes under the seats. If we entered a combat situation, loading the weapons would take considerable time before we could defend ourselves. This was typical of trips between the Cu Chi base camp and Saigon. Thay say there is the right way, the wrong way, and the military way. This sure did not seem like the right way to me. Unless the troops were headed to Saigon, they always left the Cu Chi base camp with multiple fully loaded magazines including one in the weapon. When I got to the Cu Chi base camp I was assigned to the Medical Platoon, Head Quarters Company, 1st Battalion, 27th Infantry Regiment (H/1/27 "Wolfhounds"), of the 25th Infantry Division.

This is when I became a "Wolfhound," which is the 27th regiment's mascot. This assignment was fortunate as the 27th had trained at Schofield Barracks in Hawaii and been in Vietnam for one half of a year. They were a combat hardened and capable fighting unit with a good spirit. In addition, our sector of the base camp was in an abandoned rubber plantation, so we had shade unlike most of the base camp. When we had inspection, I would use sap from the trees to glue on the missing patches on my uniform. There were always missing patches.

The Medical Platoon is one of the several units in Headquarters Company of the regiment. It consisted of approximately 36 medical personnel with one medic assigned to each of the four platoons in the three rifle companies, Alpha, Bravo and Charlie. The rest of the medics had various specialties including that of a pharmacist. This Medical Platoon staffs the dispensary in the base camp and the Forward Aid Station (FAS) on military operations in the field. The constant operations against the enemy required the Aid Station to be in the field with the infantry about 25 out of every 30 days.

The Medical Platoon Leader is the Battalion Surgeon who is a medical doctor (MD) and a captain in the Medical Corps. The next officer is a lieutenant in the Medical Service Corps (MSC). Among his other duties he is the Evacuation Section Leader responsible during field operations for bringing the wounded from where they were wounded and treated by the platoon medic to the aid station. Thereafter, further stabilization is performed, if necessary, and then evacuation by helicopter to a Surgical or Evacuation Hospital for advanced medical care. When I arrived in the platoon, the Battalion Surgeon was Capt.

Qwie T. Chew, the MSC officer was Lt. Paul T. Scott and the platoon sergeant was Staff Sgt Bernabe Cenal.

Our Medical Platoon's Aid Station - 1966

Beginning Tour At Headquarters

When I arrived at Cu Chi base camp I was promoted to private first class. The rule was that they could not send a man into combat before he had been promoted to PFC. The hooches we lived in had wooden floors and 2 by 4 walls with bed high wood siding and screen above. When I arrived the heavy canvas roofs were sweltering hot, but they were soon replaced with corrugated steel, which helped a lot. During the monsoon, shoes left on the floor for a long time would grow mold on the soles. We slept under poncho liners and did not get cold, as long as we stayed dry. Fully loaded ammo belts and weapons hung on the walls next to family photographs and playboy pinup pictures. Things on the walls often rattled when 105-mm Howitzers were fired and with the whopping vibration of incoming Huey helicopters being a common occurrence.

We learned to appreciate the Huey's deep rhythmic sound. Riding them was sure preferable to humping rice paddies. Besides, some of their maneuvers fed my hot rodder spirit. On my first Huey ride I was sitting beside the door gunner and toward the back of the chopper. I was enjoying the ride but when we reached several hundred feet, I realized there was nothing to hang on to. I decided that if we banked and I started to fall out, I would grab the pole the machine gun was mounted on. Later I learned you are swinging like a pendulum from the rotor. We could have boxes stacked high in the helicopter and bank at about a forty five degree angle and they would not fall out. After I was in the field for a while, I would sit Indian style in the open doorway just behind the pilots. When we landed, I was the first one off and I would run for cover, until the rest of the platoon caught up. On one trip back to our basecamp, we were cruising at several thousand feet. I was dropping empty C ration cans out and watching them land in the rice paddies below. I let one leg hang out too far and the wind started pulling me out. I only had the aluminum floor to hang onto but luckily was able to get my leg back in.

The Medical Platoon was looking for someone to fill a Rest and Recouperation (R & R) slot early in my Vietnam tour, so I accepted the weeklong R&R to Bangkok, Thailand. Bangkok looked a lot like Saigon. The people's straw hats had a little different shape and many of the better buildings had more modern architecture but there was still poverty next door to them. More of the stores had glass windows. Saigon showed more scars since Vietnam had been at war for most of my life, starting with the overthrow of the French. The Bangkok floating market was interesting. I visited the huge Reclining Buddha and the Golden Buddha. The Golden Buddha was about seven feet tall and the largest piece of gold I have seen. We drove on the wrong side of the road on my tour to the River Kwai from World War Two fame.

Assigned to an Infantry Platoon

In October, I was assigned to the second platoon of Bravo Company 1/27. At first the men in the platoon were rather unhappy since I was not carrying a weapon. This meant less fire power for the platoon. After a few weeks they were resigned to the situation, and I did not hear any more complaints. I think they decided that I would not play favorites and would support them wherever they went. One night a squad was going on ambush. The machine gunner told me he would feel better if everyone had a weapon. He wanted me to carry his .45 so I did that one time. I never fired a military weapon until a few years ago when I fired a friend's M-1 Garand, and that was a fun weapon.

I was soon promoted to the rank of E-3 after being assigned to Bravo Company. On operations I caried an aid bag which was made of green army canvas with a shoulder strap. It contained scissors, a probe, long forceps, an airway, various bandages, tape, band aids, ace wraps, morphine syrette, bacitracin ointment, an albumin IV, and aspirin. I also carried a flashlight with a clip attached to the shoulder strap. In my ammo pouch I carried an instamatic camera wrapped in the plastic wrap from a military radio battery. Often on patrol when there was no action, I would be taking pictures while the rest of the platoon carried their weapons.

One day while we were waiting for a Huey ride, two men were playing "stick 'em." They would stand facing each other and take turns throwing a knife into the ground. The man that did not through the knife had to stretch one leg to the knife without moving his other leg. One knife throw hit the edge of the cloth bag that carries M79 (grenade launcher) rounds. One of the grenades shot out of the bag. I do not remember a big explosion so maybe the grenade did not travel far enough to arm itself, but one man received several puncture wounds. I bandaged the wounds and soon the Huey arrived and we headed home. This was the first wound I treated in the field.

The first time I landed in what was believed to be a hot landing zone (LZ) I was with several platoons on Hueys.

The door gunners were lighting up the LZ and adrenaline was running high. We landed in a rice paddy and swept right into a rubber plantation and then turned left into a pineapple field. The platoon leaders decided we were going in the wrong direction, so we turned around and headed back into the rubber plantation. The helicopter crews thought we had moved on, so they came back shooting up the rubber plantation. We dropped to the ground and tried to line up with the eight inch diameter trees. I was worried for my own safety but that was somewhat muted as I was also worried about my troops. I did not want any of them hurt and I did not want to have to move around while the bullets were flying. Luckly no one got hurt.

The Battalion Commander, Major Guy S. Meloy III, initiated Eagle Flights with much success. I enjoyed the Eagle Flights. We would come in fast and low in Hueys to start a patrol. A second flight would come onto the rear of the village and capture anyone running from the area. Anyone who started running was considered to be a suspected VC. Coming in fast and low reduced the ability for the VC to shoot at the choppers and gave a surprise start to our patrols. Often, we would receive a few sniper rounds but would not find the sniper. There were many tunnels and hidden trap doors for them to hide in. The book "*The Tunnels of Cu Chi*" by Tom Mongold provides an understanding of the lengthy and elaborate tunnel system throughout this area.

The Battle Of Attleboro

In August 1966, the 196th Light Infantry Brigade arrived at Tay Ninh and started building a base camp and began patrols. In late October they found indications of North Vietnam Army (NVA) and Viet Cong (VC) operations north of Dau Tieng. The NVA's official name was People's Liberation Armed Forces Viet Cong (PLAF) and the VC's official name was the People's Army Vietnam (PAVN). After receiving intelligence that the 9th VC Division was advancing toward Dau Tieng, the 25th Infantry Division placed the 1/27 Battalion under the command of the 196th Brigade. On November 1, 1966, the 25th Division ordered the 1/27 Battalion to move from our Cu Chi base camp to Dau Tieng. The first two nights we slept by a large, abandoned house on the old Michelin rubber plantation.

On Thursday, November 3, 1966, the 196th Brigade sent two of their battalions attacking northward into the jungle. Twenty minutes later Bravo Company, 1/27 flew to an LZ east of these companies and swept northwest. The LZ was covered with a thick stand of elephant grass that was several feet above our heads. The blades of grass were sharp, so we tried to avoid getting cut. We worked our way into the nearby jungle and came to a worn path at a small river crossing. There was a small plastic shelter with a gunny sack filled with grub hoe heads stamped *Made in*

China. We turned left and headed away from the river on this trail which was wide enough for a jeep.

Thirty minutes after we landed, Charlie Company 1/27 landed in an LZ about three kilometers northwest of Bravo Company 1/27. It was also in elephant grass next to the jungle. When they advanced toward the jungle they came under intense fire power from the jungle. This was the beginning of the Battle of Attleboro.

With the intensity of the fight Major Meloy called in Alpha Company, 1/27 to join Charlie Company 1/27 and then he joined them on the ground. Capt. Fred Henderson and Sgt. Sam Solomon the command structure of Charie Company 1/27 were badly wounded and eventually died before they could be medevaced. The 196th Brigade commander sent in three of his own companies to join the battle. By late afternoon with air and artillery support, Major Meloy was able to drive the enemy out of their position and move into the jungle. He now had a secure LZ to bring in supplies and medevac wounded. Major Meloy now brought in the 1/27th Battalion Aid Station plus more mortars.

The next morning, November 4, 1966, Alpha Company 1/27 led the battle group farther into the jungle. After advancing 200 meters they ran into the enemy's bunker line and were pinned down under intense fire power. The bunker line stretched for almost 1,000 meters. They were well fortified concrete bunkers and well concealed by the dense jungle. To suppress the enemy, friendly bombs and artillery fell within 10 meters of the US perimeter. The enemy was returning mortar rounds on our lines. The same day the 2/27 battalion was moved from our Cu Chi Basecamp to Dau Tieng. Charlie Company, 2/27 was deployed into the battle but due to the confusion of battle, ended up on the far side of the enemy bunkers, pinned down behind enemy lines.

I knew little of what was happening to anyone except for Bravo Company 1/27 until I read about it later in Captain Robert P. Garrett's book titled "*A Wolfhound Reminisces.*" Captain Garrett was a West Point class of 1962 graduate and my company commander. I am sharing what I have since learned of these events to give context to my experience. Although Bravo Company engaged the enemy along with the other rifle companies, it suffered fewer casualties. Captain Gerrett's calm, superb leadership was likely a factor.

Word came down that Charlie Company 1/27 had been pinned down under heavy combat. It was apparent that they were substantially outnumbered. The next day we learned that with reinforcements they had fought their way out of the grass and into the jungle. The jungle was so thick we could not hear the combat three kilometers away. I did not know most of the men involved in the combat except for the 1/27 medics. I was a member of that platoon and was assigned to the second platoon of Bravo Company 1/27.

On the first day in the jungle, November 3, Bravo Company 1/27 came to a large, burned area where a rice cache had been destroyed. In another place there was a large tin roofed enclosure which stored rice. The jungle canopy was so dense this cache could not be seen by flying over the area. Travel was slow since we walked in the jungle off the road to avoid possible mines or an ambush.

On November 4 we enlarged a clearing so Hueys could resupply us. When the first helicopter started to descend into the jungle, its rotors hit some of the top branches of the jungle canopy, so the pilot climbed above the jungle canopy and dropped supplies from above. The water jerry cans would dent a little when they landed but none of them ruptured. Since water was very limited, our platoon sergeant watched as we filled our canteens. If we spilled any water, he ended our turn. It was hot and I sure would have liked more water.

That afternoon we formed a column to turn left into the jungle. My platoon leader, Lt. Slavey, told me he wanted me in the middle of the column and if anything happened, he wanted me to get to the front. This confirmed that we were headed toward the battle. In a short distance we were pinned down by small arms fire. In the thick jungle you could not see where it came from. It was turning dark when we turned back. That night we were spread out in ambush positions along a crossroad. During the night we eliminated a column of enemy reinforcements headed toward the battle.

The next day, November 5, we again formed columns and headed toward the battle. After a while, the jungle opened into an area with paths and round holes in the ground. So, we knew we were in an enemy base camp. A little farther we found US soldiers lying on the ground. They told us to get down, or we would get shot so we took cover behind ant hills and downed trees. Soon both sides started shooting. Lt. Slavey later told me he saw a VC eating his lunch in one of the holes as he walked by. Later that day replacements were brought in and we evacuated to Tay Ninh Basecamp. As we left the jungle, F-4 Phantoms were flying low toward us. Their bombs would separate just before they passed overhead. Since then, I have learned that our other flank was able to encircle C Company 2/27 and help get them from behind enemy lines as we swept from our original position to friendly lines at the battle site.

We stayed in Tay Ninh several days to rest before resuming patrols near Tay Ninh. During one of these patrols, we set up camp in a thick jungle. One night, two men from my platoon were forward observers stationed outside the wire. During the night, they were scared and whispering on the radio that the VC were making animal calls, trying to locate their position. Thankfully, the VC were unsuccessful, and the men returned safely the next morning.

That same night we had incoming mortar rounds. One of my men received a broken leg and a few shrapnel wounds. His pulse and breathing were good. Since he was not going into shock, I gave him a shot of morphine. One of the men in my platoon held a flashlight while two other men helped cut branches. They helped me splint his leg and we made a litter out of two branches and our shirts for webbing. We took him to the 1/27 Aid Station. When we got there, a man was laying on a litter. His head was completely covered in a white bandage. He had reached for a radio outside of his fox hole without putting his helmet on. A mortar round had destroyed the back of his head. When we got back to Cu Chi, the Bravo Company medics obtained a resupply of liters to carry on patrols.

After we had been in the field for about a week, we came across an abandoned road in the jungle. The water in the adjacent ditch was clean but clouded by the bottom sediment. As soon as I stepped in, it provided me with one of the most enjoyable baths of my life.

One day on patrol we were in thick bamboo stands. Part of the way we crawled on hands and knees through the bamboo. There were a lot of leeches on the ground. They were a couple inches long and moved like inch worms. When we stopped in a clearing for the night, my men asked me how to get rid of the leaches. Medic school did not address this problem but being the medic the men looked to me for the answer. I spent my younger years in the John Day Valley of eastern Oregon where sage brush grew as high as the roof of my father's pickup cab. Many ticks lived in the sagebrush. The local remedy for ticks was to light a match to their backside, and they would pull their heads out. I gave this as a remedy for the leaches and fortunately it worked. I remember the look of horror when one of my men found a leach on his private parts. I unrolled my poncho that night to sleep on and was glad to be leech free in the morning. The Vietnamese kids were not as averse to leaches. They would come out of the canals with leaches the size of large slugs attached to them. They would call the leeches number 10 and throw them back into the canal before diving in again. Number 1 meant very good, and number 10 meant very bad.

Back at our Base Camp

The latrines at Base Camp were nice wooden structures on concrete slabs. There were small doors in the back that opened the area below the seats. Fifty five gallon barrels were cut around the middle and placed under the seats for receptacles. Each day the barrels were removed and burned with diesel fuel. Being a medic I was assigned to oversee this operation. On Christmas Day two new soldiers burned the barrels. They could hardly believe this was their Christmas activity.

Late New Years Eve, the second platoon was awakened for formation. I learned that we were back-up for another platoon on ambush and they were hit with enemy fire. I may have been the only sober person there. One of the squad leaders counted his squad by facing each man like you would for an inspection. He would continue counting several positions past the last man. Even with several attempts he was too drunk to count his squad. I was very worried about going out of the wire with men locked and loaded while in their condition. Before we headed for the wire, the platoon on ambush radioed back that they had the situation under control, so we went back to bed.

That same squad leader would get drunk the first night we were back at basecamp after living in the field for a while. At these times he would want to fight and would go through the hooches grabbing weapons from the walls while the other soldiers wrestled them away from him. Yet he was a seasoned troop and one of the best men to be on patrol with. The sight of dead VC lying on the ground bothered me at first, but I rationalized that once they were dead, they were no different than a dead animal. This helped me adjust to combat.

One day Bravo Company was on patrol, we surprised four VC who ran from us as we came to the edge of the jungle. They ran across a small grassy area. Two of them dove into a ditch on the far side of the clearing and the other two kept running onto the rice paddy berms beyond the ditch. They were a few hundred yards along the berms by the time Bravo Company lined up along the ditch and started shooting at them. They just kept running single file until they entered the jungle about a thousand yards away. I was quite surprised that no one hit them. After the runners were gone we pulled two men out of the ditch and started bandaging the bullet wounds we had inflicted. I think we used all of the bandages we four medics had and yet there were still unbandaged wounds. We took the wounded VC with us back to our Cu Chi Base Camp for further medical treatment and for interrogation.

The VC had been mining the bridge over the Rach Vam Trang River just south of Trang Bang. One rainy night we set up an ambush to catch them. We left the Trang Bang soccer field and circled around the outskirts of the city starting on the northern edge. To avoid revealing our position we were not allowed to smoke or wear our rubber ponchos. Ponchos would make noise and reflect light. Our mood was further enhanced by the eerie oriental music coming from town. The river was flooding at the ambush site, so we set up a few hundred feet away on higher ground next to some banana trees. We were wet, some were chilled all night, but our native guide and his interpreter slept in their ponchos. We did not see any VC so just before dawn we blew the claymore mines before leaving. When the guide and his interpreter heard the explosions, they dove into a couple of shallow ditches full of water. I couldn't help but laugh since they had been toasty all night while we had been chilled.

I was on another squad sized ambush where we were laying in a ditch beside a road. I had fallen asleep and when I woke up, the rest of the squad was asleep also. We had been on patrol that day, so we had very little rest before going on ambush. Being the medic, I had to go on every patrol and on every ambush. It could be a challenge to stay awake on a night ambush after a day patrolling. If my platoon was not on patrol before a night ambush, then I was given the day off to rest for the ambush.

The southern tip of the Iron Triangle was several miles across rice paddies from our Cu Chi Base Camp. Every time we entered the Iron Triangle we expected to have a fight on our hands. It had been a strong hold for the Viet Minh while fighting the French and now it was a VC stronghold. After entering the Iron Triangle one of the 1/27 companies was pinned down for the rest of the day and much of the night but was able to flush out the small village. The next day they moved on and Bravo Company replaced them. We spent that night in that village.

The following morning, we walked on rice paddy berms as we turned toward our Cu Chi Base Camp. Artillery rounds started falling behind us. We could tell the next round would be too close, so we dove off the berms into the rice paddies. The mortarman's radio man was behind me and the mortarman was behind him. I and the mortarman dove to the left and the mortarman's radio man dove to the right. I heard the call for medic, but when I got up I found the mortarman's radio man face down with a large steam of blood pumping from the left side of his buttock. I put a compression bandage on him and started an albumin IV. Soon we had a medevac flight. He was alive when it arrived but showed no signs of regaining consciousness. He did not survive. The attack had ended and we were no longer under the pressure or in the chaos of battle. I had time to think and to feel. After the medevac, I wondered happened to the radio man and it really dampened my spirits.

The VC often mortared the Cu Chi Base Camp from the Iron Triangle. One afternoon 2nd Platoon of B Company went on an ambush to intercept them. Their base camp was several miles north of the Cu Chi Base Camp and barely inside the jungle along the rice paddies that separated our base camp from the Iron Triangle. The man watching the compass heading was right on but the man counting the clicks let us go too far. Just before dusk we saw two VC run into the jungle. We followed them and found worn paths and tunnel entrances. They took a few shots at us as we walked through their small camp. We turned left and spent a quiet night behind rice paddy berms. The next morning the platoon left the machine gunner and two riflemen to cover our evacuation until we were out of rifle range. I started leaving with the main body of the platoon but realized my most vulnerable men were the machine gunner and the two riflemen left behind. I stopped several hundred yards from them and crouched behind a berm as the rest of the platoon continued evacuating. That was a little uncomfortable since I was by myself without a weapon. I joined the machine gunner and riflemen as they evacuated. Even though the VC took a few pot shots at us, no one was hurt.

One day, we were on the Trang Bang soccer field waiting for transportation. A tank recovery vehicle passed going north on Highway One. As was common, there was a group of villagers standing along the other side of the road. After the vehicle passed we noticed the group was excited and standing around a preteen girl. She had gotten too close to the vehicle and had been hit so I and another medic checked her injuries. She was standing but in considerable pain and she was traumatized. She was bloody but had no apparent broken bones. We bandaged her wounds and gave her a shot of morphine before medevac'ing her and her mother to Cu Chi Base Camp.

Occasionally one of my men would ask me about some disease. Usually, I had heard the name before but knew almost nothing about the disease. Our medic training did not cover diseases. I believe the man had a relative or friend dealing with the disease and knew more about it than I did. I talked to them until I understood what they knew about the disease and then I would agree with what they knew. This led them to believe I was a good medic and knew more than I did.

One time while on patrol we found some children in a remote farming area. We asked them, "Are you South Viet or VC?" They said, "When South Viet come, we are South Viet and when VC come, we are VC." If they did not want to be a part of the war, they had no other choice. If we found them with a weapon, we would take their weapon and bring them in for interrogation. If the VC found a weapon, they would take it from them and possibly conscript them into service. Unless the Vietnamese were in uniform or had a weapon you did not know which side of the war they might be on. It was like walking down a US street and trying to determine whether a person is a Republican or a Democrat by their appearance.

One day Bravo Company was in Trang Bang waiting for a convoy to start heading back to our Cu Chi Base Camp. We were loaded in the back of deuce and a half trucks. Across the two lane paved road was the school. It had a fence along the road and about 50 feet of courtyard between the fence and school. The school was a long one story building with an exterior door to each classroom but no windows facing the road. We threw a full C ration can against a door. A minute later, the door swung open and the students rushed out to get the C ration. The teacher came out and sternly herded the kids back in. Just before closing the door, she turned and gave us a big smile so of course we threw more C rations. Each time we got the same response.

One of the 1/27th companies did an air raid into Cambodia looking for a POW. Bravo Company landed in a grassy area next to the boarder of Cambodia and waited as a backup for the raid. We were told to remove our dog tags and leave all identification back at Cu Chi Base Camp. If we had entered Cambodia, I am sure they would have recognized who we were any way. In training we were told that if we were captured, we were to only tell our captors, our name, rank, and service number. The dog tags would have only provided this information plus our blood type and religious preference. I did not hear of any casualties and I do not think they found the POW.

During the dry season, we occasionally walked through a hot pepper field while on patrol. I would pick a pepper to add to my C rations. That was a good boost to the flavor. A glob of fat floated on the liquid in the main C ration entrées. I would melt the fat by burning the C-ration box around the entrée can. This made the food much more palatable. I learned that it was easier to wade through flooded rice paddies if you step on the rice plants. You would not sink as deep in the mud. If we did not return to basecamp, we slept with our boots and wet socks on. The jungle boots had two one-way valves to drain water and a double layered screen insole, which helped. I would rather keep wet socks on than try to put wet socks back on in the morning. Some of the men were also worried about not having boots on if there was an enemy attack at night. However, it was my job as a medic to encourage the men to change into dry socks. During the monsoon it was hard to keep a pair of dry socks. Wet feet caused a lot of ringworm and jungle rot infections. Sometimes the ring worm would get up to the waistline. The loose shirts did not provide the environment for it to progress higher.

When camped in the field, occasionally men would make two men pup tents by tying two ponchos together and supporting them with rope and short sticks. During the monsoon season, our air mattresses usually kept us above the water flowing through the tent. That was pure luxury.

I encouraged the troops to take a daily quinine primaquine pill, a large orange horse pill, as a prophylactic for malaria. I also encouraged the men to take salt tablets to counteract electrolyte loss through sweat. The 1/27 Aid Station at Cu Chi used a jeep to carry a Mighty Mite Fogger around Base Camp to kill the abundant mosquitos. Even so, in Base Camp we often slept under mosquito nets over our cots. I treated a few other combat wounds and other problems from living in the jungle and wading through rice paddies but none of them were life threatening. I received the rank of specialist 4th class (E4), February 16, 1966, while in the field with Bravo Company.

Back at Headquarters

In April 1967 I was reassigned to the Aid Station in Cu Chi Base Camp. They gave me the job of pharmacist. I had taken one year of biology in college, but I surely was not a pharmacist. However, the Battalion Surgeon was a good coach. He wrote prescriptions and I filled them. It was my responsibility to procure the medical supplies from the base hospital supply facility. If narcotics were needed the Battalion Surgeon would come along to sign for them. The field medics bags contained several surettes of morphine and none of them signed for the morphine.

One time a pet monkey got into the pharmacy. He was up on the shelves tearing open sealed sterile bandages and other packages. When I tried to run him out, he bared his teeth and lunged at me. He proved to be a true combatant, but I finally got him out without getting bitten. That ended his time as a pet.

The part of the Aid Station that stayed at Cu Chi Base Camp functioned as a day dispensary. Medivac flights from field operations usually went directly to either the 7th Surgical Hospital or the 12th Evacuation Hospital at the Cu Chi Base Camp. We treated infections, especially ringworm and jungle rot. We provided many shots and kept vaccinations current. Sometimes rats would bite soldiers while they took their turn sleeping in the perimeter bunkers. When this happened, we gave them the painful fourteen shots for rabies at the Aid Station. They received one shot per day in the flat muscle of the stomach. Cleaning and rebandaging wounds was a common activity at the Aid Station. I remember working on a few ingrown toenails. I did several sutures under supervision.

Me at our Wolfhound Aid Station at Cu Chi Base Camp

One of the E-6 medics would have new medics practice inserting needles into his veins to prepare them for giving IVs in the field. Each new medic had done this in training, but a refresher was good preparation for combat situations. After he had been poked a few times, I would let them practice on me.

Occasionally we would go on Medical Civil Action Program (MEDCAP) trips which provided free medical care for villagers to generate goodwill and to learn who was mining the roads. We were accompanied by an interpreter. The villagers would line up in single file to be checked by the medical platoon doctor. I would dispense medicine from a footlocker, and another medic would give each person a bar of soap. One day we found out how valuable the soap was. We had a half box of soap left over. The soap dispensing medic started passing our soap without making the villagers line up. Soon they were rushing him from every direction. He threw the box and fled. The villagers of all ages ended up having a tug of war over bars of soap.

The ARVN compound where we held MEDCAP visits

The 12th Evacuation Hospital had a separate supply office for MEDCAPs. Their only penicillin shots came in large glass syringes with huge horse needles. When I had to give a baby a shot of penicillin, I would have several medics hold the baby stretched out face down while I quickly jabbed the needle halfway into its buttocks, stopping before I hit any bone. The baby would squirm, so we tried to hold it still to reduce damage from the inserted needle. Children often had small scabs on their legs. There were puss pockets under the scabs so instead of leaving the scabs to heal as you would for a normal wound, we picked the scabs and cleaned under them before bandaging. I wondered if this problem was partly due to their lack of soap to clean their wounds.

There was a small ARVN camp a little north of Saigon. The south Vietnam government provided medical care for the soldiers but not their dependents that lived with them. Occasionally, we provided MEDCAP treatments for the dependents. One day while I was in the MEDCAP supply office, the supply medics were playing with a grenade. One of them pulled the pin and dropped the grenade. After I recovered from face down on the ground outside the office, I realized the grenade did not explode. Evidently, they had previously removed the cap from the grenade and exploded it away from the grenade, making it a dud. Halfway through my time back at Headquarters we remodeled the Aid Station and completely sided the walls with wood. This provided more privacy. It was attractive but it stopped the air flow which increased the temperature inside.

One day our medical platoon sergeant asked us to tell him if we were eligible for a promotion. Danny Rousseau and I were both eligible for promotion to E-5 at the same time. Danny talked to the platoon sergeant who sent him to the first sergeant. The first sergeant told Danny that if he went back into the field with an infantry company, he would give Danny the E5 rank. Danny did not plan to be a career man and did not feel it was worth it. I felt the same and did not talk with our platoon sergeant. I retired an E-4.

One of the new medics wrote a letter to his parents and placed it in his footlocker at the Medical Platoon. He requested that I mail it to his parents if he was killed In Action (KIA). It just seemed morbid to me. He was killed while assigned to an infantry platoon. It took me several days to decide to send his letter. The new medic that replaced me in 2nd platoon B company was KIA several months after I returned to the Aid Station at Headquarters Company.

The canvas jeep roofs were removed during the dry season so they would not get baked in the sun. Rain returned several weeks before the official date for the end of the monsoon season. During this time, it would pour buckets of rain for an hour or so. Since the monsoons had not officially started, we could not put the jeep roofs back on. I was not caught riding in a jeep during one of these downpours, but I let it irritate me that we could not put the jeep roofs back on yet.

One day I helped take the trash from the mess hall to the dump. We had several fifty five gallon drums of trash in the back of a deuce and a half truck. They were full of what looked like pig slop with a few pieces of good food. At the dump, Vietnamese were scrounging through the trash. They wore their conical straw hats, and many wore what looked like long wool socks without shoes as they waded through the muck. We tried to get them to move away from the back of the truck before we tipped the drums over so we would not cover them with garbage. They would not move so we turned our heads and dumped the drums anyway. Somehow, they got out of the way just in time.

Treating some young Vietnamese children at our Aid Station

Sometimes I would have guard duty at the sandbag bunkers on the perimeter. In the rainy season when things were quiet at night you would hear splashing. It would make me wonder whether someone was walking around the perimeter fence or if it was just frogs jumping. I was never sure someone was out there, so I never responded. Since I was unarmed, I would have awakened one of the armed guards sleeping in the bunker.

One night a soldier went missing, having left the Cu Chi Base Camp to talk with a Catholic priest because the atrocities of war were bothering him. I was on duty at the headquarters bunker where there was a switchboard for the telephones. The switch board was a wooden peg board with one wire attached to each plastic fitting that had a male and a female terminal. To connect the lines, you plugged the plastic fittings together. I was receiving calls in rapid succession from excited officers and NCOs. In the dim light I was trying to determine which plastic fittings to stack together. I made some incorrect connections which added to the excitement. After a while they brought a tank along the outside perimeter of the fence. Its huge headlight above the gun lit up the night. Finally, everything returned to a quite night. I think they finally found the missing soldier.

Medic, Dennis Mason, was due to replace me as the pharmacist when he returned from the field to the 1/27 Aid Station. He was close to getting a degree as a pharmacist before being drafted and would replace me as the pharmacist. He extended his stay in the field by two days and lost both legs on the second day. I felt guilty that I was still in the pharmacist position. If he had been back in that position, he would not have been injured. Years later at a Wolfhound reunion he told me that he stayed in the field longer to take the place of one of the medics under him that was sick. I do wish that I had visited him while he was in the 12 Evacuation Hospital in Cu Chi Basecamp. Dennis passed away on October 22, 2023.

The showers at Cu Chi were usually invigoratingly chilly. There were several shower heads in a head high enclosure that were fed from a large airplane wing tank on stilts. It would take a few days for the water to warm up after the tank was filled with well water. Iodine was used to purify the well water. At the mess hall you could drink coffee, orange juice, chilled well water, or sweet tea. Chilling the water increased the flavor of the iodine. If orange juice was not available, I drink water but I did not care for the iodine taste, so I finally adapted to the flavor of sweet tea. The laundry and barber shop were staffed by Vietnamese. They took our laundry home to clean it. Some of their houses would have our laundry hanging along the road to the town of Cu Chi. During the monsoon muddy water from our vehicles would splash close to their clothes lines and during the dry season dust would fly everywhere yet our returned clothes always seemed clean.

Several times while in Saigon, I took taxi rides from Tan Son Nhut Air Base to the Cholon PX. I was not good at bartering, so one time I asked another soldier what the fare to the PX should be. I handed that amount to the driver without discussing price when he dropped me off a short distance from the PX. I headed for the PX as he followed me for half a block, saying something in Vietnamese. Did I cheat him? I don't know. I hope not. Cab drivers would often try to sell you alcoholic beverages, connections with women or get you to buy things from the PX which they could sell on the black market. One time I was in a cab with a soldier I did not know. The driver kept trying to get us to buy him a small refrigerator at the PX. The other soldier finally took his money. We went into the PX but left by another gate and took a different cab back to Tan Son Nhut. We did not buy a refrigerator. One time I was riding in a rickshaw like taxi, but the seat was in front between two wheels and the driver was on motorized cycle attached behind. We came to a large roundabout where there was a traffic jam as usual. As soon as a hole opened, another driver would crowd in. I was surely uneasy being crowded between cars a couple feet away.

My Return Stateside

Short timer's sticks were Vietnamese made canes with dragon heads carved in the top. I still have mine. I had a fifty caliber shell casing, with the bullet, that had the primer end cut off. I put this on the lower end of my stick. Looking out of the airplane window I saw a string of red tracer rounds in the distance just after lifting off from the Tan Son Nhut Airbase. I was glad to be leaving Vietnam. It was good to be going home. Before I left Vietnam, I was asked my preference of duty stations to finish my six months of required service. I chose and received orders to Fort Lewis, located just south of Tacoma, Washington, since this was close to home. My orders were missing the date for my assignment to Ft. Lewis. Officially this made me attached to, instead of assigned to, Ft. Lewis. I learned that this kept me off of the duty roster, so I was free from kitchen police duty (KP), and I skipped police call, which was mostly picking up cigarette butts.

I worked in the main post dispensary, duplicating paperwork for physicals. Soon after leaving active duty, I saw a sequence of pictures in a magazine. They showed two American advisers and several Army of the Republic of Vietnam (ARVN) troops in a ditch. The pictures started with the troops receiving small arms fire. The Americans immediately moved to the side of the ditch toward the incoming bullets and returned fire. The ARVNs crouched to the other side of the ditch. Later pictures showed them, one by one, joining the American troops and began to return fire. These pictures made the hair on my neck stand up straight. Cowering to the wrong side of the ditch was so dangerous. The wrong side of the ditch does not provide as much protection and if you do not return fire, you are at the mercy of the enemy.

The draft obligations were two years of active army duty followed by two years of active reserve duty and then two years of inactive reserve duty. Soon after I got out of the active army duty, I received a letter saying they would notify me when and where to start my active reserve duty. That was the last I heard from the army. During the Vietnam War, the reserve units were full. On March 22, 1968, I was once again a civilian. If I had served all the reserve time, it would have ended March 22, 1972. Instead, I graduated with a bachelor's degree in mechanical engineering from Oregon State University in June 1972.

After graduation, I worked for Texaco for several years and then contracted house framing around Portland, Oregon. I then moved to Anchorage, Alaska, on June 21, 1984. Here, I worked for the construction branch of the

Army Corps Of Engineers as an inspector and as a project engineer. l retired on September 30, 2015, about a month before I turned 70 years old. This work took me to much of the southern half of Alaska. I enjoyed Alaska so much that I still live in Anchorage today.

A U.S. Army Medic's Story
J. Richard Claywell, U. S. Army

Our company supplied medics to F Troop, 17th Cavalry, 196th Light Infantry Brigade, the Americal Division. I was a combat medic with F Troop. The life expectancy of a combat medic during a firefight was 6 seconds. In June of 1970, Jerry Foley, John E.S. Mitchell, and I volunteered to do temporary duty ("TDY") with F Troop. On July 2, 1970, John E. S. Mitchell was on an armored personnel carrier that hit a land mind and after being with F Troop for just ten days, was killed. His total time in Vietnam was sixty days. On July 8, 1970, I was on an armored personnel carrier that hit a land mine. I received a Purple Heart.

Dustoff – Unarmed Medical Evacuation Helicopters

I did some research on the Internet and saw where the life expectancy of a Dustoff crew in Viet Nam was 19 minutes. I also found that the life expectancy of Dustoff crew, having landed in a hostile Landing Zone, was 30 seconds. I was a Dustoff medic in Vietnam from December 1970 through August 1971. I flew with the 236th Medical Detachment in Danang, Viet Nam. Our call sign was Danang Dustoff and our field site call sign was Charger Dustoff. I also did temporary duty (TDY) with the 571st Dustoff in Phu Bai. These were medical evacuation crews that were all voluntary. These dangerous missions were flown under the call sign "Dustoff" and were unarmed Huey helicopters flying and landing in the middle of battles to evacuate wounded soldiers. We also evacuated civilians, Viet Cong, and North Vietnamese soldiers. The Geneva Convention stated that we were non-combatants. As a medic I could carry an M-16 to protect my patients and a pistol for my own protection. We were shot at on a regular basis by the Viet Cong ("VC") and North Vietnamese Army ("NVA") soldiers.

At the age of twenty-one, I was making life or death decisions on which patients to work on. It was common for the Dustoff helicopters to be shot at and receive battle damage from automatic weapons fire, RPG's, and landmines. Our unit had six helicopters. If we received battle damage resulting from missions, we could borrow a helicopter from a different unit. There was a battle in Hiep Duc Valley that lasted approximately two days. We had to replace nine helicopters as a result of battle damage. Do the math, we only had six but had to replace nine helicopters.

During my tour, I had five helicopters receive extensive battle damage. I was told that these helicopters could not be repaired and would either be sent back to the US to be rebuilt or would be taken offshore and dumped into the South China Sea. From 1962 to 1972, there were 496,572 of these types of missions and they evacuated over 900,000 wounded or injured all over Viet Nam.

Casualty Rates

The Dustoff missions were different than all other types of missions using helicopters. When a US unit would engage the enemy, gunship support was normally already involved supporting a different US unit engaged in a firefight. This meant that most of the time, we were landing in the middle of a firefight with no gunship support. Most of the time our only support was what the ground unit could provide. These incredibly dangerous missions were flown by unarmed Huey helicopters. Of the approximately 3 million US troops that served in Viet Nam, only about 3,000 volunteered and flew Dustoff. The casualty rate for these crews was 3 times that of all helicopter units in Vietnam. Flying as a crewmember of the medical evacuation helicopters meant that you had a one in three chance of being killed or wounded during your tour. The motto for Dustoff was "so that others may live." When we arrived on site the pilots would talk to the ground unit and assess the tactical approach needed to land inside the Landing Zone ("LZ"). With or without gunships, we were going to land in the LZ and pick up the patients. This is why we had such a large casualty rate.

Types of Missions

These missions were almost always as a single unescorted helicopter that flew into the middle of firefights to extract the wounded. Waiting for gunship support could easily mean death for a patient. In today's world, the military requires that Dustoff crews be escorted by two gunships. This has resulted in unnecessary death of US soldiers. Where most helicopter units flew during the day and in favorable weather conditions, these medical evacuation missions were flown 24 hours a day no matter what the conditions (weather or enemy fire) – conditions that often grounded all other aircraft. Lives were at stake and we would do our best to evacuate them and treat the patients with lifesaving procedures until we arrived at a hospital.

Missions in the mountains meant that these helicopters came to a stationary hover over the treetops and lowered a cable to extract the wounded while perilously exposed to enemy fire. While hovering, we were a static target and again often took enemy fire. Depending on the terrain, the pilots would sometimes be able to lower the helicopter down into the trees. This would involve cutting trees with the mail rotor and tail rotor blades. This is an excellent way to crash a helicopter. Someone here in the US will tell you that this maneuver is impossible. My comment to them would be to talk to a Dustoff crew and ask them how many times they did this.

Been there and done that

Whenever a ground unit radioed that they had wounded casualties, these crews unhesitatingly answered the call. During daytime missions, a ground unit would pop a colored smoke, which would be identified by the pilots and that would indicate where to land. The night missions were extremely dangerous and the ground units could not pop a colored smoke because the Dustoff crews could not identify the smoke from the air. Some ground units had strobe lights that could be easily identified. So, the question becomes, where do you land, in the middle of complete darkness? Some missions were guided by ZIPPO cigarette lighters.

Landing in a hot LZ

The approaches varied by pilots. Some would low level from a distance traveling over 100 miles per hour, turn the tail of the helicopter 180 degrees and drop the helicopter into the LZ. I remember several comments where the ground unit thought we were going to crash. Another technique was to position the helicopter so it would seemingly just drop from the sky from about 1,000. The G forces were so strong that I could not move when we started the landing approach from the ground. These techniques were honed by the pilots, and they were excellent at using their craft. The military tracked the number of hours flown and the number of patients they picked up. This type of information was not maintained for the crew chief or medic. Based on my flight hours, I estimate that I flew over 800 missions. For me, the most significant thing I have ever done was to be a Medic in Viet Nam and keep soldiers alive long enough to get them to a hospital to get the care of a physician.

[CPA J. Richard Claywell was a medic in Vietnam from November 1969 through August 1971. He was assigned to a battalion aid station at Tam Ky where he learned from physicians how to perform lifesaving procedures which he used throughout his entire time in Vietnam. Today Richard works as a forensic CPA, working on many cases that involve millions of dollars. Richard is a recipient of the Congressional Gold Medal for Vietnam Dustoff crews signed into law September 26, 2024.]

Medic Dennis Mason, U. S. Army
My Special Guy

by Juliet Mason

Dennis D. Mason and I met in October of 1973 at dinner where I was with my sister and her husband. They knew him from high school. Den was having dinner with some friends and he came over to our table to visit. He was on crutches. I knew from my sister that he was an amputee. We started talking and he asked if he could call me. I said yes. That was the start of our 49 years and 10 months together. We married in January of 1974.

Like all newlyweds, we spent our first years getting to know each other better. Den was teaching and I was working at a bank. We visited my parents on a weekend at their river place at Weeki Wachee River. Den loved the area and fishing with my dad. We bought a place nearby on a canal off the river and started our 10-year adventure on the Weeki Wachee. We had many wonderful weekends with family and friends – river fishing, tubing, fishing out in the Gulf of Mexico. We bought a boat and Den was the captain.

He loved driving our boat and was very good at it. My parents had a 24’ float boat and he always drove the boat for my dad. He taught all our nephews and nieces how to fish, to crab, and how to drive the boat. They all loved their Uncle Den. He was their super Hero. Den had been drafted in 1966 and completed his Army Basic Combat Training (BCT) at Fort Bragg, NC and then his Advanced Individual Training (AIT) at Fort Sam Houston, Texas. This was the Medical Field Service School where he earned his Military Occupational Specialty (MOS) as a medic.

In January of 1967 he was assigned as a Spec 4 medic with the infantry in 1st Platoon of C, Co. 1st Battalion 27th Infantry Regiment “Wolfhounds” of the 25th Infantry Division in Vietnam. Dennis was the senior medic in his company and had been on the line in his platoon for six months. He was badly injured on June 26, 1967.

There is an email dated March 2, 2010, from former Medical Service Corps Lt. Allen Hinman to Wayne Steelman, C Company Commander, and William “Easy” Smith, C Company Infantryman: “Thank you for the kind words about medics. I agree. This email is also going to

Dennis Mason (email – Julden) who is the medic who lost his legs. He and I reconnected at each of our first reunion in Atlanta. He just retired as a high school history teacher and department head. If you google "Dennis Mason + wheelchair softball" you will see that he is semi-famous. He had finished his time in the field and was the aid station pharmacist (who invented a cream that actually cured crotch rot but the formula left with his wounds). For a reason I forget the newer medic for his old platoon was gone and Dennis volunteered to go back out with his old platoon.

The Chaplain, known for carrying no weapon except a giant bowie knife, was shot at the lunchbox where we were receiving ineffective sniper fire and when crossing a canal he stayed behind to give the troops a hand, climbing out. Dennis Mason, I believe, pushed his guts back in and then he and I carried the chaplain to medevac bird. The chaplain told me he would be doing sit ups in no time. He said that was going slowly as he was just up to lifting his head. Both of Dennis's legs were heavily injured when he stepped on a booby trap or mine while his unit was on this operation. He was fortunate that there was a chopper nearby that landed and picked him up for transport to a surgical unit. There, the surgeons amputated both legs above the knees. He then spent two months in Japan at the US Army Camp Zama Hospital in Honshu, located about 25 miles SW of Tokyo. He then spent over a year and a half at Valley Forge Medical in rehabilitation and getting fitted for prosthetics. When he was better, he came home to Florida and finished his college at University of South Florida, and he became a high school teacher embarking on his long teaching career.

On July 10, 1967, the battalion chaplain, Capt. John K. Durham, wrote Dennis's mother, Mrs. Myrtle Boron, a letter. The letter is reproduced here:

10 July 1967

Dear Mrs. Boron

Until the 20th of June, I was the Chaplain assigned to your son, Dennis's unit, the 1/27th Inf of the 25th Inf Div. On that date I was hit by a sniper's bullet which entered above the left hip and came out the right front groin. I had no more than hit the ground when Dennis was beside me working with the professionalism which had earned him the job of senior medic in "C" Company. During all the time he was working on me, he kept encouraging me with conversation. At one point, as soon as it had been determined, he said, "Good sign, Chappie, it's not bleeding." I knew what he meant and he had known I would know – a short time earlier "C" Company had lost a Lieutenant when a piece of shrapnel entered him just about where this one came out on me. It had cut some important arteries and he bled to death quickly and easily. You can imagine how reassuring his words were to me.

Having known Dennis for some time, there was no thought in my mind to doubt what he was saying. Mine was a serious wound and several doctors have indicated I probably owe my life to Dennis. One person just can't owe another anymore than that. Despite the seriousness of it at the time, I am well on my way to recovery and will be functioning as well as ever.

It was the following week sometime then when Dennis was hit. We were both in the 12th Evac Hosp in Cu Chi, but in different wards and I did not get to see him. Then we began our evacuation trip to Japan together and we had beds next to each other much of the time. Even now we are in the same ward, separated by about 4 beds. We get to visit each other. Dennis tells me you know he has lost both legs. I want you to be assured that the same wonderful, victorious, selfless spirit which had marked him before his injury is still characteristic of him. He's talking of finishing school and is planning for the future. And he'll get it done!!

He had asked, if I felt like it, to write a note to you just reassuring you that he's going to be alright and he is doing fine. Despite the tragedy of his injury, I don't know of anyone I speak those words of, with more meaning, than of Dennis.

I don't know when he'll be coming back to the States. None of us have much advanced knowledge of this. I would encourage you, his family, and his friends, to be prepared to accept him without a feeling of pity. This, of course, will be difficult for you. But this is Dennis – he doesn't ask for pity – he only offers strength and encouragement and this is what is going to see him through.

May God bless you in these days.

Sincerely,

John K. Durham (CPT)

Chaplain

During his teaching career, a student interviewed him about Vietnam:

These are the student's notes:

1. Flashbacks – sounds & smells bring back thoughts but no real flashbacks.
2. Most common injuries were caused by booby traps.
3. Did not really mind going when drafted.
4. Booby traps made even from "C" rasons (sic: c-rations). Take can and fill with nails, glass, metal and put up with a trip wire.
5. No real regrets about going to Vietnam. I would do it again . . . knowing what I know. It made me what I am today.
6. Sea Rasions (sic: c-rations) dated . . . some back to the 1950's. Not bad tasting.
7. Helicopter allowed them 1 hot meal a day in the field.
8. Each Company (150 men) broken down to 4 platoons (45 men); each platoon had its own medic. Dennis was the senior medic for the entire Company.

Den did not talk about Vietnam until he started going to the Wolfhound Reunions. He enjoyed visiting with some of his buddies at them. One evening when we had returned from a reunion, he told me of a terrible night for him. He said it was his worst experience in Vietnam. He was 22 years old, the senior medic in his company, and he was sent on a recovery mission. He described what had happened to 22 soldiers who were killed. They had been overrun by the enemy.

The medics had to place all the soldiers in body bags with their names, a complete list of all the injuries they had suffered and what had killed them. Den said it was awful for him to do this. Many had their throats cut. Only two soldiers had survived, but they were seriously injured. He said it shouldn't have happened. Reinforcements did not arrive and they had been overwhelmed by superior numbers. Den said he and others in his unit could hear the soldiers calling for help. But, those in command said they were mistaken and there was no enemy in the area. The officer in charge was later relieved from duty. Dennis and others in the recovery group received Bronze Stars with a "V" device for their valor. The VC were indeed still in the area and the recovery was not only emotionally taxing, but dangerous.

Den always told me he could do anything; it just might take him a little longer – or might take time to adjust. I never saw him unable to do anything an able-bodied person could do. He never suffered from PTSD and always maintained his calm.

We enjoyed the river for 10 years and then we changed direction. Den started playing doubles tennis with my sister, brother-in-law, and me every day. He played in a special sports chair for tennis. He loved that sport! Soon he was taking lessons and we started going to tournaments all over Florida and then all over the USA. His high school asked if he would coach the boy's high school team and he said, yes. He taught at Lakeland for 22 years, was Department Chairperson for Social Studies and was the boy's tennis coach. He was recruited to open the new school, George Jenkins High School. Den then became Department Head of Social Studies there. He finished his teaching career at George Jenkins in 2008, retiring from the school system after 37 years. He was voted Teacher of the Year at both schools and was inducted into Jenkins Wall of Honor in 2017.

He was voted All Area High School Coach of the Year 1986, '88 and '89. He was selected Teacher of the Year at Lakeland Senior High School in 1989. Den always loved sports and he was just as supportive in my sports and activities. I played tennis and was a runner with my sister. He went with me when I ran my only marathon: Marine Corp in Washington, DC. He accompanied me and my tennis team at regional championships. He was always there cheering us on.

Den took up wheelchair softball for the Tampa Bay Rays in 2004. He and his teammates played together for over 10 years. We traveled to different cities. The men would play softball tournament and exhibition games. He loved team sports. He was the pitcher and won awards for his pitching. We met many wonderful friendly people. Some of the guys and gals were vets and some had been injured in different ways.

Den was wonderful with my sisters and me and we went on many pleasure trips together. He took us to Niagara Falls, an Alaskan cruise, and a Canadian cruise. He never got mad when we asked him to stop or couldn't decide where or what we wanted to eat. He was our Hero!

Dennis and I traveled most of the times in the summers when he was off from teaching. He loved history. So many trips were to historic areas: Williamsburg, DC, Charleston, SC. Den loved to drive and we would put 90,000 miles on our trucks in 4 years. After his retirement in 2008, we spent every Veterans Day and Memorial Day in DC at The Wall. He wanted to pay his respects and visit with those memorialized there. He loved meeting and visiting with his Wolfhound Brothers there. We became friends with the Park Volunteers. These were special times for us. Den and I were married for 49 years and 10 months. There was nothing Den could not do. His handicap never held him back. He was a top-rated wheelchair athlete in tennis and softball. He loved to fish and was an excellent swimmer. He was a very special man. He was loved by our families and friends and he loved his Wolfhound Brothers.

Den passed away on October 22, 2023, my birthday. He was truly the best and I could not have had a better husband. He was an awesome Teacher, a terrific Uncle to our nieces and nephews and most importantly my Sweetheart! We had a wonderful life. We didn't argue or have any major problems. I was so lucky to have him in my life.

Den always told me – there were guys worse than he was and he was happy to be alive. I miss him every day. But I know he is watching over me and our family from above.

Juliet Mason

*Editor's Note: Spec 4 Dennis D. Mason was also awarded the Silver Star for Gallantry in Action in the Republic of Vietnam on 16 May 1967 and a Purple Heart medal for his injuries on 26 June 1967.

Dennis Mason, One Fine Medic

by
Command Sergeant Major Johnny M. Langford,
U S Army, (Ret)

I was drafted as a 24-year-old in 1966, went to Fort Bragg, NC, for my basic training and, thereafter, to AIT (Advanced Infantry Training) at Fort Jackson in Columbia, SC. My MOS (Military Occupational Specialty) was infantry. Even though I was a draftee, I made a career out of the army and retired as a Command Sergeant Major in 1994. I arrived in Vietnam on January 5, 1967, and was assigned as a rifleman to C Company First Platoon of the First Battalion of the 27th Infantry Regiment (the Wolfhounds) of the 25th Infantry Division, nicknamed "Tropic Lightning."

Lieutenant William I. Brown was my platoon leader at the time. He was later wounded evacuated and a replacement assigned. I was a Spec 4 (Specialist 4th Class) acting in a sergeant's position. I had occasion to observe Spec 4 Mason perform his duties well as a medic over several months. He was always calm under fire, would go to the injured grunt (nickname for infantryman) no matter how risky, stop the bleeding and bandage their wounds. All the while he would talk to them to keep them calm. He treated wounds from mortar rounds, booby traps, and small arms fire frequently in the legs and arms. We often experienced casualties after we jumped from the helicopters as we ran to the wood line. At these times we'd often receive shrapnel wounds from mortar fire. We saw some tough times.

It was on June 26, 1967, early a.m., we broke camp and started moving out on a search and destroy operation. This was a company operation and my platoon was one of them. We immediately began receiving rifle fire. One of the wounded called for a "Medic" and Specialist Mason ran about 50 feet toward the wounded grunt to a ditch line adjacent to a bush. As he jumped into the depression, he hit a booby trap or mine and was badly injured in both legs and part of his body. He was still talking and conscious when the dust-off medivac helicopter arrived. He even gave his replacement medic instructions before his evacuation. He was taken to the 12th Evacuation Hospital at Cu Chi.

After the operation, I took the occasion to visit him there. He looked bad. I did not think he would make it. He was later moved to a US Army Hospital in Japan for a period of two months and, thereafter, stateside for more recovery. It took a year and a half for him to recover from his injuries. Having lost both legs from the knees down, he was a paraplegic and used prosthetics, crutches, or a wheel chair for the rest of his life.

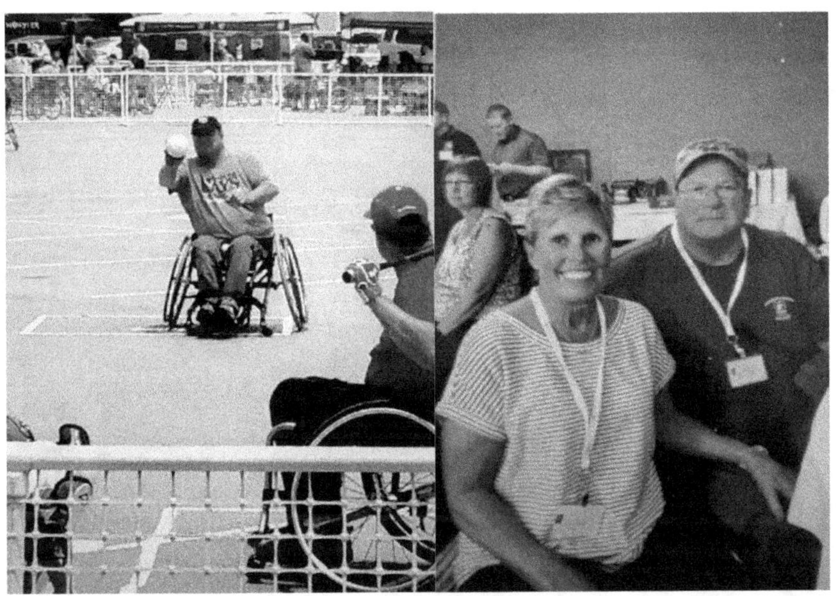

We stayed connected. It was special to see him and catch up at the annual Wolfhound Reunions. Dennis passed away on October 22, 2023.

SP-4 Gerald (Gerry) Randazzo, U. S. Army

Small Pox in the Village

Wolfhound Medics Reunion 2018

[L-R: Kathy Cirtaus, Steve Cirtaus, Roberta Laskowitz, Neil Laskowitz, M. Kinman, Allen Kinman, Neil Laskowitz, Lyden Belin, Juliet Mason, Gerry Randazzo, Dee Scott, and Paul Scott.]

In 1966 I was a medic with the First Battalion of the 27th Infantry Regiment of the 25th Infantry Division with the rank of Specialist 4th Class. During my tour of duty in Vietnam, I was assigned as a medic to a rifle company. However, at this particular time, I was in the medical platoon in Headquarters Company.

In addition to supporting the infantry on operations as a forward aid station, the medical platoon went on Medcap (Medical Civic Action Program) operations. We'd go to the villages and treat the villagers for their various ailments. These usually included colds, headaches, minor injuries, and skin infections. Our interpreters, Sgt. Muc and Sgt. Hoa, helped us communicate with the people.

Capt. Donald G. Winningham, MD, from Washington State and a urologist by specialty, was the battalion surgeon. In the early spring, it was at the end of the dry season and beginning of the monsoon. We were out on a Medcap operation in a small village northeast of our base camp at Cu Chi.

I was the medic that drove the jeep and trailer with medical supplies to the villages. This was my third Medcap operation with the medical platoon. We examined and treated the children who had, unfortunately, been hit by shrapnel, were wounded or needed other medical attention. We then examined the elderly villagers. As the captain was examining the elderly, he called to me "come quick, I found something interesting." He told me to see the woman he was assisting. He determined that she was infected with the small pox virus. In the United States we were vaccinated as children, so we felt like it was safe to be near her and treat her. The villagers had partially isolated her in a separate hooch and we further quarantined her. The captain called headquarters to let them know we needed to vaccinate the villagers. A quantity of vaccine sufficient to vaccinate the entire village was sent out by helicopter. We created and sent flyers to let the villagers know they needed to get vaccinated. We set up a system to check the villagers and then vaccinate them. We successfully vaccinated over 100 villagers over several days.

Capt. Winningham saved many lives when he diagnosed the small pox and treated the villagers. To my knowledge, he never received the credit he deserved for saving Vietnam from an epidemic. He was a hero in my book.

Specialist 4th Class
Bill Hughes, U. S. Army

Specialist Fourth Class William (Bill) Hughes served as a Medic in Colonel Moore's outfit during the Vietnam War. Bill was born in Florence, NJ and grew up near a fire station where he developed an affinity for its rescue squad. As a teenager, he took several American Red Cross courses and served for three years as a volunteer aid man.

Specialist Fourth Class William J. (Bill) Hughes, US Army Medic, was one of those rare individuals who will never be forgotten by those with whom he served. He possessed nerves of steel and his expertise as a medical aid man was unrivaled. His heroism and skilled medical care were an inspiration for all of us and led to the saving of countless lives during his nearly two years in Vietnam. He was precisely the type of medic needed in our type of unit and set an extremely high standard for all who followed.

When he enlisted, the Army gained a tough kid from Jersey who quickly learned to love the discipline and camaraderie of the military. Bill was initially interviewed by the legendary commander of the 57th Medical Detachment, Major Charles Kelly, who saw that he graduated second highest in his medical training at Fort Sam Houston, so in his usual blunt fashion, Major Kelly said, “You’re going to see some pretty horrible stuff in a unit such as this, so you ought to consider going to a clinic or hospital.” Not to be outdone, Bill Hughes shot back, “Sir, I figure the bodies here couldn’t be any more messed up than they were along Route 130 in Jersey.”

Over the next few weeks, Bill’s other attributes began to surface. He was a gifted artist who painted most of the unit’s signs and designed unit patches and cartoons. With his personality and natural gift of gab, he quickly became a key source of supplies. When “hard to get items” were needed, Bill would take a jeep and drive all over Saigon trading and scrounging materials from the many Army, Navy, and Air Force contacts he had made.

The skills learned as a volunteer rescue crewman put Bill ahead of his contemporaries and we felt very comfortable having him aboard. He took incredibly good care of patients and always jumped from the aircraft to get the wounded loaded quickly. Bill was at his best in a "hot" landing zone.

On October 26, 1964, an Air Force fighter plane was shot down in heavy jungle north of Saigon. Despite enemy6 fire, Bill walked several hundred yards into the jungle to reach the crash site only to find both pilots dead, the aircraft burning, and the area covered with unexploded ordinance. Without regard for his own safety, Bill pulled both men from the wreckage. For his actions that day, he received the Army Commendation Medal with "V" for valor, an extremely high award at that early stage of the war.

Another of his heroic acts occurred in February of 1965 when the Viet Cong began their second major attempt to destroy the predominantly Catholic village of Binh Gia. A Vietnamese infantry battalion was lifted in to save the village and four Army helicopters were shot down. A regimental sized enemy force then attacked and began throwing gasoline torches into the heavy grass covering the landing zone, so when Bill's crew went to help, his pilot had to land more than a hundred yards away from one of the downed helicopters. Undeterred, Bill jumped out and ran through both the grass fire and heavy enemy fire. After pulling three crew members from the downed Huey and loading them aboard his helicopter, Bill returned to extract the dead pilot who was trapped in the wreckage. Although the downed helicopter was burning, Bill climbed into the cockpit and began cutting the pilot out. Numerous rounds struck the aircraft and followed him as he carried the dead pilot to his own aircraft. At that point, the enemy directed heavy automatic weapons fire towards him. Three more airlifts were conducted that afternoon and Bill repeatedly exposed himself to enemy fire while recuing eighteen more wounded. Bill was recommended for a Silver Star for his heroic actions that day.

On March 1, 1965, Bill was driving into Saigon when he heard a thunderous explosion. Without hesitation, he sped to the scene and found the front of the American Embassy had been blown off by a massive truck bomb. Since he was one of the first there, he began triaging dozens of patients who were lying in the street and in the blown-apart building. He separated those needing immediate care from the dead and began using their clothing to make tourniquets and dressings. As others began to arrive, Bill had the presence of mind to use his own uniform shirt to cover the face of a dead embassy worker so that she could not be photographed by gathering media. After all the patients had been evacuated to the US Naval Hospital in Saigon, Bill drove there and volunteered his services. He was later honored by the American Ambassador and his heroic actions were depicted in a book entitle, "The Chronicles of the Vietnam War."

When his first tour ended, Bill asked to extend. On November 12, 1965, after 20 months of combat, his helicopter came under heavy fire while picking up several wounded Vietnamese near the village of Bau Bang. During take-off, Bill was firing his weapon at the enemy when a bullet ripped the rifle from his hands and then another tore through his knee and followed the bone into his upper thigh where it ruptured the femoral artery. Bill Hughes almost bled to death before reaching the hospital and became the first Dustoff medic to be severely wounded and evacuated from Vietnam.

Bill spent several months recovering at the Valley Forge Army Hospital, but his wounds proved to be so severe that he had to be medically retired. He went on to obtain a master's degree in fine arts and taught at the high school and junior college levels for many years before his health began to fail because of his wounds. Bill Hughes was inducted into the Dustoff Hall of Fame in 2006 and we lost him on September 2, 2017.

[With permission from Colonel Douglas Moore's book: *A BULLET THROUGH THE HELMET: A Vietnam Dustoff Pilot's Memoir.*]

A Medic's Memories from Vietnam
Neil Laskowitz, U. S. Army - 1967

I was inducted into the United States Army on the 10th of December 1965 and was honorably discharged on the 8th of December 1967. With orders for Vietnam, I flew from Los Angeles International Airport, and arrived in Vietnam in August 1966, I'm just not sure of the exact date of my arrival.

Initially, I was sent to a reception area before getting orders to report to the 25th Infantry Division, 1st Battalion, 27th Infantry "Wolfhounds" who were located at Cu Chi. I spent a few days at the headquarters company before I was assigned as a "line medic" with Bravo Company, in the 1st Battalion.

While I'm not certain of the dates of the following incidents, I can say that not everything that happened was always serious. I do not remember being scared most of the time that I was there, just during several isolated incidents.

I can remember one time when Bravo Company flew into a supposedly hostile Land Zone (LZ). The helicopter pilot refused to land, and we were told to jump out of that chopper, which was about 10 to 15 feet off the ground. The person before me jumped without any problems, but as luck would have it, I jumped next and landed on top of him. Luckily, we were both fine on landing.

Bravo Company was involved in a sweep when a shot rang out. It was then when I heard someone call "Medic" for the first time. I ran as fast as I could in the direction of that call. Fortunately, the soldier was not seriously wounded. As I walked back to my platoon, I felt my chest, where I had kept all of the letters I had received from home, tucked inside my shirt. They were gone. When I returned to my platoon, I learned that one of the guys had found my letters and returned all of them to me.

I recall walking through the jungle with my platoon. As we continued to advance, one solemn sight struck me right between the eyes. It was seeing the bodies of dead VC lying before me with the Ace of Spades playing cards placed upon their heads. The Ace of Spades was considered to be a negative entity when placed on the head of the Vietnamese soldier.

I was a line medic with Bravo Company, 3rd Platoon, when we were camped outside of the Michelon Rubber Plantation. That night, we were ordered to go out on a night ambush inside the plantation. It was known that patrols that went into the plantation did not always survive the ordeal. Just before we entered the plantation, I gave my wallet, with all of my personal items in it, to our senior medic. My reason for doing this was in the event that I didn't make it back, he would be able to send my personal items back to my family. Thankfully, all of the members of the platoon made it back safely.

I believe that the following incident took place during Operation Attleboro. Somehow, I became separated from my platoon and found myself in an open area with some of our wounded guys. As I looked around, I heard someone call my name. It was one of our wounded, although not from my platoon. I walked over to him and all he wanted was for me to stay with him and hold his hand. He was scared, and talking to him and holding his hand helped to calm him down. I'm not sure, but I believe he made it. I returned to my platoon.

Bravo Company was out in the field, and we had established our base camp. Then, shortly afterwards, "All Hell broke loose." It felt like it came out of nowhere. Artillery rounds were landing near us, and I remember yelling to one of the guys in my platoon, "throw me a rifle." The rounds ended pretty quickly and thank God no one was hurt. It seemed that we were experiencing "friendly fire." If I had never believed in luck, I did that day!

Not everything about Vietnam was filled with fear and death. There were times that actually made me smile.

I was back in HHC, and I had become very friendly with one of my fellow medics, and Dennis Mason was his name. We talked about where we were from, and Dennis had told me that he was from Florida, and I mentioned that I was from Brooklyn, New York. Dennis was amazed that not only did I not have a driver's license, but U+I had never learned to drive a car. One day, Dennis got ahold of a jeep and he decided that he was going to teach me how to drive. This turned out to be an experience that I would never forget. I sat in the driver's seat, turned on the ignition, and proceeded to move forward. It wasn't long before I drove that jeep into a ditch. I thought that I was going to have to pay the Army back for a new jeep! I don't know how Dennis did it, but he got that jeep back to the motor pool and I did not have to pay for anything. This experience caused me to wait many years before I would get my driver's license.

Dennis had a way with words, and he was able to convince me to do things I probably would not have done on my own. Our battalion was in the field while Dennis and I were assigned to HHC at the time. Dennis had heard that a religious service was being held in one of the company areas. Dennis said, "Come on, Neil, let's go to the service." I had never been a very religious person, so I asked Dennis what kind of service was being held. He replied that it would be a Protestant service. I said, "You know, I'm not a Protestant." His response was, "You're going!' So, for one afternoon, I was a Protestant.

Events

The Dustoff Crews
An Overview

During the Vietnam War, "Dustoff" crews were Army helicopter pilots, and medics, who flew unarmed medical evacuation (MEDEVAC) missions to rescue wounded soldiers, often under fire. Operating in dangerous conditions, these pilots and their crews flew nearly half a million missions, saving over 900,000 lives using their motto, "When I have your wounded". The bravery and life-saving actions of these crews have been formally recognized, including being awarded the Congressional Gold Medal in 2024.

- **The mission:** Dustoff crews flew to retrieve wounded soldiers from the battlefield, including in dangerous remote areas and during intense combat.
- **The risks:** The job was extremely dangerous, and the UH-1 Huey helicopters were often targeted by small arms fire, rockets, and missiles. The Red Cross insignia on the helicopters did not provide immunity.
- **The crew:** A Dustoff crew typically included a pilot, co-pilot, crew chief, and medic, who provided immediate medical care in flight.

- **The impact:** The revolutionary aeromedical evacuation system pioneered by Dustoff crews significantly increased survival rates for wounded soldiers.
- **Recognition:** In 2024, Congress passed the "Dustoff Crews of the Vietnam War Congressional Gold Medal Act," awarding this highest civilian honor to the crews for their "extraordinary heroism and life-saving actions".

Huey Dustoff Helicopter

WO-1 Douglas Petersen, U. S. Army

It was late 1970 and I was 1st up out of Long Binh. A hoist mission came for an American soldier who was wounded. My crew and I sprinted to the helicopter, and we were off, heading east, and our missions often took us over active artillery fire bases. It was important that we would not be flying through their firing mission. We would radio each one that was in the vicinity of our flight path to make sure our route was clear. Radio calls were made and we were good to go. The concept of "big sky, little bullet" would be a gamble. Once we got in the vicinity, I contacted the unit on the ground and asked about the patient and any enemy contact. They replied the patient was stable and had no enemy contact in the last hour. Still at 1,500 feet AGL (above ground level), I asked them to pop smoke.

We could see red smoke coming up from the jungle. I radioed back to them, "I see Choo-Choo Cherry." They confirmed. Looking at the landmarks around the area, I was evaluating the route in and the route out and briefed the crew. I could see a clearing west of the PZ and made a mental note. We now made a rapid descent from our altitude to the top of the jungle, using terrain references I saw from above, and we began searching for the smoke, all the while talking with the ground unit. Once we approached the top of the jungle, the crew chief and medic would put their intercom on "hot mike" meaning they wouldn't have to press the "talk" button on their microphone (mike) cord to talk. The noise in out helmets was now loud with all the external noise of the helicopter.

I was hovering over the thick green jungle, and I thought I was close to the unit where the red smoke had filtrated up, and the injured soldier, then suddenly, we began taking enemy fire and the rounds were hitting the aircraft. Since the crew was on "hot mike," you could clearly hear the loud crack of an AK-47, in the automatic mode, and the rounds hitting the thin metal of the aircraft. The crew shouted, "WE'RE TAKING FIRE! WE'RE TAKING HITS!" I immediately began a sharp left bank away from the gunfire to get away. I remembered that clearing a couple of kilometers away. The ground unit shouted, "GET OUT OF HERE DUSTOFF 34!"

We had flown directly over the Viet Cong, and he, or they opened up with their AK-47 to bring us down. As I turned the aircraft, I could see our red WARNING lights coming on and it was apparent that we were losing oil to the engine and transmission. The mission now changed; now it was to get my crew to safety before the engine quit, and before we would crash into the jungle. "MAYDAY! MAYDAY! MAYDAY! DUSTOFF 34 GOING DOWN IN THE VICINITY OF YT 320190. MAYDAY! MAYDAY! MAYDAY! DUSTOFF 34 GOING DOWN" was transmitted on the emergency frequency. We made it over to the clearing I had seen earlier. We didn't know if it was occupied by the enemy or not. It was my only choice. On edge about where we landed, we were alert to any movement or activity. It was clear that the enemy was in the vicinity, I just didn't know if I had landed in the middle of them. About 15 minutes later, American soldiers in APC (Armored Personnel Carriers) were coming around us and we had other helicopters overhead. We felt a little more secure.

While waiting to be picked up we counted 25 bullet holes in the aircraft, and several in the cockpit where me and the other pilot were sitting. One of the rounds had penetrated the instrument panel and was lodged in one of the instruments, the airspeed indicator, I think. We could see the round in the broken glass of the instrument. If the round had any more velocity, the trajectory would have missed the armored chicken plate of my copilot, and he would have been shot in the head. To say the least, he was pretty shaken up.

About an hour later, we had one of our other crews (probably 2nd Up) land and take us back to Long Binh. Once we landed, I got another helicopter and another crew, and we went back to get the injured soldier. He was still injured and in need to be taken to a medical facility. As I was flying back out, there was a Chinook helicopter with a sling load aircraft I left out there below it and was bringing it back to the unit. Following the same procedure, the same route, but a lightly different approach path to the PZ (Pick Up Zone), we were able to complete the mission, and we got the injured to the hospital. END OF MISSION.

A little side note to that mission, years later, back in the states, newly married I made a trip to New England for a wedding of one of my wife's cousins. While sitting across the table at the wedding reception, I struck up a conversation with another Vietnam veteran and (long story short at this point), and by our conversation, he was in the unit that I had pulled that guy out of the jungle. He was not the injured soldier but was there on the ground as I lifted his buddy out of there. Small world wouldn't you say?

WO-1 Stephen Peth, U. S. Army

The year was 1966 and I was entering the second semester of my junior year at Ithaca College in upstate New York. I was studying to be a music teacher and my major was piano. The Viet Nam war was reaching a high point in terms of numbers of troops deployed to South Vietnam. Some of my high school classmates had volunteered for Viet Nam and others were being drafted. I had a student deferment and few thoughts about the war. I had just completed my first semester of student teaching. I did not like it and planned to switch from music education to applied music which would result in a loss of two semesters. Someone suggested that I should check with the local draft board. I did and was told that if I lost one single credit hour I would lose my student deferment.

I kept thinking about my classmates serving in Viet Nam and had some nagging guilt about my status. But more than anything, I always had a strong desire to become a pilot. I headed for the Air Force Recruiting office in Elmira, NY. They were not interested in me because they required all recruits for pilot training to have a four-year degree. I walked down the street to the Army Recruiting office and they told me about the Warrant Officer Candidate (WOC) flight training program. Given how many pilots they needed at the time, I think the only prerequisites were a pulse and correctible vision. Of course, I really had no idea what I was getting into.

I joined the Army on March 27th, 1967. I went through Fort Polk, LA, for basic training and then off to Fort Wolters, TX, for primary helicopter flight training. Training was completed at Fort Rucker, AL, where I received a promotion to Warrant Officer One and the wings of an Army Aviator on May 7th, 1968. While in flight school I married the love of my life, Beth, and started the beginning of an exciting career in the Army.

Near the end of flight school, we were asked to fill out a 'dream sheet' for our first assignment. I can't remember exactly how I filled it out, but I am confident it went something like this: 1) Cobra Gunship Training, 2) Chinook Training, 3) Scout Training 4) Assault

Helicopters, in that order of preference. The next thing I know, I get orders for Essential Training for AMEDS Aviators. What the heck is that? That was not on my preference list!

I did pretty well in flight school and it turned out that the Army Medical community had a high priority need for aircraft and pilots. I think they took the top fifteen warrant officer pilot graduates from my Warrant Officer Class and sent them to train for a month at Fort Sam Houston, TX, to become Dustoff pilots. It never occurred to me that I would be assigned to one of the most dangerous jobs in all of Viet Nam. Even then, I had no idea just how dangerous being a crewmember on a Dustoff helicopter was. So, in July 1968, I headed to Viet Nam for my first operational assignment. Hello, 159th Medical Detachment in Cu Chi, South Viet Nam. Little did I know when I signed in to the 159th that my life was about to be changed forever. I was starting an adventure that proved to be the most satisfying experience in my life. Nothing came close to the satisfaction of spending eleven months in the 159th with some of the bravest and most dedicated men I have ever met.

Major Doug Moore was the 159th commanding officer when I arrived, and he was still the CO when I left. Doug had a huge influence on my life. He encouraged me to get a commission and provided the kind of leadership that I wanted to emulate. My decision to stay in the Army was largely influenced by Doug. I started out as a co-pilot. You know how that goes: “Buckle in and don’t touch anything.” I wanted so badly to do a good job. Demonstrating piloting skills, earning respect, and learning how to conduct a mission became the highest priorities. The first time I really began to think I was getting good at tooling around in a Huey was after getting the full treatment by Tony Peters. Tony taught me to be smooth on the controls. Thanks to Tony, I developed what pilots call “good control touch.”

Speaking of Tony Peters, I believe I was flying as his copilot when I lost my ‘cherry.’ We were flying low at tree top level to make a pick-up at an outpost near Cu Chi. We were doing 90 knots when a bad guy fired a clip of AK-47 rounds up at us. We must have flown directly over the top of the guy because the jungle was too thick for him to shoot at us unless we were directly above. We took five hits: two through the instrument console on the floor between the pilot and copilot; one through the floor between the crew chief and medic; one through the transmission compartment; and one that came up through the engine deck, through the tail rotor drive shaft and all the way through the diffuser section of the engine and out the top. We landed at the outpost and left the engine running. Tony gave me the controls and jumped out of the aircraft. He looked at the damage in the engine compartment and then ran back to my window and asked how the gauges looked. I told him everything was green. He jumped in the Huey and said, “let’s get back to base before this thing quits." We made the short flight back safely, and I gained a huge amount of respect for the resilience of the Huey.

On another mission with Tony, we landed in a hot landing zone on a road. We were at a hover with Tony at the controls when the bad guys brought AK-47 fire on the aircraft. One round hit the bulkhead behind Tony's seat on the left side of the aircraft, striking a glass bottle of saline solution the medic had stowed there as usual. The bottle exploded behind Tony's head and tilted his helmet down over his eyes. Suddenly his control of the aircraft was erratic, so I took control while Tony tried to regain his composure and eyesight by pushing his helmet back. We exited the LZ as quickly as possible with the whole crew laughing at how funny Tony looked with his helmet pushed down over his eyes. Danger and a sense of humor can coexist. During my tour with the 159th, I remember taking actual hits on the aircraft 9 different times. I have no idea how many times the enemy fired at us.

After about four months of flying as a copilot, Doug selected me to be an aircraft commander (AC). I don't remember my first mission as AC (aircraft commander), but I do remember how nervous I was to have all of that responsibility. To this day, I cannot understand how those brave medics and crew chiefs could tolerate sitting in the back while some young pilot was upfront making life and death decisions and, hopefully, not making pilot errors.

I had been flying into the same area repeatedly because a unit was in heavy contact to the North of Cu Chi. The unit was configured in a large horseshoe shape over about a half mile with the enemy pinned up against the south side of the Saigon River. I was flying the 'first up' bird and all of the missions were mine. We landed on one side of the LZ and picked up several wounded. As we took off, a different unit on the other side of the horseshoe called in an urgent mission. We immediately landed, picked up a litter patient, and took off. On the way out of the LZ, the bad guys started shooting at us. We took hits in every single fuel cell but managed to fly our patients to the 12th Evac Hospital in Cu Chi. The aircraft was grounded for a long time for repairs. As we arrived at the hospital pad, we quickly discharged patients and were met by Major Moore in a jeep. He told us to grab our stuff and he would take us to our back-up aircraft. Sure enough, we arrived at the aircraft no sooner than missions started coming in.

I knew they were going to be at the same location where we just took hits. I did a quick preflight and noticed my hands were shaking. Then I realized that the crew chief for the new bird was not there but the one from the damaged aircraft was getting the aircraft ready to fly. I asked him where the assigned crew chief was and he said he had sent him back to the barracks and he was going to fly. I quickly told him he did not have to fly and to get the other crew chief. His response humbled me. He said, "Mr. Peth, if you are going back to that LZ then I'm going, too."

As soon as the engine started and the blades were spinning my hands stopped shaking. The rest of the missions were completed without taking on any more hostile fire. I will never forget the bravery and dedication to the mission of that crew chief. In my mind he served as an example of the bravery of all of those enlisted crewmembers exhibited during my tour with Dustoff.

A mission that I was particularly proud of took place near Tay Ninh at night outside of a fire base. I arrived on the scene for an urgent Dustoff. Gunships, command and control aircraft, AF Forward Air Controllers were already flying in the dark above the fire base. I arrived on the scene and started making radio calls to gather necessary information to ID the LZ, the locations of the enemy and friendlies, and the status of fires, when I started receiving what appeared to be 51 cal. fire. I was about 2000 feet above the ground and immediately turned off my lights. The enemy was engaging all of the aircraft overhead. We were all turning our lights on and off trying to avoid the enemy fire but also to figure out where the other aircraft were to avoid a midair collision. After a few radio calls to the other aircraft, we all set up orbits at different altitudes with our lights off. It turned out that a friendly unit was on patrol outside the fire base when the enemy attacked the fire base. The patrol unit must have been very large because the casualties included a company commander and a first sergeant.

The fire base was under heavy fire and I could not figure out if the patrol was taking friendly or enemy fire. The enemy seemed to be all around the base and we were being asked to land outside the fire base. The patrol had managed to move to a bomb crater surrounded by tall trees and filled with snags and stumps. They turned on a small strobe light and asked us to hover in the bomb crater while they lifted the casualties into the aircraft. So, with my lights out I headed down without really knowing where the enemy was in relationship to the bomb crater. As I approached tree top level, I had the copilot turn on the search light. As soon as the light came on the radio lit up with calls from the orbiting aircraft to turn it off before we got shot out of the sky. Of course, we could not turn it off. The crater was littered with stumps and partial trees. I hovered and put my tail either near or between two trees. The crew chief and medic stood on the skids and gave me directions: They were calm, cool, and professional. The jungle was lit up by our light. The copilot was on the controls waiting for me to get shot. The radio was going crazy and we were still trying to get lower in the crater. We could not land, only hover. After what seemed like an eternity, the crew on the skids said we could not go any lower and to hold our position. To this point, I thought I had done my best flying ever. Then the guys on the ground started raising litters up to the aircraft and the crew was trying to guide me and pull the litters in at the same time. The guys on the ground could only reach one side of the aircraft and, of course, the lateral center of gravity was constantly being shifted in a dramatic way. Then my skills at holding position were really being tested.

We got all of the casualties on board and then had to work our way back up through the trees with the crew still on the skids yelling directions. As soon as we hovered up to tree top level, we turned off the lights and headed to the 45th Surgical Hospital. It is good to be lucky and that was the toughest mission I have ever flown in terms of maneuvering the helicopter and crew coordination. The entire crew gave me exactly what we needed and their bravery was amazing. I don't know what happened to the soldiers on the ground that night. I'm sure they never had a chance to think about recognition for the helicopter rescue, and rightly so. The fighting was furious all around the fire base and we made numerous landings inside the wire at the fire base to evacuate casualties. What a night!

Finally, my luck and skill ran out with approximately thirty days until DEROS. I was flying 'first up' with Denny Derber as my copilot. The mission was to evacuate South Vietnamese casualties near 'Dodge City.' The location was known as a hot bed of bad guy activity. After take-off from Cu Chi base camp we stopped in Cu Chi City and picked up a US advisor, an interpreter, and an RTO. We then proceeded to the pick-up zone. While enroute we were told that the unit was retreating from north to south from a heavy engagement with the enemy. They claimed they were no longer receiving fire and it was safe to come in. I elected to treat it as a hot LZ. Denny was in the left seat getting used to flying from that seat in preparation for becoming an AC. I was the AC but flying in the right seat. I elected to make the approach and landing with Denny close on the controls. The approach would be from south to north. From about 2000 feet, I zeroed out the airspeed and then dropped the collective and nosed into a steep dive. We rapidly lost altitude and sped up to 120 knots. When I got to tree top level I made a steep right turn to final. I looked up through the greenhouse over my head and could see people standing up in the LZ. That is usually a good sign. While still in the turn with the right side of the aircraft facing the ground and the air speed still above 100 knots, the earth lit up with small arms fire. We were taking multiple hits from the enemy on the south side of the LZ and I immediately started a climb to safety.

After getting a good climb initiated, I realized I was hit in the right arm. I told Denny I was hit and he said he was hit, too. I kept flying and then Denny said he was OK. He took the controls and I reached down with my left hand and grabbed my right arm to see how bad it was. About one-and-a-half inches from my elbow on my forearm I could see daylight through my arm. I thought that did not look good and I set my arm back in my lap. I experienced no pain. It turned out that when the bullet went through my arm it passed behind Denny's head and lodged in the bulkhead behind his seat. Part of the bone from my arm went into Denny's right shoulder. It turned out to be a superficial wound and he was able to fly the aircraft. I started trying to make radio calls to let the guys on the ground know that they were surrounded. Safely at 2000 feet above the ground I looked up and Denny was orbiting. I asked him what he was doing and he was waiting for me to tell him where to go. I think I yelled, "take me to the hospital." Poor Denny, I'm sure he did not want to leave the area while I was still trying to communicate with the guys on the ground. He flew me to the hospital but while enroute, the crew popped my seat releases and pulled the seat back and down to treat my wound. I was facing the ceiling and yelling "put me back," which they did. I guess I was pretty worked up about trying to communicate that the guys on the ground were retreating right into a large enemy unit.

Later I was told the aircraft took thirty-nine hits. It flew us back to the hospital pad and then had to be towed away. When Denny safely landed us at the pad, I got out and walked into the hospital while holding my arm. I immediately noticed I was walking with a limp and had pain in my right foot. I had been hit by a bullet that passed from the right side of my boot arch to the left side and out. While the bullet never hit my foot, it had caused the metal arch to bend up through the leather and press against my arch causing a contusion on the bottom of my foot. Someone, I don't know who, saved that boot for me and the outer copper casing of the AK-47 round that likely went through my arm and into the bulkhead behind Denny's head. I still have the bullet casing and boot.

I had two operations at the 12th Evacuation Hospital in Cu Chi and after brief stays at hospitals in Long Binh and Japan I ended up at a Hospital in Fort Devens, MA. Another operation resulted in a pin, the diameter of a pencil, being inserted through my ulna starting at the elbow and going all the way to my wrist. The pin lined up the two pieces of bone and the space was filled with a bone graft from my hip.

It all grew back together and after six months I was back to duty as a flight instructor at Fort Rucker. I still have the pin in my arm and consider myself to be extraordinarily lucky. I had no permanent nerve or vascular damage and could pretty much do what I wanted. That included playing the piano and drums, again.

And, true to form, I went on to have a full career in the Army with many unique assignments, including another tour in Viet Nam in 1972. I also had very successful 10 years with the Raytheon Company before I retired. However, none of those experiences came close to the satisfaction I felt while serving with the 159th Medical Detachment rescuing casualties from the battlefield. It was an honor to serve with the men of the 159th .

[Stephen Peth, born on April 18, 1946, in Seneca Falls, N.Y., enlisted in the U.S. Army in 1967. While on active duty, he received a Bachelor of Science degree from Cameron University and an MBA from Auburn

University. He is a graduate of the U.S. Air Force Air Command and Staff College and a 1985 graduate of the Program Managers Course at the Defense Systems Management College. Steve retired from Raytheon August 1, 2004, as Vice President of Air and Missile Defense Programs, US Business Development. Steve is a recipient the Congressional Gold Medal for Vietnam Dust-Off crews signed into law on September 26, 2024.]

From Revival to Survival

Jerry M. Free
B Troop 1967-1969

[Major Jerry M. Free of Irmo, 86, was honored with the prestigious Order of the Palmetto on Friday, Oct. 25 at the Brookland Baptist Banquet and Conference Center. SC Representative Nathan Ballentine made the presentation in front of Free's family, friends and neighbors including the Mayor of Irmo, Bill Danielson. The Order of the Palmetto is the highest civilian award in South Carolina and is presented in recognition of a lifetime of extraordinary achievement, service, and contributions on a national or statewide scale.]

My memories of the time I spent in Vietnam are reflections of long ago. But sometimes, it seems like it was only yesterday. Memories of days past give pause to daily flashbacks of what might have been. Vietnam in many respects was a beautiful country as seen from the air as we flew from our home base at Vinh Long to our area of operation each day. Lush and green as far as the eye could see. It was easy to get lost in the solitude of the moment considering how peaceful and cool it was up in the air. Yet just a few thousand feet below lurked death and destruction. I found solace in the words of the poem, "High Flight" by John Gillespie McGee Junior as he penned; "***Oh, I have slipped the surly bonds of earth and danced the skies on laughter-silvered wings; Sunward I've climbed and joined the tumbling mirth of sun-split clouds and done a hundred things You have not dreamed of-***" Just a few moments to be lost in thought away from the war.

January 4, 1969, dawned the same as many other countless mornings. Awake before daylight ready to face another day not knowing what might be in store for any of us. We went to the mess hall for a quick breakfast and then went down to the flight line in the dark. After making sure all personnel were present and accounted for, we checked our equipment and did our preflight inspections of the aircraft. At the designated time we started our engines, did our radio checks, and announce, "flight up, everyone ready for takeoff."

We departed Vinh Long at O-dark-thirty and climbed to cruise altitude. We proceeded south into the heart of the Mekong Delta. The area was mostly flat, consisting of scattered rice paddies bordered by thick jungle that followed winding drainage canals. The trees were only about fifty feet tall. Hidden among the dense undergrowth of the trees were small villages scattered throughout the area. There were few roads, and the only forms of transportation were by foot, small boats, or aircraft. January is the dry season in Vietnam and the area we were working was a hotbed for the Viet Cong.

The flight was not very long. After landing at a South Vietnamese airfield called Vi Thanh, we refueled and waited for the flight leader to be briefed on our mission for the day. At approximately 7:30 a.m., we took off for the first mission to scout an area southwest of the airfield. Our "Hunter Killer" teams consisted of two 0H-6A Scout helicopters called Loaches, two AH-1G Cobra gunships, and one UH-H model Huey Control and Command (C&C) helicopter. The Huey was flown by Major David Thompson. His crew chief was Mike Thompson, and his co-pilot was CW2 Louis Schantz. I can't remember who his gunner was.

I flew the lead Scout Loach, and my observer was Sp-4 Gary David Falk. Warrant Officer James Hilton flew my wing and James L. French was his observer. Dick Fedorowicz and Joe Klesen flew one Cobra and Capt. Ed Hinderks flew the other one. I can't remember who Ed's co-pilot was.

The beginning of the mission went fairly smoothly, and we located very little activity. As I scouted a small stream surrounded by thick trees and banana palms, I came upon a village consisting of approximately twelve to fifteen thatched huts. The village had a sewage canal dug around the outside with a small clearing in the center. I didn't see anyone in the village. At first, everything appeared normal, except for the absence of people. Then I saw enemy bunkers and firing positions hidden among the trees. I reported my sightings to Maj. Thompson in the C&C ship. Then I saw several individuals running through the undergrowth toward the bunkers. They were dressed in black VC pajamas and carrying weapons.

I quickly flew away from the village. The Cobra gunships rolled in firing rockets and miniguns at the bunkers. When they finished their gun run, we came back in to do a damage report. As I came around the edge of the village at tree-top level and slow speed, all hell broke loose. I received heavy automatic weapons fire as rounds penetrated my Loach. I radioed, "Taking fire, taking fire."

Jim Hilton was right behind me and later told me that the engine cowlings blew open and the engine was blown right out of my helicopter. He believes an RPG hit me. I didn't have much time to react as we nosedived into the trees. The last thing I remember was tree-limbs flashing by as we crashed to the ground. I was knocked unconscious on impact.

While I was unconscious, James Hilton tried to rescue me. As soon as he arrived at my downed helicopter, a VC jumped up with an AK-47 and opened fire on him. James was shot through both legs and his finger was shot off. A round penetrated his helmet, nicking the side of his face and shattering his face shield. The round sprayed blood and Plexiglas in his eyes temporarily blinding him. Hilton would have crashed too if it hadn't been for his observer, James French. "Frenchy," as we called him, hadn't been in the Scouts long enough to fly the helicopter by himself. He directed Hilton toward a large field and literally talked him to the ground with a perfect landing. As soon as Hilton's Loach was clear of the area, Richard Fedorowicz and Joe Klesen came in and hovered above me in their Cobra. They fired rockets and miniguns into the tree line where I had taken fire.

I don't know how long I was unconscious. When I came to, my neck and face on the left side were burning. I believe the heat from the flames is probably what woke me up. Everything was hazy at first, as if I were in a twilight zone. The helicopter was burning and filled with smoke. My helmet and the glove from my left hand were missing. The cockpit was completely smashed.

I looked over at my observer, Gary Falk. He had been killed on impact. Gary was a good man, a good soldier, and totally fearless. At twenty-one years of age, he had three sisters, and a younger brother. My heart filled with grief. For some strange reason that is still a mystery, I couldn't move. I felt at peace and resigned myself to die. My first thoughts were, '*You're not going to get out of this mess.*' *You've lived a good life, but this is the end for you.*

I've heard it said that when a person is facing certain death, their entire life flashes before their eyes, but that was not the case for me. After a few seconds of contemplating my fate, I heard a voice speak to me as clearly as a bell. "*You have a son you haven't yet seen. Get out of there, get out of there.*" Upon hearing that voice I regained my senses and somehow scrambled out of the wreckage. By then, I was badly burned and had lacerations on my leg from the crash.

I made it out of the helicopter and stumbled toward a drainage canal a short distance away. I waded through chest deep water and scrambled up the other side trying to make it to a rice paddy. It was tough going with a wounded leg and the heavy chest protector still strapped on. Luckily, the rice paddy was dry. As I ran, I heard gunfire behind me. A round tore through my right forearm. It felt like I was struck with a baseball bat as I went down. I was totally exhausted from the ordeal but continued crawling out into the rice patty.

Dick Fedorowicz and Joe Klesen saw me running from the wreckage and someone chasing me. At first, they thought it was my observer, Gary Falk. When they got a better view, they realized it was a VC shooting at me with an AK-47. They rolled in and killed him. Hilton later told me that he was sure that it was the same VC who had shot him. While the first Cobra put down protective fire, the other Cobra gunship flown by Capt. Hinderks landed in the rice paddy next to me. His front seat pilot climbed out and opened the ammo bay door on the side of the helicopter. This door is about four feet long and eighteen inches wide and supported by cables at both ends. The co-pilot helped me up onto the door, then climbed on beside me. I don't remember who was holding me on to that Cobra, but I will be forever indebted to him and Capt. Hinderks for saving my life.

We both hung on for dear life while Capt. Hinderks flew us to another area a short distance away where we landed. I was transferred to the C&C helicopter and Maj. Thompson flew me to the hospital at Can Tho. Capt. Hinderk's Cobra escorted us to the hospital. After arriving at the hospital, I was rushed inside for treatment. I remember the doctor asking me if I was allergic to anything. I told him I was allergic to pain. My face felt like it was on fire. My arm and leg were also hurting. The pain was almost unbearable.

The next thing I remembered was waking up. The doctor that had told me that I needed to go to surgery right away was standing over me. I reached over and felt my arm and realized that I had already been to surgery. I was taken to the ward for recovery and went into shock. I started shivering. I kept telling the nurses, "I'm cold, I'm so cold." I couldn't stop shivering. This wasn't normal because it was always hot in Vietnam plus the hospital wasn't air-conditioned. The nurses brought me some blankets, and after a while I was all right.

When Maj. Thompson and Hinderks left the area, Dick Fedorowicz couldn't find James Hilton's helicopter. Fedorowicz couldn't make radio contact with Maj. Thompson or Hinderks to determine where the other Loach had gone. The talk channel on the C&C ship had been shut off or switched to another channel. Fedorowicz and Klesen searched the area and located Hilton's Loach sitting in a rice paddy about a thousand meters from the village with the rotors blades still spinning. Frenchy had dragged Hilton free of the aircraft. Dick Fedorowicz landed his Cobra next to the Loach. Joe Klesen got out of the front seat and helped Hilton onto their ammo bay door. Frenchy got in the front seat of the Cobra. Joe sat beside Hilton to help hold him on the helicopter ammo door.

As they took off, Klesen's mouthpiece was blown off his helmet by the downdraft. He held on by bracing his feet on the skids while holding on to the cables and ammo box to keep Hilton and himself from falling off. Hilton held on to one cable with his good hand and grabbed the back of Klesen's collar with his injured hand.

There were no other Huey helicopters in the area to transport Hilton to the hospital. Fedorowicz flew the helicopter at an angle to keep his passengers from falling off while he transported them to the hospital at Can Tho. His low fuel light was on most of the way. He landed on fumes and the helicopter ran out of fuel. The helicopter had to be re-fueled before they could take off again.

When the medics put Hilton on a stretcher, they attempted to put Joe Klesen on another one believing he was also wounded. He was covered in Hilton's blood and so cramped from holding on that he couldn't move. Klesen finally convinced the medics and nurses that he wasn't injured. He and Fedorowicz followed Hilton into the hospital where they saw me lying on a table talking to the doctor. They heard the doctor ask me if I was allergic to anything and my reply, "Yes, pain!" I didn't know they were there, but they knew I would make it after hearing me talking to the doctor.

I spent a week in the hospital in Vietnam being treated for the gunshot wound in my arm, second and third degree burns to the left side of my forehead, and deep lacerations to my left thigh. Because of the concussion, I went temporarily blind, but my eyesight came back after a couple of days. After a week in the hospital in Vietnam, I was evacuated to Japan where I spent a week. They did a closed reduction on my right arm and treated my burns. I was then returned stateside via Andrews Air Force Base and completed my recovery at Fort Jackson. While at Fort Jackson, I underwent more surgeries to set the bones and to have a metal plate put in my right arm.

I petitioned to remain on active duty and my request was granted. After spending several months at Fort Jackson, I was transferred to Fort Knox. During my career, I served at several other bases, including two years in Korea, before retiring from the Army in 1978. I will always be grateful to the brave men with whom I served with in Vietnam, especially those who saved my life. The Blackhawks will forever be my brothers and I love seeing them at the reunions.

[Captain Jerry M. Free served in the U.S. Army as a helicopter pilot, retiring with the rank of Major in 1978. He served two tours in RVN with the 188th Airmobile Company 1965-1966, B Troop 7/1 Air Cav 1968-1969. He was awarded the Distinguished Flying Cross with 2 Oak Leaf Clusters, Air Medal with V & 22 Oak Leaf Clusters, the Purple Heart, Bronze Star, Army Commendation with 2 Oak Leaf Clusters, and the Vietnamese Cross of Gallantry, among many other awards and certificates.]

Neal Caspersen – Dustoff Crew Chief

I was a helicopter crew chief flying with the 45th Air Ambulance, Dustoff, and in December 1970, we were on standby flying out of Tan An down in the delta when we got the call. The mission came about midday, and it was a beautiful cloudless blue-sky day, too pretty of a day for it to become a bad day. When we got on station a C&C, (Command & Control) ship had us hold in place as they were conducting an airstrike on a thick tree line boarding a large rice paddy. In the rice paddy, about 50 yards from the tree line, was a dirt berm shaped like an eyebrow approximately 30 feet long and 8 feet high, sticking up out of the flooded rice paddy, and a platoon of ARVNs were huddled behind it.

The C&C bird informed us they would conduct another airstrike and we were to follow. A pair of F-4's took the lead followed by a pair of A-6's and following them were a pair of A-1's. Next were a pair of Cobra gunships, then a smoke ship laying down smoke was followed by us tucked in on the friendly side of the smoke.

The aircraft commander, Mr. Brian Prahl, brought the aircraft to approximately 50 feet of the berm. The rice paddy being flooded, Mr. Prahl kept the aircraft at a hover, our skids were under water but not low enough to get the deck underwater. Four ARVN's carrying two wounded came quickly to our right hand side, which was my side of the aircraft. The water was greater than waist deep on the ARVNs. No litters, the first wounded was loaded onboard and the second one was almost loaded feet first when his body jerked hard in my hands. He took a round right in the top of his head splattering his last thoughts all over me. At the same time the audio warning blared through my helmet.

The protective smoke was gone, the airstrike aircraft had not come back around yet, and we were now exposed to the enemy. Mr. Prahl dropped the collective and the deck was awash in about two or three inches of water. Sitting in the wide open taking rounds Mr. Prahl shut down the aircraft and told us to make for the berm. I exited the helicopter and opened Mr. Prahl's door, and one of the ARVNs who was carrying the wounded was now face-down in the water. He was another headshot victim and the back of his head clearly showed.

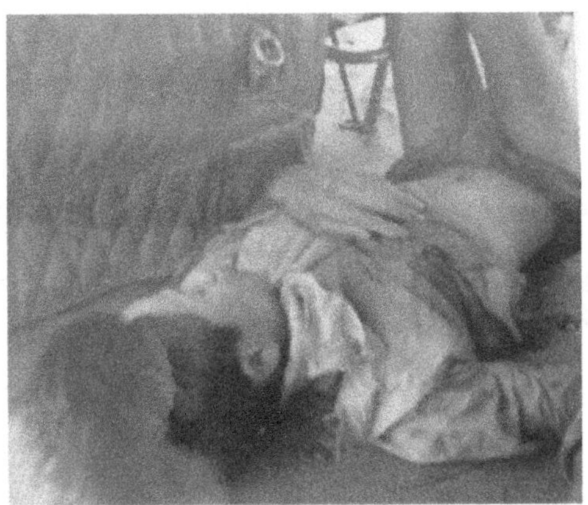

The water was nut to waist deep, sticky thick mud clung to my boots making movement a great effort and slow, geysers made by bullets where erupting all around us as we struggled to the berm, half way to the berm I went into a hole and went completely under water. Wearing my chicken plate and carrying my M-16 I don't know how I got out of the hole. Just as we made it the berm miraculously unscathed the airstrike aircraft led by the F-4's made it back around scaring the hell out of me as I didn't know they were coming, the sound of the F-4's followed by the ordnance they dropped was, well it got my adrenalin maxed out. Being a crew chief air crew men I have never been out of aircraft in a hostile situation with air strikes, none of liked it. The bad guys heads were down with the airstrikes back in full swing.

The C&C ship came in landing out of the target zone. Mr. Prahl rushed out to our aircraft picked up the wounded

ARVN and loaded him on the C&C ship. I went to inspect my aircraft sitting in a red lake of hydraulic fluid. She didn't look to bad no engine oil coming out, no apparent damage from the swash plate up. Mr. Prahl says let's get out of here, we all agreed taking a chance with the aircraft seemed better than taking a chance on the ground. Getting in back seeing all the water and weight it represented I was concerned our skids may be stuck in the mud so I slid the KIA out next to the other KIA in the water. It was the fastest startup and takeoff I ever experienced. We were dumping water like we were firefighting. I forget if it was Vin Long or Dong Tam we flew to but they foamed the runway for our running landing. Post inspection, we took a round through the irreversible valve on the right cyclic servo, a round to the engine oil cooler, one clipped the tail rotor cable just above the 42 degree gear box and the rest of the rounds just through the skin.

Thank You Mr. Prahl for safely getting us out of there and back to the friendlies.

The Nurses: An Overview

During the Vietnam War, approximately 7,000 American women served as nurses, primarily in the Army, facing challenging conditions and high-stress environments to care for wounded soldiers. They often worked long hours in a constant influx of casualties, performing emergency procedures like triage and surgery. Despite the dangers, they worked tirelessly, with many of the nurses being young and some without extensive experience before deployment. Their service is now recognized through memorials such as the Vietnam Women's Memorial.

Experiences and duties

- **High-intensity medical care:**

Nurses worked in evacuation hospitals, often performing life-saving procedures and assisting in surgeries, and were sometimes referred to as "Pluckers" for their work in removing shrapnel.

- **Constant threat:**

They worked under the threat of enemy fire and rocket attacks, which became a part of daily life in many areas, requiring them to take shelter during alerts.

- **Long hours:**

Shifts were often long and demanding, and the constant

arrival of wounded by helicopter made it a nonstop environment.

Demographics and recruitment

- **Young and inexperienced:**

The average age of these nurses was 23, and many were recruited directly from nursing school, with only about 35% having more than two years of experience upon commissioning.

- **Male nurses:**

About 20% of military nurses in Vietnam were men, as the Army Nurse Corps had accepted men since 1955.

- **Recruitment:**

Some nurses were recruited through programs such as the Army Student Nurse Program, which paid for their tuition in exchange for their service.

Recognition and legacy

- **A largely unrecognized contribution:**

For many years, the crucial role of these nurses was not widely acknowledged.

- **Vietnam Women's Memorial:**

The creation of the Vietnam Women's Memorial in Washington, D.C., spearheaded by former nurse Diane Carlson Evans, helped bring their stories to light and ensure their contributions were recognized.

- **Saving lives:**

Nurses saved the lives of hundreds of thousands of men wounded in the war.

- **Continued service:**

Many nurses continued their careers after the war in various roles, including becoming physicians, teachers, and even the military's first female general officer.

The Nurses
Dedicated to
1st Lieutenant Sharon Ann Lane,
U. S. Army Nurse Corps
The First American Woman Killed
during the Vietnam War

Sharon Ann Lane joined the U.S. Army Air Corps Reserve on April 18, 1968, as a 2nd Lieutenant. Her first assignment was at Fitzsimons General Hospital in Denver, Colo., where she was promoted and sent off to Travis Air Force Base with orders to Vietnam.

1st LT Lane arrived at the 312th Evacuation Hospital at Chu Lai on 29 April. She was originally assigned to the Intensive Care Unit, but a few days later was reassigned to the Vietnamese Ward. Nursing the Vietnamese in Ward 4 was often physically and emotionally challenging, yet Lane repeatedly declined transfers to another ward. She worked five days a week, twelve hours a day in Ward 4, and spent her off-duty time taking care of the most critically injured American soldiers in the Surgical ICU. She thrived despite the demanding schedule and was adored and respected by co-workers and patients alike.

On the morning of 8 June 1969, the 312th Evacuation Hospital was struck by a salvo of 122mm rockets fired by the Viet Cong. One rocket struck between Wards 4A and 4B, killing two people and wounding another twenty-seven. Among the dead was 1st LT Lane, who died instantly of fragmentation wounds to the chest. She was one month shy of her twenty-sixth birthday. Though one of eight American military nurses who died while serving in Vietnam, Sharon Lane was the only American nurse killed as a direct result of hostile fire. A memorial service was held in Chu Lai 10 June 1969 and a Catholic mass followed the next day. 1st Lieutenant Lane was buried with full military honors at Sunset Hills Burial Park in her hometown of Canton, Ohio.

For her service in Vietnam, 1st LT Sharon Ann Lane was awarded the Purple Heart, the Bronze Star with "V" device, the National Defense Service Medal, the Vietnam Service Medal, the National Order of Vietnam Medal, and the Vietnamese Gallantry Cross (with Palm).

The One Who Stayed After Dark
Joanna Mae Linton,
U S Army Nurse Corps

Her name was Joanna Mae Linton, but she rarely introduced herself. To most of the wounded boys in the field hospital outside Da Nang, she was simply "Doc Jo."

Born in 1946 in Kentucky coal country, she was the daughter of a war widow and a part-time gospel singer. She had never left the U.S. until she signed up for the Army Nurse Corps in 1969. She didn't join to make a difference. She joined to escape a silence at home that was louder than any bomb. Joanna was calm. Always calm. When others panicked, she counted heartbeats. When shelling shook the tents, she pressed her hand to the wounded and said: “As long as you feel me here, you’re still here.”

But the thing that made her different was this: She only worked after dark. She volunteered for every night shift. Every overnight watch. Even when her eyes were bloodshot and her hands were raw. When asked why, she said: “They’re more afraid at night. And nobody should be alone in the dark.”

One evening, a boy named Charlie Amos was brought in — 16 years old, barely breathing, with a picture of his baby sister in his pocket. The other nurses said he wouldn’t last the night. Joanna sat by him for eight hours straight. “Tell me something,” he whispered. “Is it gonna hurt?” “Only for a moment,” she replied, holding his hand. “And after that, it’ll feel like falling asleep while someone sings to you.”

Charlie didn’t make it. But he never cried. A month later, Joanna herself was wounded while shielding a medic from an explosion. Shrapnel tore through her side, but she recovered. When she was offered a discharge, she refused. “I’ll leave when the dark feels empty,” she said. “But it’s still full of voices.” Joanna returned home in 1972 — with a limp, a box of letters from soldiers’ families, and a voice rough from smoke and whispers. She became a children’s nurse in a small clinic in Tennessee. Never married. Never told stories. But every night before bed, she lit a single candle by her window and sat in silence for 16 minutes — one for every boy she lost on her shift. When she passed away in 2007, the local paper ran a single line on the obituary page: “She was the one who stayed after dark.”

The Flight Nurse
LtCol Mary Jane Parrish, USAFR (Ret)

Mary Jane Parrish is a retired Air Force Flight Nurse who flew during Vietnam as a Reservist. Her husband was a pilot who retired after 40 years as a BGen. She went to Flight School in 1968 and then came back to Andrews AF Base. I was Chief Nurse of the Medical Air Evac Unit for many years and then was transferred to Malcolm Grow Hospital at Andrews AF Base where she retired as a Lt Col after 20 years.

When I returned from Flight School in Texas, I continued to be assigned to the 60th Aeromedical Evacuation Unit at Andrew's Air Force in Md. Shortly thereafter I received orders for a 2 week tour to Vietnam Nam. This part of my life I will never forget.

We flew into Japan and then would pick up a load of casualties waiting in Vietnam from the front lines where they had been taken care of by the Army Nurses and Doctors. After loading ambulatory and liter casualties we were off to the US. We then flew into Elmendorf Air Force Base, in Alaska and unloaded all our patients. They would then be picked up by another Air Evacuation crew and then would be transported to Medical facilities in the United States. After 4 hours of Crew Rest, we would load up another group of patients and deliver them to other Bases in the US. Our final destination was Malcolm Grow Medical center at Andrew's Air Force Base in Md Crew rest at last- this one for a few days. Then back to Vietnam again and repeat the same journey.

This was quite a challenging experience taking care of severely injured individuals. We had both litter and ambulatory patients. We, the nurses had Medical Techs assisting us with the care of mostly the liter patients. Some no longer had limbs but they were so happy that they were finally going home. They never complained and were so thankful that we were there to take care of them. They were so tired and most of them did not complain in spite of being in pain. They did their best and supported each other.

We Nurses and Medical Techs did our best to keep them as comfortable as possible. With God's help and guidance.

1st LT. Jennifer Glick, U. S. Army Nurse Corps

I had been working for a year after graduating from college with my degree in nursing. During that time, I often thought about finding a position where I could work and travel. The Peace Corps seemed like a natural choice for me. But then I heard nurses were needed in Vietnam; that the Army Nurse Corps had developed a special program for nurses who would volunteer for a tour of duty in Vietnam – 8 weeks of basic training and the standard year-long tour would fulfill your military commitment. So there I was deciding, Peace Corps versus Vietnam, Peace versus war, war versus peace.

The Army program appealed to my desire to use my nursing background to help the troops in Vietnam. They were giving their lives in service to their country. I wanted to support them as much as possible. So, I chose war. Interestingly, Army nurses who served in Vietnam averaged 23.6 years of age (I was 23) and only 35% had more than 2 years of experience. About 79% were female; and I had never met a male nurse at the time. The decision to go to Vietnam probably determined the arc of my career – away from traditional nursing as it was known at that time.

I was commissioned as a First Lieutenant and started Officers' Basic Training for nurses and doctors, at Ft. Sam Houston in San Antonio, TX in September 1970. Basic was like going back to college, except for the marching drills on the quadrangle before sunrise – we clumsily followed the Drill Sergeant's orders, often crashing into each other. We attended classes on the military way of doing things, in addition to clinical practice instruction. As nurses we learned advanced skills required to treat combat injuries, including insertion of large-bore IV's, debriding, and suturing of open wounds, and establishing emergency airways in life-threatening injury cases. We were taught how to handle firearms and how to set up field hospitals, including managing patients on hand-held stretchers – a challenging but necessary skill. There was no mental health training, which became a concern when we got to Vietnam.

Besides the usual military garb, we were issued a traditional nurse uniform of a white dress, white hat, and white stockings! I couldn't imagine wearing that uniform in a combat zone, and as it turned out, we didn't. With very few exceptions, nurses in Vietnam wore fatigues. After basic, and facing deployment to Vietnam, I felt pretty confident – that is, until the night before I was to fly out of Travis AFB in Oakland, California. That night, with a college friend, I went to see the latest movie "MASH," which as you know, was about Army medical personnel during the Korean War. While watching this tragicomedy I didn't know whether to laugh or cry. It was the first time I felt fear about what I would be facing in the coming year. The next day, I was on the flight to Vietnam, five women, all of us nurses, among a crowd of young men – a mixture of draftees, volunteers, and career personnel. None of us knew each other; headed to the war in Vietnam alone, not part of a formal unit that trained together – and when the time came we would also return home alone. This was significantly different compared to deployments in the Gulf War, Iraq, and Afghanistan.

The mood was high as most of us were fairly young and this was quite an adventure. On the way to 'Nam, we stopped in Hawaii, Wake Island, and Okinawa before landing at Tan Son Nhut AB near Saigon. As we disembarked, I remember a cheering crowd of troops boarding a "Freedom Bird," and a sign "Welcome to the Real World!" They were on their way home. I thought: So, we're entering an unreal world? And to a certain extent, we were. The movies "Apocalypse Now" and "Good Morning Vietnam" capture how bizarre the environment was. In Vietnam, there were no front lines; enemy forces could strike anywhere. Your Mama-san, a Vietnamese woman who did your laundry, or any innocent-looking kid on the street could be a threat just as dangerous as the NVA/VC.

My first duty station was the 67th Evacuation Hospital in Qui Nhon, near the large airfield there. Medical facilities were often located on airfields, near combat division headquarters, or supply depots – all enemy targets. I felt this acutely when fighting occurred outside the hospital gates or when the supply depot was hit and exploded all night long. After I came home, I experienced PTSD-type nightmares that lasted 20 years. I still react to the sound of helicopters, remembering how the wounded were evacuated to our hospital for treatment --the sound of those blades going "whop, whop" as the chopper hovered over the hospital before landing near triage. We regularly shopped at the PX for food items, liquor, cosmetics, stereo equipment.. There were hamburger joints, tennis courts, water skiing on the South China Sea, movies, and lots of parties.

Outside of work (12-hour shifts, 6 days a week), there was a very active social life– Commanders often invited nurses to parties. We were the only Western women in-country, except for the Red Cross staff and a few administrative personnel in Saigon. Most nurses in my group were assigned to medical-surgical units or ICUs around the country. I was shocked to learn I was assigned to work with a psychiatrist at the 67th Evac - certainly not what I envisioned for my tour of duty. I had little psychiatric nursing experience, which amounted to dispensing the latest psychotropic medications. Addressing the psychiatric needs of combat soldiers was not part of basic training. I thought, what about the advanced clinical skills I worked so hard to learn?

I felt a bit disheartened by this assignment – as a nurse, the field of psychiatry didn't seem well-respected, plus, mental illness was burdened by stigma and discrimination. I felt out of my element, like I didn't fit in well with my fellow nurses. It was not just that I felt inexperienced and unprepared, but that combat stress casualties that were supposedly the focus of psychiatric services in Vietnam didn't present nearly as often as the psychosocial casualties (the disciplinary problems, racial disturbances, attacks on superiors, drug abuse.) That's where the bulk of the work was.

I believe there was a reason for this. I was deployed to Vietnam at the beginning stages of the withdrawal of U.S. troops. Some hospitals had closed; equipment was being sent home. And there was a cultural polarization going on in the U.S. and Vietnam: Across the U.S., there were anti-Vietnam demonstrations. Returning troops were being greeted with insults and abuse. Replacement troops were mostly young draftees and "reluctant volunteers" many in trouble with the law and faced with a choice of going to jail or Vietnam. Their attitudes often resonated with the anti-Vietnam demonstrations back home. Increasingly, the troops questioned their purpose in Vietnam. They expressed, sometimes through psychiatric conditions, inability, or unwillingness to accept the risks of combat, or the authority of military leaders, or the hardships of being in Vietnam.

All of this contributed to a breakdown in soldier morale and discipline, and the development of a burgeoning drug culture. So, our Mental Hygiene Clinic was very busy, including emergency room coverage. We also treated some people in the Vietnamese community – my first attempt at delivering culturally competent care. I was lucky to be working with Frank, the psychiatrist. He was patient with me, as well as fair, kind, and compassionate. I reported to him and not the Chief Nurse, which exempted me from abrupt assignment changes that other nurses had to put up with. Frank allowed me to travel around the country, from the Mekong Delta to the DMZ, which was very exciting. I took advantage of every opportunity to explore the country and get to know the Vietnamese people. I also made use of the R&R benefit (Rest and Recreation), traveling to Australia, Hong Kong, and Thailand.

The clinic closed when Frank finished his tour of duty, and I was reassigned to the beach, literally, in Cam Ranh Bay, where the military set up the first drug treatment center. The military was receiving negative press about the drug culture among troops – especially those flying back to the states in detox mode. It became mandatory that everyone returning to the U.S. had to submit a urine sample, and if "dirty," had to go through detox before boarding the "Freedom Bird."

I came home in late November 1971. Leaving my boots and fatigues in a pathetic pile in Bien Hoa, I boarded a flight back over the Pacific to Fort Lewis in Washington State. There I made the decision to leave military service.

I was relieved to be back in the U.S., and finally in Connecticut, but there wasn't much of a homecoming. No one wanted to hear about Vietnam; people mainly turned away rather than acknowledge I had just been there. There was no "Thank you for your service." It was surreal, and once again I found it hard to fit in. Most of my friends had gotten married and were starting families. It would be a few years before I would enter that realm of our society.

So, I got to work - finding a job, an apartment, and driving a car again, trying to acculturate to the "Real World." I applied for a credit card – a new item back then, and I couldn't get one despite having served a year in Vietnam. I was a woman and back then, women needed permission from the right people, men primarily, to obtain a credit card. I remember feeling very insulted. But the women's movement was beginning to take off – to the point that women would soon be able to make their own health care decisions, as well as obtain credit cards.

I sought treatment for depression, plus I had a recurrent dream for over 20 years where I found myself back in

Vietnam, always running from the VC, through a steamy jungle in the dead of night, and jumping into a river to hide from them. In my last dream, I was caught and shot. The dreams ended; however the sound of a helicopter still triggers memories. Not until 1993, when I was in Washington, D.C. for the dedication of the Women's Vietnam Memorial, was I ever thanked for my service in Vietnam. A male veteran ran up to me, hugged me, and gave me his paratrooper insignia, which I still have stored with other memorabilia. I also met a few of the nurses I had worked with at the 67th Evac Hospital.

It was so exciting that day, so gratifying to finally be honored for our service. I felt proud of all the nurses. We served and we survived.

[Jennifer Glick served as a First Lieutenant in the Army Nurse Corps in Vietnam from 1970-71. Her service there led to a career in the field of Mental Health - focused on the experiences of veterans and older adults. Now retired, Jennifer lives in a retirement community in Cromwell, CT. She is enjoying new friends, writing poetry and personal essays, creating mixed-media art, morning walks to the Connecticut River, and playing pickleball. Before moving to Cromwell, Jennifer represented veterans on a local Town Commission. With her new environment, she is becoming involved with another veteran's group. She is also a member of a veteran's writing group and a veteran's kayaking group.]

Captain Dianne Carlson Evans, U. S. Army Nurse Corps
Screaming to Death

Above, in the sky, the bird wasn't going away. I knew the sound of a Dustoff, and this wasn't one. The sounds of the blades kept getting louder and the vibrations stronger. Choppers meant only one thing – more death. Moe disillusionment. More distrust of everything I'd once believed in.

By the spring of 1969, after eight months in-country, my Vietnam experience, had, if possible, turned darker. I was so tired I just wanted to go to sleep and wake up anywhere but this war-torn place that I hated so much.

I told the nurses sharing my hootch "That's a Chinook." That means dozens of wounded instead of a handful.

It was March 7, 1969: a mushrooming nightmare for our medical team. Mass casualties. A "push." In came the wounded and sick. Out went our generator – Not an uncommon occurrence, but the first time it had happened during a mass casualty situation like the one we were facing. Ventilators can't pump oxygen into the lungs when the generator dies. Pleiku's dust turned the chopper's landing zone into a whirl of crimson fog. Litter-bearers shielded their eyes as they ferried their wounded buddies into our heavily bunkered emergency room for triage.

Then came the final indignation, the sky began raining enemy fire. In Vietnam, army field hospital wards were uniquely spread apart so that one rocket couldn't destroy the whole complex.

The first mortar round hit close to my ward. A series of incoming rounds landed. Exploding mortar shells sprayed shrapnel and dirt. We grabbed our helmets and flak jackets enroute to our duty posts. Shaos laughed in the face o9f whatever sanity was left.

I was ordered to open up the spare ward. What hours earlier had been an empty room and it was suddenly filled with groaning bodies. I felt a sense of dread. I yelled for a Corpsman to bring a flashlight.

I knew the drill, as did all the other doctors, nurses, and Corpsmen already in the emergency room or setting up the OR. Dazed from the load-in, the Corpsman and I did a quick assessment. "Twenty-eight," said the Corpsman after a quick count. Something more was happening here.

I asked my medic if he saw what I saw, "No boys full of holes. This is really strange."

I did a quick assessment: weak pulses, low blood pressure, exhaustion. The patients were drained of color, struggling with life-threatening dehydration. They were going into shock soon. I couldn't diagnose them, but I knew they needed fluid resuscitation – and fast.

A harried doctor appeared and took a quick look. "Start Ringer's lactate on every one of them. Two liters over the first two hours, then one liter over two hours. I'll be back later."

Thanks to heroic pilots and their choppers ready to lift off at any given moment, most soldiers arrived at a field or evac hospital within hours, sometimes minutes of being wounded. But these mud-crusted and disoriented soldiers appeared to have been days in getting here. It was impossible to know their back-story. Nobody was talking. Some were moaning and a few were so hypertensive they were bordering on what we called "expectants," those certain to die.

Compartmentalize, I told myself. Trust the process. One step at a time. One soldier at a time. I breathed deeply. By now, Vietnam had pretty much blotted out any faith I'd arrived with, but I was desperate.

Thank God for the ward master, a crusty sergeant who'd served in World War II and Korea as a medic, who seemingly always knew exactly what to do and was always one step ahead of me. He had set-up all the IV poles, tubing, and a bottle of fluid hanging from every one of them. As the last litter-bearer came in I said to my Corpsman, w3e're3 ready . We're going to get fluids in these men before they dry up and blow away.

I soon realized the numbers, the darkness, and the whistling of the mortar shells above us weren't the only concerns. The men were so dehydrated that their veins were collapsed. I had trouble finding them to insert the needle and get the life-saving liquid going. By now I had started hundreds of IV. I was good at this. I knew what to do. Touch the soldier on his hand as a means of connecting with him. Choose the arm with the most probable vein. Wrap the tourniquet around the arm. Scrub the entry point. Insert the needle. Release the tourniquet. Run the fluid. Repeat.

The guys with the painful abdominal cramping worried me, but they even settled down as the intravenous fluids took hold.

About a third of the way through the twenty-eight men, we found one who seemed mildly lucid. His eyes widened when he saw the flashlight beam. "Soldier," I asked, "what happened?" He stared right through me, eyes fixed. "Food poisoning?" my Corpsman asked. "Water poisoning?" No response.

Hours passed. The shelling stopped. My eyes scanned the bodies for those who may be in distress, those slipping into some degree of unconsciousness; we would never find out what happened to these guys.

Twenty-eight soldiers arrived. Twenty-eight still have measurable pulses. We mirrored quick smiles. I shook my head sideways in wonder and weariness. “Good Work,” I said to my Corpsman. “Uh, good enough for your usual reward, ma’am?’ “Sure!” We slipped into the supply room. Whatever faint light was still left in his flashlight, he shined on a tier of shelves, one of which contained something I’d baked the night before, a batch of cinnamon rolls. “Oh my God,” he said, these are heaven.” A week after the mortar attack, at just after four in the morning, all was quiet in the compound. Every building was dark and I had a fleeting image of our hands-on-hip nursing supervisor, a woman born sometime before Attila the Hun – and with the same disposition. Our shift was over.

I slept for four hours, but it seems like four minutes. Back on our post-operative unit by 6:30 am, we evac’d out most of our patients. I checked on a Montagnard child burned by napalm – to make room for the newly wounded. As darkness fell, the skies lit up; in Vietnam, the night belonged to the enemy. A shell ripped into the earth just outside our ward. The NVA was targeting the Pleiku Air Base and the radar placed alongside our hospital buildings.

We needed no coaching – nor did the patients. They hit the floor, yanking out blood lines and IVs. We grabbed their empty mattresses and threw them atop the patients who couldn’t move – those connected to chest tubes, tracheotomies, malaria ice blankets, and ventilators. It was a sorry way to protect them, but it was all we had.

While reconnecting tubing and blood lines, I heard it, a child's scream. In the faint glow of the flashlight, I found her. She was perhaps two or three, face wet with tears, hands over her ears. It was the little Montagnard girl. I couldn't pick her up; she was burned too badly. God, what had we done? Her parents had been killed in their village. She was terrified and in extreme pain. More shells. More screams from the little girl. I had done all I could, now I got under her crib and reached up to hold her hand. And I prayed to take away her pain, to stop the shelling and stop the suffering. Don't let them die, not here, not now.

"It's OK., I've got you." She heard the comfort in my voice but kept screaming. Just when you thought you'd seen it all – necklaces made of human ears and all the rest – something such as this would remind you that, when it came to war, the potential for man's inhumanity was immeasurable. A few moments later the little girl screamed herself to death. Literally. One minute you were enjoying a cinnamon roll with your Corpsman, the next realizing a little girl whose had you held – the girl you'd promised to protect – had gone limp as a rag doll.

Moving to the 71st Evacuation Hospital at Pleiku, I felt like flying directly into a storm, but that's what I needed. I was wiser, smarter more confident than I'd been when first arriving in Vietnam. Less trusting, yes but no less intent on looking for the good in people, be it Americans, Vietnamese, or Montagnards. I went from being a 2nd lieutenant to a 1st lieutenant and became the head nurse of a surgical unit. I quickly formed bonds with a handful of other nurses, foremost among them Edie McCoy. We arrived about the same time, both wanting a change even though the territory looked more hostile. We realized we were both from Minnesota and traded memories. She brought a green tomato home from the mess hall and put it on her windowsill. "What's that for?" I asked. "I just want to look at something that's alive."

Beyond the combat casualties, even the jungle around us was dead, leveled by liberal spraying of Agent Orange.

We worked in wood-framed wards with glass-free windows. Choppers arrived with regularity, sometimes two or more at a time. Depending on the type of Huey, a Dustoff helicopter could bring up to ten or twelve KIA or wounded.

In February, the post-Tet offensive ratcheted our casualties to a new high. I once went thirty-two hours without sleep. Even when you dd catch shut eye, it wasn't always peaceful.

The compound was surrounded by concertina wire and guard towers housing medics or MPs with M16s. It wasn't just here that hospitals were taking heat. I got a letter from a friend in Vung Tao who said shortly after I left, they'd been hit by a rocket attack and taken mass casualties. Numbers never bled, cried, or died; however it was the individuals you remembered.

A young black-haired girl, maybe twelve or thirteen arrived, teetering toward death. A pediatric doctor,

Captain Dan Rowe, diagnosed her with plague, possibly pneumonic. Quarantine was a joke. All we could do is put up a sheet separating he from other patients. Dr. Rowe told me to put a sign above her bed "Do Not Resuscitate." I briefed our corpsmen and nurses that under no circumstance should they do mouth-to-mouth as plague can be contagious from the saliva. On the next shift, I walked in to find one of our medics, Specialist John Huddleston performing mouth-to-mouth. "Huddleston, stop!" Don't you remember what I told you? STOP! He wouldn't. I checked the little girl's pulse. She was gone. "Huddleston, it's too late." He wept…unabashedly. "You know that was dangerous. Why were you doing it?" He rubbed his hands across his face. "I just wanted to save her life," he said.

One night litter-bearers brought in a teenage Montagnard girl wrapped in a dark maroon sarong. She grabbed my arm, terrified. I noticed the pupil of one eye was huge a dilated, the other pin-point small, always a bad sign. Of course, she wanted her mother. I was "mom" for those brief moments; I comforted he as best I could, then, called Dr. Rowe with my plea for him to take a look, explaining the symptoms.

I could tell I awakened him, probably after a fourteen-hour shift. "Diane," he mumbled, "you know as well as I do, there's nothing we can do for her." What could I say? I had no response. So I held her in my arms, knowing she would likely die soon. And then, ten minutes later, there he was, coming through the door: Rowe. Hair mussed. Eyes half-mast. But there, ready to help if there was even a glimmer of hope. The girl died anyway. But he had come, a moment I would never forget.

I was far too exhausted to notice that I'd arrived at some sort of emotional crossroads. I was feeling less and less like I had a say in where I was going. I was careening unsteadily toward a choice that – whatever it was – might have more control over me than I had over it. On one hand you could say I had only myself to blame, after all, it was my decision, after six months in Vung Tau, to seek a transfer closer to intense fighting. You were always on guard for the unexpected, whether that might be an attack, an infiltration, or the Mama-San who did your wash stealing medical supplies. Or worse: passing secrets to the enemy.

And so amid the madness, I decided, rooted in self-preservation, my personal cry to refuse being so warped by war that I could no longer recognize myself if I looked in a mirror. A week after the mortar attack, just after four in the morning, all was quiet in the compound. Every building was dark. Suddenly combat boot, their owner purposely walking lightly to avoid detection, padded down a hallway and into the mess hall supply room.

I flicked on my flashlight5, startling a mama san asleep on a supply shelf in my path. She ran off. The nursing supervisor be damned; this was war. Time to make a batch of cinnamon rolls.

[Diane Carlson Evans is a former Captain in the Army Nurse Corps who served in the combat zone of Vietnam. She is the founder of the Vietnam Women's Memorial Foundation, Inc. She served as president and CEO of the foundation's board of directors for thirty years. Diane is the recipient of the Presidential Citizens Medal.]

With permission from her book: "*HEALING WOUNDS*"

The Eight Women on The Wall: Nurses Who Made the Ultimate Sacrifice
March 31, 2016
by VVMF

The names of eight women, all nurses (seven from the Army and one from the Air Force), are inscribed next to their fallen brothers on The Wall in Washington, D.C.

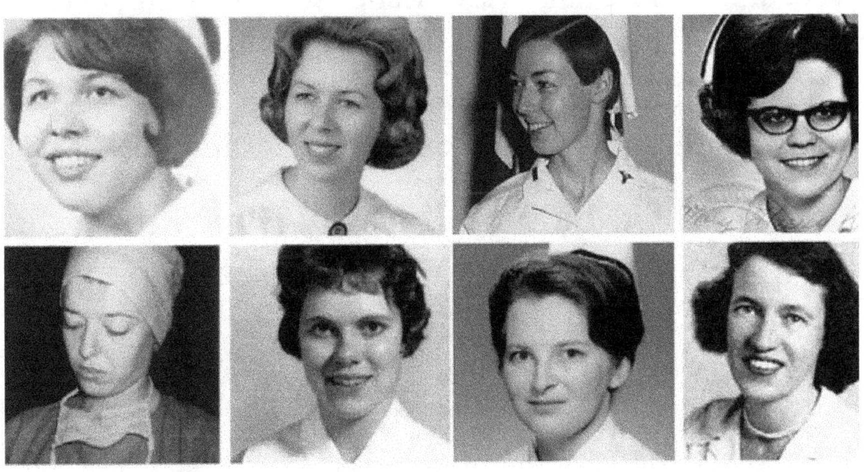

(L to R: 1st. Lt. Hedwig Orlowski, 2nd Lt. Carol Drazba, 1st. Lt. Sharon Lane, Capt. Mary Klinker, Capt. Eleanor Alexander, 2nd Lt. Elizabeth Jones, 2nd Lt. Pamela Donovan, LTC Annie Graham)

Each dedicated themselves to taking care of the wounded and dying.

See their faces and remember their names.

1st Lt. Sharon Ann Lane of Canton, Ohio.

1st Lieutenant Sharon Ann Lane, U.S. Army was killed by a rocket explosion on June 8, 1969, less than 10 weeks after she arrived in Vietnam. Assigned to the 312th Evacuation Hospital, 1LT Lane was working in the Vietnamese ward of the hospital when the rocket exploded, killing her and her patients. She was from Ohio and her name can be found on Panel 23, Line 112.

2nd Lt. Pamela Dorothy Donovan of Brighton, Massachusetts.

2nd Lieutenant Pamela Dorothy Donovan, U.S. Army died of pneumonia on July 8, 1968. Born in Ireland, she was assigned to the 85th Evacuation Hospital in Qui Nhon. 2LT Donovan is remembered on Panel 53W, Line 43.

Lt. Col. Annie Ruth Graham of Efland, North Carolina.

Lieutenant Colonel Annie Ruth Graham, U.S. Army suffered a stroke on August 14, 1968. She was from North Carolina and was the Chief Nurse with the 91st Evacuation Hospital in Tuy Hoa. Her name can be found on Panel 48W, Line 12.

Capt. Mary Therese Klinker of Lafayette, Indiana.

Captain Mary Therese Klinker, U.S. Air Force was part of an on-board medical team during Operation Babylift.

Her flight was carrying 243 infants and children when it developed pressure problems and crashed while attempting to return to the airport. Captain Klinker was killed on April 4, 1975, just three weeks before the Fall of Saigon. A native of Indiana, she is remembered on Panel 1W, Line 122.

2nd Lt. Carol Ann Elizabeth Drazba of Dunmore, Pennsylvania and 2nd Lt. Elizabeth Ann Jones of Allendale, South Carolina.

2nd Lieutenant Carol Ann Drazba, U.S. Army was killed in a helicopter crash near Saigon on February 18, 1966. Born and raised in Pennsylvania, she is remembered on Panel 5E, Line 46.

2nd Lieutenant Elizabeth Ann Jones, U.S. Army was flying with 2LT Drazba and was killed in the same helicopter crash near Saigon. She was assigned to the 3rd Field Hospital. 2LT Jones was from South Carolina and is remembered on Panel 5E, Line 47.

Capt. Eleanor Grace Alexander of Rivervale, New Jersey and 1st Lt. Hedwig Diane Orlowski of Detroit, Michigan.

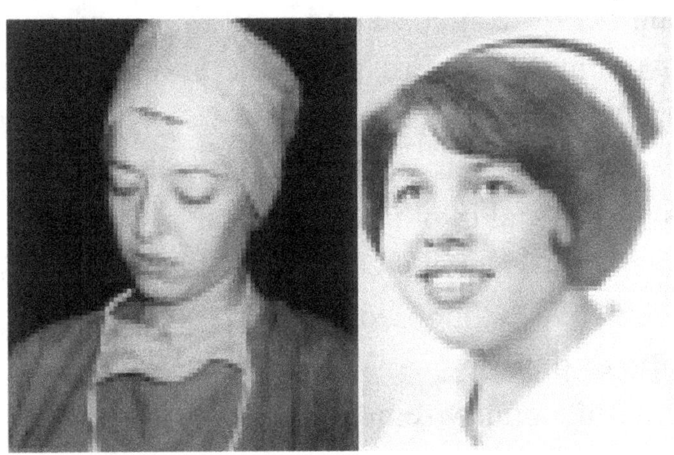

Captain Eleanor Grace Alexander, U.S. Army had been working in a hospital in Pleiku to help out during mass casualties from Dak To when her plane crashed on the return trip to Qui Nhon on November 30, 1967. She was with the 85th Evacuation Hospital. She was from New Jersey and is remembered on Panel 31E, Line 8.

1st Lieutenant Hedwig Diane Orlowski, U.S. Army was on board with Capt. Alexander when their plane crashed on its return trip to Qui Nhon. She was assigned to the 67th Evacuation Hospital, 1LT Orlowski was from Michigan. She is remembered on Panel 31E, Line 15.

These eight women embody selfless love, sacrifice, and courage. They are American heroes who volunteered to serve their country.

They joined the over 265,000 American women served during the Vietnam era. Approximately 11,000 served in Southeast Asia. Close to ninety percent were nurses. A small number of women served in civilian capacities, such as the American Red Cross and the USO. More than 50 civilian American women died in Vietnam. Others worked as physicians, air traffic controllers, intelligence officers, clerks and in other capacities.

It wasn't until November 1993 that the patriotic service of all women was honored in the nation's capital at the dedication of the Vietnam Women's Memorial.

A grateful Country remembers.

The Doctors: An Overview

Doctors in the Vietnam War were primarily military personnel who provided a wide range of care to American troops, from treating combat wounds to common illnesses such as colds and skin infections. Many also provided humanitarian medical assistance to Vietnamese civilians, sometimes through the Volunteers for Vietnam Program, treating conditions such as malaria, tuberculosis, and war-related injuries that were prevalent in the region. The doctors' roles varied from front-line trauma care to managing large hospitals and conducting medical research.

Roles and responsibilities

- **Military medical care:**
- Provided health services for American troops, including basic care and treating wounded soldiers.
- Treated common illnesses, such as colds, skin infections, and diarrhea.
- Managed battlefield injuries, often stabilizing patients for evacuation to rear-area hospitals.
- **Humanitarian and civilian care:**

- Treated Vietnamese civilians, both military and civilian, especially in areas where there were few local doctors.
- Participated in humanitarian efforts like the Volunteers for Vietnam Program, which provided medical assistance to a population struggling with diseases such as malaria, tuberculosis, and meningitis, in addition to war wounds.
- Set up temporary clinics in villages to provide care to those who cannot access hospitals.
- **Specialized medical roles:**
- Some doctors were involved in specialized work, such as surgical teams that assisted at Vietnamese hospitals or teams that developed screening laboratories to detect drug use among troops.
- Medical personnel also worked on hospital ships, in naval support activities, and in various other operational units.

Doctors
& Medical Service Corps

My Service in the U. S. Army

by Lt. Paul Tucker Scott, MSC

1966

2025

In college, I endured four years of ROTC classes and marching instruction, before being commissioned as a Second Lieutenant in the US Army. The Army assigned me to an infantry unit, specifically the Medical Platoon/Forward Aid Station of the First Battalion, 27th Infantry Regiment ("Wolfhounds"), as part of the 25th Infantry Division. I wanted to be where I felt I could do the best -- in the field, and that is how I became a Wolfhound.

Infantry training (IT) included classes on tactics and squad, platoon and company maneuvers under combat conditions, marching, jogging, rifle marksmanship courses, PT (physical training), and the use of all military firearms, including the M-1, M-14, mortars, and machine guns. This also involved breaking down and cleaning these weapons, too. I got the "M-1 thumb" as did many others. Training included crawling under live machine gun fire in the hot sun as the drill sergeant pushed me to the end of my tolerance. Training also included the use of gas masks and removing them in a CS gas (tear gas) chamber. At the conclusion of this training, , I was commissioned a Second Lieutenant in Medical Service Corps and assigned to the Medical Field Service School at Fort Sam Houston in San Antonio, Texas. The officer designation was one gold bar. The nickname was "shave tail."

Upon graduation from the Medical Field Service School, I drove to California to my next duty station at Schofield Barracks with the Wolfhounds. I stayed for several days with former friends from Fredericksburg, and I was treated to a tour of Disneyland.

The Twenty-fifth Infantry Division's base is at Schofield Barracks on the island of Oahu in the Hawaiian Islands, as Hawaii had only become a state in 1959. The division was made up of infantry, artillery, mechanized armor, JAG (Judge Advocate General), and medical units.

There were several Infantry Brigades, each consisting of two battalions. The Wolfhounds were the 1st and 2nd Battalions of the 2nd Brigade. I was in the 1st Battalion.

The regiment spent many days in the Koolau and Kahuka Mountains of Oahu. It rained heavily in those jungles. I remember the orange mud covering us and the vehicles. The training, of course, was to prepare the regiment for duty in Viet Nam

Sgt. Samuel K. Solomon was at that time the first sergeant of Headquarter Co. Every morning he'd lead the company jogging around the base. We'd enjoy "Jodie" calls as we counted cadence. Jodie calls are rhymes often laced with profanity. On December 28, 1965, I wrote to my father advising him of our division being ordered to Viet Nam.

The Cruise to Vietnam

On January 2, 1966, our battalion boarded ships and left the docks of Oahu. This was a two-week voyage. Our battalion was on the *USS Gordon*, an old WWII troop ship. There were about 4,500 troops on our ship. We crossed over the international dateline, which entitled everyone to a membership in the King Neptune's Royal Domain of the Golden Dragon.

We arrived in Vung Tau South Viet Nam after two weeks at sea. We had our weapons with us, and as we approached shore and then the landing craft gate went down, and we were met with a band and with pretty

Vietnamese girls dispensing leis and welcoming us to Viet Nam.

Our battalion had a temporary base camp set up shortly after our arrival in Viet Nam. Our unit was on the grounds of the University of Saigon, which, at the time, was empty. The rooms were used as barracks for the Army of the Republic of Viet Nam (ARVN). This was our staging area before our unit moved to our permanent base camp at Cu Chi. Being a captain, the battalion surgeon was technically the Platoon Leader and I, being a lieutenant, was the Evacuation Section Leader. During my time in Viet Nam, the medical platoon had four other battalion surgeons. So, I often became the de facto platoon leader as the doctors preferred to involve themselves with medical issues rather than running the platoon.

In those days, there was no internet, no phone service and mail call was one's only contact with home, friends, and family. Letters from home were morale boosters and it took about a week for a letter to arrive. My mother wrote me weekly, sometimes more. Her letters kept my spirits up. The Army even brought mail to us while in the field. I wrote back to her after returning to base camp from every operation.

A MSc Lieutenant's Routine

In combat, the wounded would be initially treated by a line medic assigned to an infantry platoon. My duties as the Evacuation Section Leader in that situation were to further stabilize the wounded, if necessary, and carry them by litter, poncho or over one's shoulder to the aid station. What they did not tell us in Medical Field Service School was that some of the wounded had not been treated by the platoon medic due to the volume of injured personnel. That would then be our job before moving them to the aid station. There we'd further stabilize or, if necessary, give an IV injection of glucose, saline or albumen and then evacuate the wounded by helicopter, if available. IV's were seldom given due to time constraints. My other duties when in base camp were to give shots by the hundreds, treat maladies, rashes, prickly heat, ring worm fungus (tinea pedis and tinea rubreum) and VD. Gonorrhea was prevalent – called "the clap," treated with 5 cc's of procaine penicillin in the upper right quadrant of a soldier's hind quarter. All GI's were to report to the aid station before a three-day pass or, before going to Saigon or R & R, to secure prophylactics. But, after a few drinks, they'd forget about them and come back to the aid station with the clap for treatment.

For general hygiene, my directions to the troops were not to wear underwear as it created a warm moist environment for "jock itch." My further duties in base camp were the inspection of the mess halls for cleanliness and the cooks for personal hygiene. Most of the company mess sergeants took my inspections well as I tried to be very fair and respectful. These were career Army NCO's and I was a mere Reserve Army lieutenant. For instance, when weevils got in the flour – it was not a serious concern as cooking the bread would kill them. They looked like caraway seeds, were harmless, and the soldiers were quite used to them.

The headquarters mess sergeant, Sgt Johnson, nicknamed "Sgt John," was so used to serving coffee, he'd have hot coffee in 110° weather and fresh water in a lister bag suspended in a large tripod. I bet him that if he had a cooler of orange juice next to the coffee, that line for the juice would be longer. He took the bet and the OJ line was twice as long as the coffee line. This shave tail lieutenant taught that old sergeant a lesson that day!

My duties also included inspecting the latrines. The latrine was a small building with a long shelf structure with toilet seats and a 55-gallon oil drum cut in half underneath. Access to the ½ drum was in the back of the building at ground level. Gasoline would be mixed well with the contents and lit with a match and stirred until it all turned to charcoal. This would be taken to a central location and discarded. The men who had this duty called it the "shit detail." The aid station medics treated more than one soldier for flash burns after lighting off these cans.

Mosquitoes were also a very large problem. Some carried malaria, and one of my duties was to have the Wolfhound area of the base camp sprayed with insecticide. We used a mighty mote sprayer mounted in the bed of a jeep. All of the soldiers were required to take a malaria pill and a salt tablet every day. There were no Saturdays, Sundays, weekends, or week days. All the days seemed to run together; one was just like another.

Both the First and Second Battalion troops went by two and a half ton trucks and “cattle cars” from landing at Vung Tau to Cu Chi. As we were moving in convoy to Cu Chi, my jeep driver almost struck the vehicle in front of us. As he veered to the left, my foot was caught in the doorway with the bumper of the other vehicle, mashing it flat against my shin, and it hurt like hell. We did not know if it was fractured, but it certainly felt like it. We had no x-ray facilities so, upon arrival at Cu Chi, Dr. Winningham wanted to ship me to Saigon and then on to Japan. Having just arrived, I declined and made a crutch from a tree limb. I hobbled around with an ace wrap for a couple of weeks until I could walk on it. So, apparently it was only sprained. Cu Chi was in Hau Nghia Province of Vietnam and we were in War Zone C. Later these war zones were numbered Corps rather than letters. Our area of operation (AO) was between Saigon and the “Parrot’s” Beak of Cambodia.

The Tunnels of Cu Chi

Astonishingly, the senior powers that decided the 25th Division would be located at Cu Chi did not know of the enemy tunnels there. Ever since WWII, the Viet Minh in fighting the French had dug tunnels from Cambodia all the way to Cu Chi, when the French were finally defeated at

Dien Bien Phu. After we established our base camp there, the Viet Cong (VC), using these tunnels, would come out of their "spider holes" and shoot at us day and night. It was quite hectic at first and it was referred to as the Battle of Cu Chi. One of my medics, Specialist 4th Class Stannard, took a bullet through both femurs, and it was all very unnerving. Sgt. Barker would stay outside with his shot gun waiting for VC to pop up out of these holes, but he could never get a bead on one. We slept in tents, on cots, over a dirt floor not knowing when or where a VC would pop up out of a hole (which were well concealed). I slept with a loaded pistol under my pillow. It is beyond belief that Army Intelligence did not know of these tunnels before we arrived.

The aid station in our new base camp at Cu Chi was a tent. Next to us was an 8" artillery piece which fired all night long to keep the enemy at bay. The firing was so loud it would hurt our ears. Later we had wooden frames with a canvas tent over it for the aid station. We later sandbagged around our aid station in the Cu Chi base camp to protect ourselves against incoming mortar rounds. The VC would hit us at night sometimes, usually around 0200 hours.

It was the middle of the dry season when we arrived in Viet Nam in January of 1966. There was little rain, it was very hot and the rice paddies were rock hard. I, as the Evacuation Section Leader of the Medical Platoon in Headquarters Company, went on all battalion and multicompany operations. We were not air mobile, so we walked everywhere searching to make contact with the enemy; the Viet Cong or NVA (North Vietnam Army). As I looked around me and saw the infantrymen armed to the teeth, I likened it to a big game hunt with the game being humans.

The battalion had a convoy going to Saigon once a week to take the bodies of the KIA (killed in action) to Graves Registration and to pick up supplies. It required an officer to be at the beginning and the end of the convoy. The lieutenants would often volunteer to do this because it was a way to get a break from usual duty and to visit Saigon. Once in Saigon, we had to go to the Rex Hotel and check our weapons in with the military police (MP) there. Thereafter, unarmed, we could do as we what we wished: tour Saigon, visit monuments, go to restaurants, bars, massage parlors, and other debaucheries of choice. On the rooftop of the Rex Hotel, which was several stories high, was a restaurant and a bar. There were charcoal grills around the perimeter, and we would pick out a steak and grill it ourselves.

In base camp our showers were made from an empty 55-gallon oil drum cradled on a wooden stand. It was filled with water and the sun would warm it up. Later, jet fuel tanks were substituted in place of the old oil drums. The army hired work details of village women to fill sand bags and do maintenance work around the base camp. They'd giggle while watching us take showers. I suspect that some of them were VC. Small Vietnamese businesses sprung up at the entrance to the division base camp. There were laundries, seamstresses and barbers. One was my barber. A week after my last haircut, he was killed on a night ambush. He was a VC. You couldn't tell friend from enemy among the civilian population. Some of the smaller GI's volunteered or were "volunteered" by their Sgt to be tunnel rats. I always admired the bravery and steel nerves of the tunnel rats for going down in the tunnels and hunting for VC with nothing more than a flashlight and a pistol. One such kid had been bitten by a rat in the tunnels. I gave him fourteen shots of inactivated rabies vaccine in a medium of duck embryo in the flat muscles of the abdomen once a day for fourteen days. It must be given there and is quite painful. He was so relieved when it was over, but the very next day he was killed. Until the weekly convoy to Saigon, we would accumulate the dead bodies in a small area sectioned off near the aid station. We would place them on the ground and position them appropriately. When rigor mortis set in, the body would be stiff in whatever position it was placed. We'd cordon off the area by putting ponchos on stakes to hide the bodies so they were not clearly visible. After three days the stench was unbearable and enough to make you vomit, as the smell of death is unforgettable.

I believe it was late February when we were issued M-16 rifles and turned in our M14's. Unfortunately, we were not issued enough cleaning equipment and the M-16's often jammed. There was a lot of dust during the dry season, so the motor pool would cut 55-gallon drums in half longways and fill them with gasoline. The troops would submerge the entire rifle in the gasoline to clean it.

We were on foot, until late March, walking through the jungles and across the hard rice paddies during those winter months which are the dry season there. Summer months are the wet season beginning in April. We became air mobile about three months into 1966 when we had helicopter support. The helicopter was the Bell UH-1 nicknamed "Huey" and we also referred to it as a "slick." They were flown by a pilot and co-pilot (usually captains, lieutenants, and warrant officers) and two door gunners with M-60 machine guns. Dustoff's (medivacs) would be unarmed medical Hueys marked as such with Army medics aboard, and the large rotor blades made a loud recognizable "whomp, whomp" sound. Dustoff pilots frequently risked their lives to pick up the wounded.

On one operation in late Spring, we came across a Nuoc Mam factory way out in the country. Nuoc mam is the Vietnamese fish sauce and is clear, orange, and it stinks. It is initially stored in crockery jugs. The Vietnamese would catch minnows from the rice paddies and then pulverize the minnows into a paste. They'd put the fish paste in the crockery jugs and let it ferment when it would be bottled and sold in the local markets. With the beginning of the rainy season in April, there would not only be rain but severe thunder storms. The grunts learned to keep their weapon with the muzzle pointing down and rubber butt plate up so as not to attract lightning. The lightning could hit the ground and then move horizontally until it struck something – sometimes that being a person.

During the daytime, we rolled up the sleeves on our jungle fatigues to bear the heat. At night, however, we'd roll down the sleeves because it would get surprisingly cool. On many occasions, when on operations, I'd look up at the stars and wonder what my family members were doing since it was daytime back in the States.

Many of our operations were in known VC strongholds such as the Ho Bo Woods, the Boi Loi Woods, and in the Iron Triangle. On some operations, the battalion came across large caches (bushel bags full) of rice. This, obviously, was to feed the Viet Cong and NVA in their base camps. Our troops would destroy the rice every time it was found. On one operation, a soldier with the NVA (North Vietnamese Army) had been caught in a village and shot by our men. He was biting through a banana plant to stifle the pain. His right arm had been shot and he was bleeding badly. Some of the men wanted to let him die, but I chose to treat him. I stopped the bleeding and gave him an IV of albumen. I learned later that the authorities obtained some valuable intelligence from him. I also thought that a medic on the other side might follow this example and treat our wounded. Who knows? It was a judgment call.

Mines and booby traps were always a problem. One day in the early spring 1966 we were on a battalion operation and found ourselves in the middle of a mine field. For some reason, the engineers had not checked it. We looked for newly disturbed ground where a mine could be buried. A mine went off about 20 feet from me taking a soldier down. I ran over to him and found his foot blown off at the base of his lower leg – his boot with it. I bandaged the stump quickly as there was not a lot of blood. I then retrieved his boot with his foot still in it, sock, and all. He was now on a stretcher, and I handed it to him and told him to hang on to it – the docs may be able to reattach it. I doubt if that occurred. But I always wondered whatever happened to him as he boarded a dustoff medical helicopter.

We routinely treated bullet wounds and shrapnel wounds from mortar rounds and enemy hand grenades. The headquarters medics set up the aid station tent only a third of the time as we were usually on the move. We'd sometimes be walking through a semi-wooded area with the tankers. Often, they would offer us a ride, but I always refused these offers. I had seen guys wounded in the legs if they were hanging over the side of the tank. I always walked a safe distance from them since they would blow all the mines and booby traps nearby. At other times we'd be walking through bamboo thickets, which were very hard and often full of red ants that would fall down in our fatigues and bite and sting us.

On March 18, 1966, we were in the field and Pfc James Williams' remains were brought to me. I was told that he'd been hit by a claymore mine. There were only some bones, hair, teeth, and his dog tags left of him. I carried him in an empty sand bag tied to my belt for several days before I could give it to a helicopter pilot to take to Graves Registration in Saigon.

During another mortar attack, in the spring, at about 0200 hours, we were in the rice paddies and I was hugging the ground, sucking in water when a round exploded about 6 feet from me. It hit just on the other side of the paddy berm, protecting me but hitting my medic, Spec. Clevester Davis, in his gut. I treated him on site with a compression bandage. The next day I dug up the tail fin of that mortar round. I have it as a souvenir today on my office desk. It reminds me that no matter how difficult a day may be, at any one time it could be much worse.

On April 20, 1966, we suffered another heavy mortar attack. We were in the field, and again in the rice paddies. It had been raining heavily and Doc Winningham was treating the wounded in an APC (Armored Personnel Carrier.) I was running around tending to the wounded when I heard another call "medic" and ran over to two wounded soldiers. It was very dark, but I could tell that they'd taken a direct hit and their legs were blown off from their torsos. They kept begging me to help them and I could only assure them that I would take care of them and they'd be alright. There was so much mud and blood I could not get the bleeding stopped to bandage them as their lives drained away. I'll picture that night in my mind forever as though it was yesterday. About this time the battalion was out on another operation. The battalion surgeon was not with us for some reason, and I was the only medical officer there. Someone yelled "snake" after a soldier had collapsed in the heat. I ran over and asked, "where is the snake?" No one knew or had actually seen one. I examined the collapsed soldier and he had no fang marks if poisonous or bite marks of any kind. I concluded it was heatstroke, got him hydrated and cooled down. In a while he was okay.

There were no doors on the choppers for easy entrance and exit. There was one row of seats and flooring between the seats as the pilot and co-pilot, sit forward. That floor space is where litters and the wounded were placed. After my first ride, I always rode on the Huey's edge because it was quicker to get out when it landed. Some men were too slow to get off. During each air assault, not knowing how it would go, or how I'd perform my duty, I'd not allow myself to think about it but adopted what I called "calm reserve."

As we walked through some of the remote sparsely populated villages, we would see the older women with black teeth. This came from chewing betelnut, which is a fruit and comes from the Areca palm tree. It is known for its stimulating effects similar to caffeine, but it would eventually turn their teeth black.

One midsummer morning the battalion was preparing to go out on an operation. One by one the men of Headquarters Company (HHC) developed severe gut pain. They were lying on the ground between the HHC mess hall and the aid station, writhing in pain – throwing up with bloody diarrhea. The operation continued by helicopter without these HHC men. But, one by one, it hit the soldiers in the field more. After three days in the field, I succumbed and had to have myself evacuated by helicopter. I was admitted to the 12th Evac and put on IV's. We later determined it was the shigella bacteria causing shigellosis from spoiled potato salad in the headquarters mess hall. Tetracycline was the treatment prescribed.

Tarantulas

About that time we were located in heavy jungle and actually had set up an aid tent. At night we could see these huge images crawling up the mosquito netting of the tent. We could then see them crawling back into a hole in the ground toward morning. The next day we dug them up. About a foot down there would be a large tarantula. We dug up as many as we could out of the holes and stabbed them with our bayonets. During the same time period, we were on a battalion-sized operation. The helicopter I was riding in took fire and had to put down in an area away from our unit. Fortunately, it was among an American unit, and after two days of moving through unit after unit, I was able to get back to the aid station at our base camp.

As I walked in the door, Spec Paul Balch exclaimed "Why, Lieutenant, we thought you was dead."

We were out on operations about twenty-five out of every thirty days. I recall one operation during the summer in which I was in a long line of soldiers crossing the Saigon River, which was about 100 yards wide. I had my aid bag and rifle over my head. While walking through the muddy river, about to step in over my head and waiting for the VC to open up on us, I thought, while looking in front and behind me, "This is serious stuff." "What was I thinking when I turned down a desk job?" About two months before, after having received good OER's (Officer Efficiency Reports) sent up to the brigade headquarters, I was offered a desk job. This would be to move to brigade headquarters and be the personal assistant to a Major Otterstedt. I was actually comfortable where I was and not wanting to leave my platoon and knowing that my men did not have the same opportunity, I declined the offer. There were also times thereafter when things got really tough that I asked myself "What was I thinking?" All kidding aside, I would have been miserable behind a desk. I was content where I was and where I could do best. My platoon of medics saved a lot of lives.

We had one fragging during my year. That's when a disgruntled soldier would throw a live grenade into the hooch of the officer he wanted to get even with. This instance was when the "A" Company commander had disciplined a private in the morning, and that evening a grenade was tossed into the captain's hooch, but fortunately, he was not there. The shrapnel from the grenade hit one of my jeeps parked nearby. And, although it was never proven, the other grunts knew and referred to the "fragger" as "Bomber Brown" thereafter.

Major Guy S. Meloy, III

In July of 1966, Major Guy S. ("Sandy") Meloy, III was named the Commander of the First Battalion, which was normally a colonel's slot. However, since the division commander, General Fred Weyand, had not been happy with some of the previous colonels and was not impressed with those colonels who might be available, he appointed a major to take command, and Major Meloy ended his career retiring as a two-star general.

Before Major Meloy took command, the entire unit had been standing down for several weeks while General Weyand searched for a new commander. When Major Meloy arrived on the scene, he had all of the companies in formation at attention while he addressed the entire battalion. We knew from that time on we had a very good commander, and the battalion was in good hands. He was a West Point graduate and had been to the Command and General Staff College and had all of the requisites including, most importantly, good judgment. The day Major Meloy took command was July 31, 1966. He was the first battalion CO to include me, as the medical officer, in the pre-operation briefings. No one had ever done that or even included the battalion surgeon after Dr. Winningham left us. I recall several pre-op briefings in the TOC (Tactical Operations Center), when Maj. Meloy would give his description of the upcoming operation and go through each of his company commanders asking for comments and responses as to how each company could contribute. After these he would then call on me, “Scotty,” (my Army nickname) as to my comments, the number of medics I would take from headquarters, whether or not I would set up an aid tent, the amount of medical supplies I would take and the number of litters. If he had any changes, he would give directions or make suggestions. He would usually rely on my judgment.

Early in his command, I recall on one occasion when I said I would have every other man carrying a litter, and he said, “double it.” I thought to myself, “uh-oh, it was going to be a bad operation.” It was from that point on that I felt a real part of the outfit because the medics were informed and treated as important. So often the medics were discounted until the casualties started, then we were really appreciated and Major Meloy changed that.

Litters

My personal observations about litters: Litters were, of course, perfect for carrying wounded soldiers who were unable to walk. In most situations they were very useful. The wounded would be brought into the aid station tent on litters and placed on a special stand like a saw horse. The litter would then become an operating table. I called the stand "legs." Sometimes, however, they could be awkward to carry. In dense jungle, the litter would get caught on anything and everything and was extremely unwieldy. In those cases, we preferred to use ponchos to carry the wounded, or if we could even partially stand up, we would carry the wounded over our shoulders. Litters required two medics to carry any wounded soldier, thereby tying up two people. Litters would be placed on the helicopters with the wounded and would end up at whatever hospital or medical facility where the wounded soldier was taken. Those facilities would literally have hundreds of litters stacked up. During heavy engagements, the medical platoon would, of course, soon run out of them. From time to time, I would fly by helicopter to these facilities, load them up and bring back a stack of litters to our medical platoon. They don't teach you this in Medical Field Service School. On one occasion, I arrived during lunch time. After filling my tray, I walked into the mess hall and looked for a place to sit. A little dark-haired nurse indicated there was a seat opposite her. I was grubby from the field but I sat where she motioned. She was cute and one of the first American girls, or "round eyes" as we called them, I'd seen in a while. We had good conversation. I don't remember her name or anything else about her, but I was "in love" on the chopper ride back to our base camp.

The Tank Rescue

In those days, I could carry a man twice my size over my shoulder. I believe it was in July, and we were on an operation in the field. The aid station received a call over the radio that a tank had blown up in the middle of a mine field. They asked for medics to go by chopper to retrieve the injured men. Staff Sgt. Bernabe Cenal and I grabbed our aid bags, jumped on the chopper, and flew out to where the tank was disabled. The pilot set us down about seventy yards away in the adjacent field because he did not want to explode any other mines. We ran across the field and crossed an extremely wet area. Bernie sank up to his hips in it. (I grew up by the water and lived adjacent to a marsh, and I knew how to walk through marshes without sinking). With some effort, I pulled him out and we went on our way. We ran over to the tank, climbed up on it, and strained to pull two men up out of it. One was unconscious and the other was conscious. Both had blood coming out of their ears from the explosion. We each carried a wounded man over our shoulders and to another field where the chopper had moved and was waiting. We put them on the chopper, and while in the air, I placed an airway down the throat of the soldier who was unconscious and I began to breathe for him. From the running, the carrying and breathing for him, I became dizzy and began to fall to my left out of the chopper. Ever alert, Bernie grabbed me and pulled me back in, saving my life. He had been giving life-saving treatment to his patient and he proceeded to continue to breathe through the airway for my soldier. About that time we landed at an evacuation hospital. The medics there took them from the chopper and we often wondered how those two men fared. We never knew, as we headed back to our unit.

On August 29, 1966, we were in an operation in the jungle with an aid tent set up. B Company took some casualties and Captain Bob Garrett was hit in the leg by a Chicom (Chinese Communist) grenade, and Sgt. Alameda was also wounded. Lt. Carter Ashcraft had a gut wound when he came into the aid station. I cleaned it up and put a compression bandage on it and then he climbed back on to the same helicopter with the others and was taken to the 7th Surgical Hospital for treatment.

On another occasion in the fall on an operation, the battalion surgeon and I were in the aid station. We had a wounded soldier who had blood all over his upper extremities. He was brought in on a litter and we put it on the stand. We cut off his fatigue shirt and saw that he was fading fast. He actually had a "sucking chest wound" but we couldn't see it because the bullet had come in through his upper right arm just below his shoulder and exited underneath his armpit and piercing his chest. His lungs had collapsed before we could save him. I always felt particularly bad about that casualty. Maybe he could have been saved had we been able to diagnose it quicker, but it was dark, we were on light discipline and only had small lights in the aid station with the sides of our tent rolled down. This was another one of my life's regrets.

A Jeep Ride to Cambodia

In October, I was visiting another medical unit in Tay Ninh, when I came across Capt. Rich Foss and we had a beer in his hooch. He was a West Point graduate and is mentioned frequently in Gen. Robert F. Foley's book "Standing Tall." He was the former CO of "C" Company and by that time the Brigade S-2 (Intelligence) officer. He had a contact he wanted to make in Cambodia and asked me if I would like to join him. I agreed and we got into his jeep with a couple of M-16s, some extra ammunition, and headed off. We arrived, parked in Viet Nam, and walked over the border into Cambodia. We walked to a tent city, which was a huge black market called "Free City." There was no border guards, just an open gate. As we walked through it there were black-pajamaed Vietnamese and Cambodians all around us. I had my right hand on the trigger of my M-16 and my left hand taking pictures with my camera. Rich made contact with his VC informant and we walked back to the jeep and drove back to Tay Ninh without incident. Looking back, that was quite a dumb thing I agreed to do. But, apparently, Rich knew that the enemy was no longer in that area and he felt it was okay to go.

The Sniper

I believe it was in October when our battalion was in a blocking position on a large operation, and we had set up an aid station tent about thirty yards from the jungle. Nothing much was happening and I was sitting in a camp chair beside the entrance to our aid tent. A soldier approached me and was about five paces away as he said "Lt. Scott . . . " to get my attention. Just then he was knocked hard to the ground and the other soldiers nearby knew immediately what had happened. They ran into the jungle and came back with a dead Viet Cong sniper. He had shot at me, an officer. Just then, the soldier who wished to speak with me stepped between me and the bullet, and he was struck in his right shoulder from behind. The sniper was likely aiming for my chest. Now was that luck or what? The soldier who took my bullet was treated and survived and I expect it took him out of commission as an infantryman and may have earned him a trip back to the states.

Tu Dia

In my photograph album is a flattened tin can with the word "Tu Dia" written on it which means "danger" in Vietnamese. It was to warn the villagers of any nearby booby traps. These signs were placed on a little bamboo stick and stuck in the ground where the grunts wouldn't see them. The booby trap would be a tin can with a hand grenade in the can with the pin pulled from about 10 feet away. There would be a strand of clear fishing line that no one could see running across the path. When the soldier walked into that line it would pull the hand grenade out of the can and explode. In this album, there's a Presidential Unit Citation awarding "A" Company First Battalion 27th Infantry Company for its action on July 19, 1966. That was the day that the company got out beyond artillery range, was ambushed in the open rice paddies and practically destroyed. In my album there is an "Eyewitness Account by Lt. Peter Schnizer" of the debacle on July 19, 1966, involving our medic, Pete Rios. Pete had been shot in the back while loading wounded into a helicopter and was paralyzed; now relegated to life in a wheelchair. Pete told me that he'd played dead while the VC walked all around shooting those they thought might still be alive. Pete was eventually sent to the Army's Walter Reed Medical Center where his physical therapist was a high school classmate of mine named Beverly Clark. Bev and I had also crossed paths while training in our respective fields at Ft. Sam Houston.

The Battle of Attleboro

This operation began as part of the 196th Light Infantry Brigade's probing for the enemy near Tay Ninh. The operation was named after the town of Attleboro, Massachusetts. (The 196th was organized at nearby Fort Devens). Upon making contact, the Wolfhounds joined them. Elements of the 1st Infantry Division, 173rd Airborne

Brigade and several ARVN units were also engaged and it was the largest US operation of the war to that date.

On November 3rd, Charlie Company of the First Battalion of the 27th Infantry Regiment was ambushed in the jungles near the Village of Dau Tieng. The company had run into heavily reinforced group of Viet Cong and North Vietnamese Army (NVA) regulars. There were concrete bunkers in place and Charlie Company sustained severe casualties. It's captain, Fred Henderson, a West Point graduate, his First Sergeant, Samuel K. Solomon, and one of his platoon leaders, Lt. Clyde Perkins, were killed along with several other soldiers. After Fred was killed, another West Point graduate, Lt. Norm Gill, took command of the company while under fire. Norm was shot in the foot as he crawled through the jungle to take command. Sgt. Solomon was pure Hawaiian and said to be descended from royalty and his nickname was "Mongoose." Dick Siebel, Henderson's RTO, was so saddened by Solomon's death that he, years later, had a medallion made with Solomon's image on it. He made a gift of one of these medallions and presented to me. Norm Gill also gave me a small photo album of Sgt. Solomon and him and they are in my home and treasured.

On Nov. 4th, the rest of the regiment, including the medical platoon and battalion surgeon, Dr. Qwie T. Chew, were lifted in by helicopter. Just prior to us boarding the choppers, we had mail call and I received a long letter from my dad. As was his habit, he used a fountain pen. After I read it, I put it back in the envelope and put it inside my fatigue jacket. After the battle was over days later, I retrieved it. It was soaking wet from my sweat and the ink had run over each page making that letter illegible. I somehow credit his letter for keeping me safe those several days and I wish I had kept it, as wet as it was.

The medical platoon manned the forward aid station for the regiment and Doctor Chew was always concerned that should he be captured he would be tortured because he was of Chinese ethnicity. He was from Chinatown in New York City and the Vietnamese and the Chinese have been traditional enemies. There were eleven rifle companies in this battle and our medical platoon was the only forward aid station servicing the entire battle. Of the U.S. troops, there were 155 killed and 494 wounded. The enemy casualties were 2,130 killed, many more wounded, and 44 NVA taken as POWs.

As we would be on the move, I had elected not to take an aid tent and to carry as many medical supplies as possible on our backs. I had directed Sgt. Cenal, to remain in the base camp at Cu Chi in order to keep us well supplied. He knew people with the Medical Battalion and the 12th Evac and how to beg, borrow or steal whatever we might need. He was not happy that I had him to stay behind as he felt his place was with the aid station in the field, however, he knew the supplies and how to get them to us better than anyone else.

As we walked into the jungle, the battalion began taking automatic weapons and small arms fire coming from bunkers and snipers in the trees. The jungle was so thick one could rarely see any light through it or above it. The rifle platoons returned fire. I had walked out ahead of the rest of the aid station medics and treated the wounded in place. Although difficult under these circumstances, I was able to give an IV to one soldier who was severely wounded and going into shock. Upon stopping the bleeding and getting the IV flowing, I could see his color returning, and later that day, I, along with the wounded, made it back through the jungle to the rest of the aid station medics. The medics there had also stayed in place once the firing started. We set up no tent, just a spot in the jungle next to an open space for eventual helicopter Dustoff's to evacuate the wounded.

Over the next two days, several medics and I went back and forth between what had been established as the front line and the Dustoff landing zone (LZ). Due to the volume of wounded, some of the casualties had not yet been treated by the platoon medics, and that became our job prior to moving them. At first we used litters to carry tin he wounded, then used ponchos, then we carried them over our shoulders, as we ran out of the litters to the first incoming Dustoff Hueys. We loaded the helicopters with so many wounded; they had difficulty getting off the ground. Several times I literally had to throw reporters off the Hueys; those who had come to get their photographs and stories and then tried to hop aboard the Hueys to get out. They were taking space for the wounded but they didn't care.

On one of my trips between the front line and the Dustoff LZ, I passed by the TOC (Tactical Operations Center) from where the battle was controlled by radio. The battalion commander, Major Meloy, motioned me to the ground beside him. Since wave after wave of the enemy kept hitting our lines, he was concerned about the possibility of the battalion being overrun and the lack of ammunition was becoming critical. The major had been instructed by the Division Commander not to lose any battalion surgeons and he told me to put our doctor on the next helicopter going out and get him to safety. I ran back to the aid station and told Doctor Chew that the major said he was ordered to leave. He was uneasy with leaving and then I put him on a helicopter, but after he was on the bird he asked me if I was going to join him, and I responded "No, my place is here. This is about you." He then jumped off the helicopter and said he, too, was staying. I ran back to the major, and I told him of the doctor's refusal to leave. He muttered something unintelligible, but I do not recall what it was. He had too much on his mind and had to get back to his radio because had so many rifle companies under his command and at that point he, too, had been wounded by a mortar round.

The enemy attacked our battalion's lines, coming on in wave after wave. Under huge stress, our guys held the line over and over again; their stamina was heroic. Years later, captured intelligence indicated that the NVA soldiers had been told that the Americans were cowards and would not fight. The NVA kept charging and a distinct recollection of mine is the loudness of the bombs dropped by our close air support. Just a split second before the sound of the explosion I'd hear the crack of metal, followed by the explosion. It was so loud my head felt as though it would explode, and these were "friendlies." Some of the trees were mahogany and the root structure was such that a large portion was above ground which provided some cover from the shrapnel.

Knowing he was concerned about the doctor, I radioed Major Meloy, during a lull in the fighting and assured him that the Doctor Chew was okay. As it was not the custom for a lieutenant to talk to the battalion commander, he did not recognize my call sign: Mustang 1-6. Usually the platoon leader would radio his company commander first, but the company commander for headquarters company was not present at this battle. There was no reason for him to be there and the immediate chain of command for the medical platoon was directly from me to the battalion commander. This was a first, as we had not been in this large of a battle before and I had to identify myself and I assured the major that the medics had the wounded under control.

The wounds during the Attleboro Battle were horrific. One I recall was of a soldier whose eyeball had been blown out of its socket by an enemy grenade. His eye was hanging by tubular tissue out of his head. All I could do was gently put it back into its socket using my palm and put an ace wrap around his entire head. Since he was now completely blind, I assigned a walking wounded soldier to hold him by the arm as we put him on the Dustoff chopper. He was also to continue to help him until arriving at the hospital. Another GI had taken a bullet in his helmet. His helmet had stopped the bullet but it and the helmet were stuck into his skull. There was little blood and it could not be removed in the field. I again assigned a "buddy" to watch out for him on the chopper until they arrived at the hospital. One of my medics assigned to "C" Company was Spec 4 Albert Gosling. He suffered a severe wound to his arm which had to be amputated. Sgt. Lester Davis, a Senior Medic in the Aid Station, was invaluable here and also acted as my RTO.

By the last day of the Attleboro Battle, I had given all of my water and C-rations to the wounded. I spied the olive drab rim of a C-ration can in the mud and being thirsty and hungry, I looked around to see if anyone else had seen it. No one else had, and I slowly crawled over to it and picked it up. It was an unopened can of peaches. I took my P-38 and opened it. I inhaled it – peaches, juice, and all, and to this day, peaches have a special place in my heart.

There is a tape recording of a crucial segment of the Battle of Attleboro. How did this tape come about? One of the reporters who crawled toward the front lines stopped at the TOC where Major Meloy was located. From there the major directed the battle with all of his rifle companies by radio. The reporter stuck a tape recorder on the back of his radio, and it recorded several hours of the battle. A week or so later, when the battle was over and the regiment was back in our base camp, the reporter came into the major's hooch and retrieved the recorder from the back of his radio. All of this had been unknown to Major Meloy until this time. Many years later, Major Meloy, as a retired two-star general, mailed a copy to his former Wolfhound officers who were involved in Attleboro. I had my copy of the tape converted to a CD a few years ago, and there is a photograph of Major Meloy on the ground at the TOC. His right arm is bandaged from the 60 millimeter mortar round that exploded very close to him. The tape recording also contains an interview by the reporter of Captain Richard Cole, Commander of A Company, and also one of the wounded at the Dustoff LZ prior to being evacuated. Toward the end of the battle, Major Meloy had the most forward rifle company pull back as artillery rounds pummeled the area, and as the next company pulled back, it was followed by the next one, and this continued until all of the companies were withdrawn. As we loaded the helicopters leaving the jungle, I looked back and I could see broken weapons and discarded equipment and gear strewn around, with bandages, and broken trees. This reminded me of the old photos of the aftermath of the

1860's Civil War battles, my being a student of that war. We then flew to Tay Ninh for recuperation.

On or about the 12th of November, General Westmoreland came to Tay Ninh; he gave our battalion a pep talk, we took showers and enjoyed a steak dinner. Then he sent us back to continue to chase the NVA and VC north through the jungles, and as usual, we set up no tents. I had gathered soft leaves to sleep on and used my first aid bag as my pillow. At 2300 hours I was awakened by Sgt. Major Jack Eakins, the battalion Sergeant Major. He had crawled through the jungle from Major Meloy's TOC and said, "Lieutenant, the Major wants you and bring your first aid bag." I crawled back through the jungle following the Sergeant Major and found Major Meloy in pain because his wounds had begun to fester. He said, "Scotty, take this shrapnel out of my arm." He had been wounded in the right elbow, shoulder and behind his left knee. His elbow wound had been bandaged by his RTO (radio telephone operator) shortly after he received it. It was from the 60-mm mortar round fired by the enemy back on November 4th.

Because of light discipline the Sergeant Major had a flashlight and held a poncho over the two of us. I took the probe out of my first aid bag and probed into his arm next to his elbow until I heard the "clink" sound of metal on metal. I reached in with long forceps and pulled out a small piece of metal. I probed some more and saw that there was nothing else. I am sure it was quite painful for him to endure as his wound was well inflamed and I had no anesthetic. The Sergeant Major said, “Let me see that piece of shrapnel.” I had it in the forceps and dropped it into his hand. It bounced from his hand and fell onto the jungle floor. We looked for it but couldn’t find it, and the Major was not very happy about this as he wanted to keep that piece of metal as a souvenir. I packed the wound with bacitracin and bandaged it up, crawling back to my spot in the jungle and went to sleep.

What always puzzled me was why did he have me, a lieutenant, remove the shrapnel from his arm deep in the jungle a week after he had received his wound? He had been to Saigon; he had briefed generals and had plenty of opportunity to have the battalion surgeon, Dr. Chew, or any other physician remove the shrapnel from his arm. For years it was a mystery to me, and it was not until 55 years later that I learned the answer. Retired Col. Arno Ponder and I had seen each other at a Wolfhound Reunion and been in touch on other matters. I took the occasion to ask Colonel Ponder who had been the XO (executive officer) of the battalion. Why would the Major not have had a physician remove that shrapnel early after the battle? Col. Ponder said, “I know. It was because he knew any of the medical officers who were captains or above could put him on light duty and remove him temporarily from command. He knew he had to continue the battle chasing the NVA and VC north through the jungles after Attleboro. He purposely did not have Doctor Chew, the battalion surgeon, come on the follow-up operation. His intent was to have you as the sole medical officer of the battalion in the field during that time. He had confidence in you and knew you could do the job. That's why he had you do it and no one else. And he knew you, as just a lieutenant, could not put him on light duty and take him out of command." There was a method to his madness and the mystery was solved after all these years.

The next few days we were in heavy jungle in the semi-swamp Prek Klok area of very dense foliage with lots of standing water. The jungle floor was crawling with leeches which would fall from the trees and on to us, which gave us concern when we slept on the wet ground. To remove them we used cigarettes to touch them and the leaches would withdraw and drop off

During this time, we were walking through bamboo thickets inspecting B-52 bomb craters, when Doctor Chew received a perforated ear drum and was evacuated for treatment. Word of Doctor Chew's departure saw Dr. Mitchell A. Aboussie, from the 12th Evac Hospital, who volunteered to fill in. We had used much of our medical chest, and Dr. Aboussie replenished and reorganized our pharmacy.

On November 23rd, we had our first aid tent sent up, and that was the night of a heavy enemy mortar attack. The darkness was lit up like daylight from all the explosions. Mortar rounds were even hitting the branches and trunks of the huge jungle trees. Fortunately, the medics had constructed a bunker of sandbags about 10 meters from our aid station, and at the beginning of the attack, we ran straight toward the bunker. Earlier, we had treated an injured Sgt. and he was lying on a litter about five meters from the aid tent. He had a leg wound and could not walk. He was struggling to get up so I stopped and put my left arm around his waist with his right arm around my right shoulder. We were making our way toward the bunker when a mortar round slammed down immediately in front of us. Had it been a few inches closer, it would have physically hit us. Waiting for it to explode, we stood there motionless. Miraculously, no explosion occurred as it was a dud. With my two good legs and his one good leg, we hobbled to our bunker for protection.

That night, one poor soldier, Pvt James N. Cagley of "B" Company, had been close to the entrance of his platoon bunker and took a direct shrapnel hit to the back of his head. He was brought to the aid station on a litter. The litter was placed on the stand to create an operating table. I placed my helmet underneath the head of the litter so that I could work on him more easily. So much blood was coming out of his head that Doctor Aboussie and I had difficulty getting it stopped. Pvt Cagley died on the table as there was nothing else we could do. I put my helmet back on, and it was full of his blood, as it drained down over my head and saturated my fatigue jacket. So ended the Battle of Attleboro for the Wolfhound medics.

In early December, Lt. Rick Clark and I were sitting on the sand bagged walls of his 4.2 mortar platoon. Having not yet decided to make the Army a career, we talked about what we were going to do when we returned to the States. Rick said, "I've been thinking about going to law school." I responded, "That's funny, so have I." As it turned out, he went to law school at the University of Arizona and I went to the law school of the University of Richmond. He had a private practice for forty-seven years in Scottsdale, AZ, and I, for forty-four years in Fredericksburg, VA.

Coming Home, Christmas, 1966

I had been in country with my unit since January and my replacement had been assigned. But on December 15th, Major Guy S. Meloy, III, the Battalion Commander, called me into headquarters. He gave me the bad news that my replacement had been directed to another duty station to replace a wounded MSC officer. I went to my hooch and wrote my parents that I would not be home for Christmas again this year. That news, however, changed on December 23rd. I was on an operation in the field when Major Meloy personally flew out in his "bubble" helicopter. He told me to get my gear because I was going home. He flew me back to our base camp where I bid goodbye to the rest of my men. Apparently, a Lt. Allen Hinman from Brigade Headquarters had volunteered to replace me so that I could go home. Many years later at a Wolfhound Reunion, Allen reminded me of our meeting in my aid station as I bid my platoon goodbye, but I had no recollection of it whatsoever. He was later wounded in the shoulder and evacuated first to Germany then returned to the States. He later became an Episcopal Priest.

Major Meloy had also arranged a helicopter flight for me to Ton Son Nhut Air Force Base near Saigon. There I then began the military processing to leave country, but soon after, I developed a high fever and felt extremely ill. This risked my being able to leave Vietnam, so I kept it to myself. One of my classmates at the Medical Field Service School, Alex McCauley, had left his .45 cal pistol at my aid station during a visit. With my fever rising, I took a lambretta motor scooter across town to his office and delivered it to him. During the required medical physical before leaving country, I didn't place the thermometer under my tongue so it would not register my temperature. After standing in processing lines, I boarded a civilian 747 aircraft contracted by the military. Dorsey Weeks, "C" Company tunnel rat, was also on that flight and he later became president of the 27th Infantry Regiment Historical Society. The pilot took off under "lights off" discipline to reduce the risk of being hit by enemy fire. As the plane took off and gained altitude, I saw from the window firefights and tracer bullets on the ground below. I felt empathy for the men on the ground still in the fight, yet I was leaving. When the plane was out of range and over the South China Sea, the pilot announced, "Boys, you're going home," and turned on the cabin lights. All of us let out tremendous cheer. By this time, my fever was raging and it continued throughout that long flight. As was the custom in those days, smoking was allowed and most lit up, but the smoke made my fever almost unbearable.

We reached Okinawa and had a short layover. During the layover I walked around the tarmac. The Sgt. who I had helped to the bunker when the dud hit was there also. After recognizing me, he walked over, shook my hand, and thanked me and the medics for all we'd done. Then began the next leg of my journey to California. Little did I know there would be more obstacles ahead before returning to Virginia. After processing through Oakland Air Force Base, I caught a cab to the civilian airport. On seeing soldiers hitchhiking as we left Oakland, I paid the $20 fare for the whole cab and had the driver pile in as many soldiers as he could to give them a ride.

With my fever pitched, I booked a hotel room before my flight home. I had decided that if I still had a fever the next morning, I'd stay in California until I was well. However, I awoke soaking wet the next morning to find my fever had broken sometime during the night. I felt drained but so much better. I showered, put on my uniform, had a quick breakfast, and headed to the airport. Having made it this far and having made up a day traveling east, I decided not to call my family and to surprise them upon my arrival.

During the flight to Washington, DC, on December 23rd, the pilot advised us that the entire east coast was gripped by a blizzard. It was dark when I stepped off the plane around 6:00 pm, into the worst snow storm I'd seen in a long time. The only coat I had on was my cotton field jacket, which I wore over my regulation tropical worsted short sleeved shirt. No tee shirt underneath as I had discarded all of them in the tropics. I had on Army issue low top shoes and thin socks. During the entire slow two-hour ride, the doors continually flapped open letting ice and snow spit through the gaps onto me. I shivered the entire way.

After arriving at the Fredericksburg Greyhound Bus Station, it took me a while to find a cab with chains willing to carry me in the storm. The cabby drove me to my parents' home, where I expected my family would be gathered for the holiday. I finally allowed myself to be excited about actually being home. After the cab driver dropped me off at the end of the driveway and with my duffel bag on my shoulder, I walked through the snow to the back door and rang the doorbell. I then heard my Grandmother Tucker say, "There's a stranger at the door Babe, don't open it!" But mom turned the light on and looked out. She immediately recognized that it was her son, home from the war, and opened the door. Mom shrieked "Paul's home!" for all to hear as I walked through the door and she threw her arms around me. The rest of the family rushed from the living room to the family room to see for themselves. Every close member of my family, mom, dad, granddad, grandma, brother, sister-in-law, and my sister, crowded in and we enjoyed hugs all around. Mom stayed close to me the whole evening, not letting me out of her sight.

My Dad offered to get me anything I wanted. He was surprised when I told him I wanted a vanilla milkshake, assuming they had the ingredients. I had warmed up from all the excitement. Even though they didn't, Dad insisted on driving his car to Earl's Food Market in the snow for the necessary ingredients. That was the grandest reunion and the best Christmas anyone could ever imagine.

Dr. Gus Kappler, M.D.
(Major U. S. Army)

"LEAVING ON A JET PLANE"

*As I was preparing to leave for the Dallas Airport my wife Robin was softly weeping, flooding reddened eyes with tears. She appeared pitiful. My strong wife's demeanor now conveyed panic, my desertion, loss, fear, and disbelief. She expressed without words "How could you do this to me?"

I had no choice. The US Army had ordered me for a year to Vietnam as a trauma surgeon. The emotion of that moment was overwhelming. We knew this day would come but the devastation of actually separating was extremely heart wrenching. I frequently relive that moment.

*On the TWA bare bones flight I looked military in my khaki summer uniform with a caduceus on my right lapel and a gold major's leaf on the left. I was the oldest passenger. Both me and the teenage soldiers surrounding me had no idea of what was waiting for us in Vietnam's jungles. But they were optimistic about their futures.

At Bien Hoa, during my first overnight in Vietnam, I bunked with another Major who was going "back to the world," home. Small arms fire erupted about 2 am. I stood up to see what was going on. The veteran Major was on the floor - my first lesson that the enemy was there to kill Americans.

I did reference sandbags and barbed wire. This barrier was actually called concertina wire that was covered with multiple small, pointed razors.

I could not wait to get back in the operating room, my sanctuary. That said, I had never encountered war wounds and the mutilation accompanying them.

In retrospect I know I was headed for a rude awakening.

*"Phu Bai's all right" was known country wide as our mocking motto for that place was the "armpit" of Vietnam. The "5 finger discount" worked well in supplying one's needs. Stealing became acceptable in wartime.

Members of the 85th Evacuation Hospital family in Phu Bai, the medics, specialists, support services, nurses, and doctors were committed to caring for soldiers' wounds and illnesses. The wounded received state-side and at times better than state-side care. Advanced techniques in patient care and surgery were explored without fear of litigation.

During the monsoon season the sun rarely appeared. The sky was overcast and the surrounding air entombed us in constant foggy wetness. If it were not raining large droplets, we would be assaulted by a constant heavy mist. Our fatigues and bedding were always damp. This problem was solved by applying an electric blanket to our cot, keeping the bedding and our next day's clothes dry. A 100 watt light bulb in my metal locker worked well on the hanging clothes. An electric blanket in a combat zone - sounds crazy.

*"*What did I do to deserve this?*" were the severely wounded grunts' last coherent words as he lay shivering on the cold hard X-ray table. I had no answer. I would have decompensated if I had not *buried* the boy's desperation.

This patient was on patrol sweeping through an abandoned Viet Cong (VC) campsite. A piece of Styrofoam caught his inquisitive adolescent eye. Just as the enemy knew from years of fighting westerners, both French and American, this eighteen-year-old kid picked up the Styrofoam and "blew himself to pieces."

His original surgery was long and tedious. His post-op course required re-operation and additional blood transfusions. His kidneys failed and his condition necessitated kidney dialysis.

I had poured my heart and soul into caring for him. I wished to accompany him into the hospital and was rejected by the staff of the 3rd Field Hospital in Saigon. I mentally closed that patient's chapter and decided to casually tour Saigon - It was *Buried.*

"*..the people all hate our guts..*" So why the hell were we there?

Their hatred was easy to understand.

The United States-

1) invaded their sovereign country.
2) changed its leadership to President Diem and then assassinated him when it did not work out.
3) covered up the fact that we were not winning the war until the Tet Offensive in '68-'69 exposed our folly.
4) attempted to "win hearts and minds" by wantonly killing fathers, mothers, women, young men, and children and
5) burning their rice crops and villages.

The lesson not learned was that America's powerful military machine failed to best an indigenous army whose advantage was knowing their "backyard." They, more importantly, could retreat into a massive tunneling network for protection, sustenance, medical care, and rearming.

To the lethal detriment of our troops, the Pentagon leadership never thought it important to learn their enemy's history and culture.

*Our 85th Evac flag football team was undefeated versus other hospitals. It may have helped that our quarterback was Leo Flynn, MD, an orthopedic surgeon, who had been the back-up QB for Auburn University. *Leo died of Agent Orange related heart disease in his mid-fifties. One of nine from our seventeen medical staff who were affected by the Agent Orange travesty to die.*

Really happy stuff!

The 85th Evac's contribution to "winning hearts and minds" was our MEDCAP trips to Hue and the ARVN hospital. On my first trip as a naive newbie I inquired of regular Army Captain Fred Brockschmidt, RN, a world class nurse anesthetist, why he had a M16. He responded, "we are at war." *Fred also died a few years ago from an Agent Orange derived cancer.*

We would bring to Hue our outdated blood that could not be transfused into our wounded. We also brought our expertise in anesthesia and surgery that was usually waisted. We stopped going because the risk of getting killed outweighed any good we could have accomplished.

The Vietnamese Army Hospital lacked the funds to fully support any aspect of health care delivery. There were little if any anesthetic agents, gowns, gloves, drapes, and instruments. Most wounded were admitted and observed.

All the Vietnamese physicians were only partially trained. Their expertise barely matched that of our Army medics. They resorted to growing and selling vegetables, chickens and their eggs, and rabbits to buy supplies.

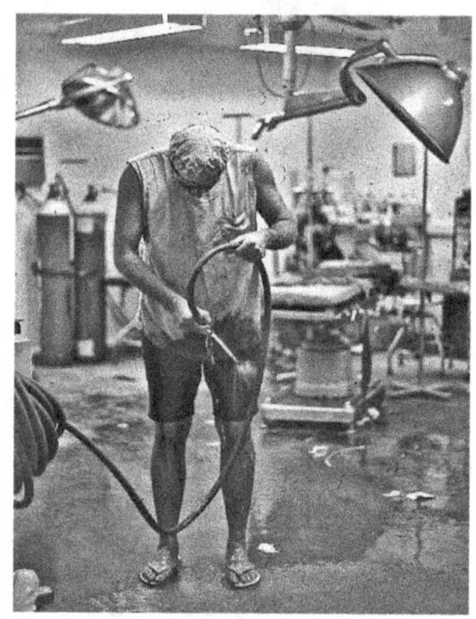

Gus hosing off the blood bath

*Our existence was periods of boredom alternating with the organized chaos of reviving and operating on multiple wounded. When finished we were covered in sticky metallic smelling blood from the waist down. The mess would fill our combat boots. The Vietnamese mamma sons who cleaned for us complained. Wearing Bermuda shorts and flip-flops solved that problem.

After surgery we partied, i.e., drinking excessively and sleeping as long as possible. In retrospect, I now realize we were ***self-medicating*** to numb any compartmentalized trauma that may have escaped its confinement in our subconscious. That issue never entered our minds. The alcohol certainly helped to ***bury*** our psychic trauma. Our PTSD was growing invasive roots.

The first face at the 85th I encountered was that of Roger King. What a miracle! He advised me that everything would be alright. And eventually, he was right.

Roger and I both trained at the Medical College of Virginia in Richmond. I chose that program because it was chaired by David Hume, MD, a young aggressive clinical and research surgeon who was active in the early days of kidney transplant surgery. We got to operate on day one.

When I was there, he and the MCV neurologists were the first in the country to redefine death as being "brain dead." The transplant surgeons did not have to wait for the heart to stop. That way the neurologically dead patient's functioning heart and lungs would continue to keep the kidneys viable while waiting to be transplanted.

We were at times overwhelmed with Richmond's trauma and given early responsibility for decision making. Roger completed his surgical training a year prior to me but was sent to Vietnam during the second year of active duty. Our time at the 85th Evac. overlapped by six months. Roger and I became the go-to surgeons. The ED and OR staff marveled at our ability to anticipate each other's moves to accomplish life-saving surgery.

Roger died last year from an aggressive prostatic cancer derived from Agent Orange exposure. That's the third Agent Orange death of my 85th Evac. colleagues I'm reminded of in the first two letters from Vietnam to my sister, Helene. We were totally unaware that Agent Orange was being sprayed. Therefore we were unaware of the extreme toxicity of Agent Orange's predictable containment - Dioxin. We never conceived that hundreds of thousands of Americans would derive major illnesses from this herbicide. In the US and Vietnam, hundreds of thousands have died from Agent Orange derived diseases.

I said goodbye to my wife and children, to be gone for a year. I abruptly flew to Vietnam and the unknown. Then there was the hot, sweaty, foul-smelling travel up-country to Phu Bai and the 85th Evacuation Hospital, halfway between Hue and Da Nang. All these experiences were mentally devastating. Yet, to my eventual detriment, my mind was capable of ***burying*** them.

During my service at the 85th Evac. Our hospital treated 50% of the American wounded in Vietnam. We were at the first exit of the Ho Chi Minh Trail, not more than 40 kilometers from Laos (look back to Principle Vietnam Landmarks). If the wounded made it to the 85th Evac. alive, they had a 96% chance of survival.

All of us at the 85th witnessed the ugly devastation of war on body, mind, and soul. We dealt with the horrors of war daily. We grew very close and shared a genuine love (brotherhood). Roger and I were a unique entity. I have never experienced a professional relationship as intense and successful. Roger King, we at the 85th Evac will miss you, especially me.

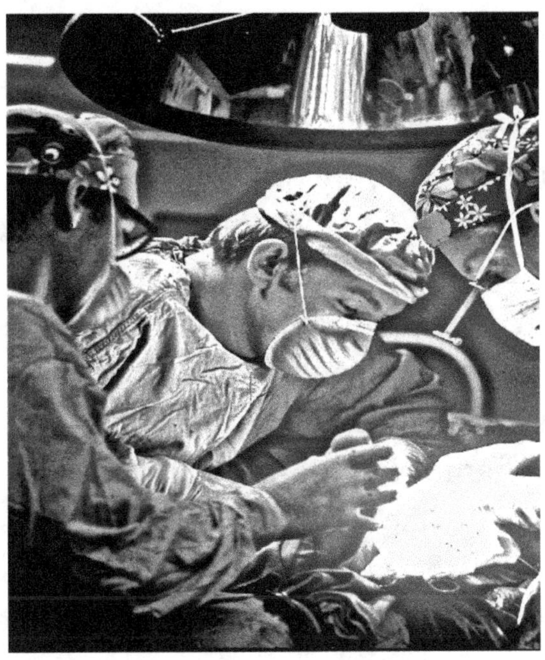

Medtec "Tree" Dave Anderson, Gus,
and Roger King at the 85th Evac

"Tree" died of Agent Orange triggered colon cancer.

*Receiving letters from home maintained our connection to sanity and comforting conversation. *Vietnam was truly an out of world experience.*

The casualties were from enemy fire, vehicle and work place accidents, disputes among soldiers (everyone was armed), attempted suicide, friendly fire, and attempted murder of leaders in the field that were too aggressive in pursuing the enemy.

Viet Cong booby traps were the majority of cases. The VC were resourceful in utilizing our unexploded ordnance - grenades, artillery shells, land mines, bullets, and bombs. The jungle was close to impenetrable and American patrols gravitated to walking established trails. A big mistake, for the VC were masters at disguising the mutilating weapon's placement.

Following the explosion, red hot fragments, traveling at 2500 feet per second and impacting with 6000 horsepower of kinetic energy, inflicted unimaginable destruction of arms, legs, torso, and genitalia. The human body is essentially the density of water and the shock wave resulting from dispersal of the kinetic energy, the *Ballistic Shock Wave*, devitalized additional tissue that required debridement.

Walking patrol was tantamount to playing Russian Roulette in not knowing if, when, and where the booby trap would be tripped. Does one bury this challenge or just accept the risk? Many grunts dealt by assuming they would be killed and no precautions could protect them. They just fought with abandon.

There were two major chapters to the Vietnam War - before and after Tet '68-'69. Before Tet, the *fabric of the Army* was intact. The chain of command was respected and the soldiers fought with purpose having been led to believe their bloody sacrifices were effectively winning the war and protecting democracy.

The Tet Offensive conducted by the Viet Cong (VC) and the North Vietnamese Army (NVA) resulted from the unrecognized (by the Americans) infiltration of enemy forces into major cities up and down South Vietnam. All their firepower was unleashed at the same time. Cites were lost to the enemy. The battle to regain the US Embassy in Saigon and the bloody urban fighting in Hue are well documented. In the end, all the enemy gains were repulsed.

The embarrassing outcome of Tet '68 presented to the world that all the American military and political propaganda was a lie. *We definitely were not winning.*

The Tet Offensive by the VC and NVA was the game changer.

Our country's leaders had decided to end the war. However, the loss would certainly tarnish political and military legacies. The drawdown was gradual and kids were still being slaughtered without an effort to win.

Following Tet '68, the politicians began the drawdown of troop numbers in Vietnam.

Norman Camp, M.D wrote in his *US Army Psychiatry in the Vietnam War* that a warrior's unit supplied strength, protection, love, stability, rationalization, a moral base, cohesiveness, and discipline. Before Tet 1968 the "fabric" of the Army was strong having been woven securely by healthy units. After Tet 1968, once the warriors learned of our government's deceit, the unit cohesion weakened considerably and the "fabric' of the Army frayed. PTS, Suicides, psychosis, racial tensions, lack of discipline, fragging, and heroin ('72: 1 in 8) usage escalated.

Discipline eroded. Who wanted to be the last to die in Vietnam? Dr. Norman Camp served in Da Nang at the same time I was at the 85th Evac.

"Friendly Fire" did not occur often but it was part of the fog of war - either by accident or on purpose. "Fragging" has become commonplace. The grunts, average age twenty-two years, realized that they would have to protect themselves. Who wanted to be the last to die in Vietnam? The grunts just wanted to go home. Self-preservation and protecting their brothers trumped the threat of becoming KIA.

They took control - "do not risk our lives needlessly." First and Second Lieutenants and senior EM's (Enlisted Men) learned to "lighten up ti-ti (a little)." If either was too risk prone on patrol a warning non-lethal smoke grenade would explode nearby. If change did not occur, the fragmentation grenade solved the problem. A M16 round in the back of a gung ho leader was not lost on others in charge.

"...these bastards aren't worth fighting for...." was a common tenant in general and on our 85th compound. We all were fearful of trusting the Vietnamese. The interpreter in the ED that befriended us was found to be VC. *He was disappeared.* The Vietnamese workers stole everything

that was not nailed down - food, tools, diesel fuel, utensils, et.al.

"This place is a damn waste!" - universally agreed to by most Americans in Vietnam. The Vietnamese on both sides hated us, we were certainly not winning "hearts and minds" when slaughtering them, burning their villages, and destroying their crops. But, our allies in South Vietnam learned how to manipulate the Americans for the benefit of themselves.

With being incarcerated on the 85th Evac. compound and time on our hands we had incentive to beautify our hooches, tape, and party at the "O" Club and in our hooch. I explored many aspects of photography. I learned about depth of field, f stops, and macro, wide angle, zoom, and telephoto lenses. Even tried to persuade my brother-in-law, Jimmy, to get involved. Photographically preserving my experiences in Vietnam was paramount in recording history for future generations. Especially in the area of battlefield trauma and the surgical techniques utilized to prevent death and maintain functionality of the victim. We repaired all vessels primarily or with a vein graft - at the time of the first surgery.

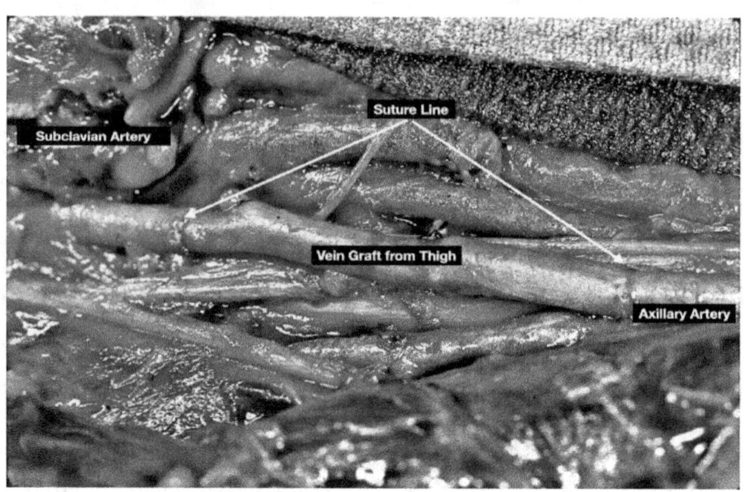

Saphenous (thigh) vein graft Subclavian Artery to the Axillary Artery, reconstituting blood flow to the arm and hand

[In WWII, the repair of injured blood vessels was discouraged. Major arteries in extremities were ligated and resulted in a twenty-five percent amputation rate. In Korea blood vessel repair was in its infancy. In Vietnam, just about every surgeon could perform this procedure. In the post 911 wars Damage Control Surgery was instituted. Initially a plastic tube was inserted to bridge the gap in the traumatically divided blood vessel to preserve blood flow to the extremity. The arterial repair was delayed to be performed in a controlled and better equipped environment.]

I wore surgical gloves size 71/2. The scrub medic would slip a size 8 over the sterile gloves so I could hold the unsterile camera. The circulating medic would then remove the bigger gloves and sterility was maintained.

Photos were taken of pre and post operative X-rays, injuries before and after surgery, the controlled chaos of the ED and operating room, and our hospital team. Our lives outside the hospital were fully documented.

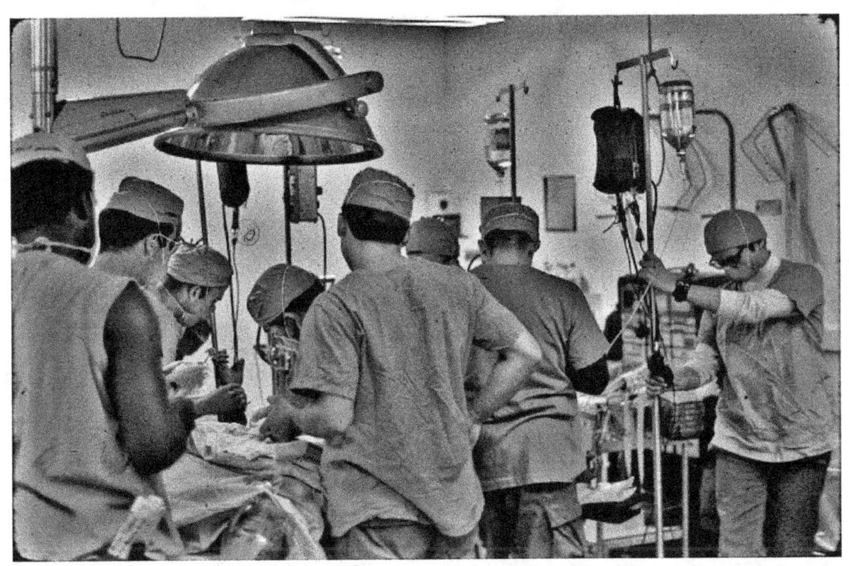

Controlled chaos in an 85th Evac operating room.
All hands were on deck

*I've shown my Vietnam trauma, 85th Evac. lifestyle slides, and my PTSD research hundreds of times over the past half century - locally, nationally, and internationally. The Hi - Bye Parties were bitter sweet. *Hi* to the newbies and *By* to the lucky ones going back to the "world" - to DEROS home (Date Estimated Return From Overseas).

The entire compound gathered in a large Army dull green painted plywood shack with a corrugated metal roof. It was elevated on short stilts to avoid flooding during the monsoons. That drab building was our officer's club but it had a nice bar and was well stocked. We loved it. Working intimately together caring for the wounded, maimed, and dying developed unbreakable bonds of love. We mourned for ourselves when friends left and felt sorry for newbies. That love is as strong as ever for those of us from the 85th Evac still alive. Our reunions are those of a loving family still looking for answers.

Why a Vietnam War? Why do our minds return there on a daily basis? Will we ever be capable of expelling our demons? After fifty-five years the reunions are sought out to "heal." Again there is reference to excessive drinking - the self-medicating was becoming more prevalent in assisting in the ***burying*** and descending into PTSD.

We could order items from Penny's and Sears to spruce up our hooch's interior. I made shelves from the wooden boxes within which mortar rockets were shipped. I could not do much with the yellowed OD green mosquito netting over my cot, but it did prevent being infected with malaria.

*Several ARVN (South Vietnamese Army) soldiers were wounded protecting the 85th Evac. perimeter. One bled out. I operated on another, repaired and removed portions of his stomach and intestines. I then resected (removed) the huge right lobe of his liver - a risky, bloody, and challenging operation requiring excessive blood with a dubious outcome. He survived. In the Post 911 wars casualties with bleeding liver injuries were packed (applying pressure with towels) to avoid resection. Most livers stop bleeding with this approach thus avoiding commitment to actual time consuming and risky surgery.

Not long after my first liver resection I successfully performed the identical surgery on a Vietnamese male whose hooch was booby trapped by the VC for aiding the Americans.

It's amazing how easily I switched from resecting portions of liver to sprucing up my hooch. *Burying again.*

Usage of the term "Gook" (originating during the Korean War) and "Dink" were associated with dehumanizing the VC and NVA - as were "Jap" and "Nip," (Japanese), "Hun" "Kraut" "Heinie" (Germans) in WWII, and "Towelhead" (Muslims and Arabs), "Hajji" (Iraqi) in our Post 911 Wars.

Enemy humans became "subhuman" and less guilt was associated with killing them. This process, according to Ed Tick, PhD, is an important factor when considering the evolution of the "moral injury" of war (*War and the Soul*).

I did not trust a single Vietnamese I met during my Vietnam service. As previously noted, our ED interpreter turned out to be VC. He was disappeared. I too was caught up in the Vietnam quagmire and used the slur.

I actually had more respect for an enemy, the NVA (North Vietnamese Army) and Kit Carson Scouts (NVA now on our side) wounded.. They were more educated, dedicated, and appreciative.

My degradation of the Vietnamese softened over the years. In 2013. I met Mytrang Do at Weill Cornell

Medicine (WCM). She was a first year medical student I facilitated in Problem Based Learning: Human Structure and Function. Emigrating at age thirteen to Louisiana she thrived, did great at LSU, and was now excelling at WCM. We bonded and she healed my war time wounds. She and Anfei, also in my WCM class, married, completed their MD-PhD degrees, love their young son, Aaron, and completed their respective residency programs. Mia in Dermatology and Anfei in Ophthalmology. Robin and I attended their wedding near New Orleans and were considered their American grandparents. I must admit that before flying there I was concerned about being surrounded by Vietnamese and what reservations some may have had. As it turned out we were treated as part of their family.

*The Army stopped the war for Charlie Carroll and I to hitchhike on C-130's from Phu Bai to Saigon to take the written portion of our surgical board qualification exam. This test was being given in the states and around the world to all board candidates. The exam was on December 2nd. We departed on November 30th with the excuse that missing the exam was not an option. We were experts in getting on C-130's stand-by and knew we would have a few days before the exam to enjoy Saigon's French restaurants, especially the Le Cave, and the bars along Tu Do Street. A few days after the exam were also added.

On the night prior to the exam Charlie and I were wandering Tu Do street in our fatigues with the medical caduceus on our left lapel and a major's gold leaf on the right side. A very professional skinny black MP very politely stopped us and inquired to see our military ID and ration card (for buying liquor). We were a little tipsy and perhaps would have given the kid some sarcasm until we spotted the two huge linebacker sized MP's in their jeep. The polite MP returned from the jeep and told us we were good to go. I then asked him, "Why did you stop us?" He responded, "Frankly sirs you do not look old enough to be Majors or act like you are." I took that as a compliment! In spite of being hung over we both passed with flying colors.

*Before I departed for my service in Vietnam, due to the concentration required during surgical training, medicine and surgery were paramount. My residency buddy, Deming Payne, referred to our existence as "child abuse for adults."

In Vietnam I experienced the separation from family, the gift of downtime to evaluate life, and the witnessing of war's devastation on body, mind, and soul. I soon realized that Robin, Kim, and Chris were the paramount considerations. Therefore, I decided to not pursue academia but to commit to solo private practice in a small community, i.e., Amsterdam. Mission accomplished!

I tore the plantar fascia on the sole of the right foot - it was painful.

A walking cast to the right lower leg and foot did relieve the pain and fostered healing. The injury occurred playing basketball in a building space we procured and renovated into a gym. A volleyball court was also delineated. It was one and a half feet short in length. We beat the Vietnamese teams (their favorite sport at that time) for their spikes were often "long."

The doctors rotated in accompanying the wounded as they were evacuated to Japan. This duty was a respite from the war and Vietnam. We would travel in our summer khakis by a C130 equipped to transport patients to Saigon. The young soldiers were then transferred to a C141 Starlifter for

a flight to the Army hospital in Tachikawa, Japan. A short train ride to Tokyo presented a view of Mt. Fuji. At six-three in my uniform I towered over the Japanese riders. I realized WWII was just twenty-five years ago and my co-riders must have mixed emotions about my presence.

We would stay at the Army's Sanno Hotel in Tokyo. Our first responsibility was to visit the huge Tokyo PX and fulfill a shopping list for stereo and photographic items ordered by the 85th Evac staff. I was relieved to be rid of the five thousand or more in cash I was carrying. Most of the items were shipped back to the "world" - home.

I was then free to tour Tokyo and the surrounding countryside. I took the tram up to Mount Mitake and wandered around stoned. All my photos were blurred by movement. The Kobe steak was delicious! I stayed as long as I dared but in the process of partying for days I lost my shot record. That folded yellow document was essentially my passport to re-enter Vietnam and return to the 85th on a timely basis and avoid being AWOL. I visited Tachikawa Hospital and persuaded a young charge nurse to forge me a new shot record.

Hitchhiking on C130's back to Phu Bai from Saigon, I encountered one of our nurses, Jeanie. At Da Nang airport we were surrounded by young, traumatized grunts. She asked me to guard the door of the nearest latrine as she made her urgent entrance.

*I visited the mail room a few days after my birthday and was presented with a mid-sized box covered with shipping paper. The return address was Helene's.

With Bob, my roommate, observing, I carefully opened my package. The contents emitted the order of a cake. Two aluminum wrapped baked cake layers appeared with a can of Hershey's chocolate icing. Everything was fresh, moist, and intact after traveling eight thousand miles over a five day period: in and out of several aircraft. My brother-in-law, Jim, was considering an executive position change with a new company. He did make the move and was extremely successful. American casualties were fewer due the heavy monsoons and the ARVNs doing most of the fighting in Laos.

Once the sun reappeared the generals would resume sending grunts to die in a war that the United States was deserting. "By February 1971, I had not seen Robin for almost six months. We had communicated by mail, tape reels, and the MARS line. My son, Chris, addressed

Robin's tape recorder as daddy for that was where my voice emanated.

This pacific reunion could have been a marital disaster. We had led disparate lives, endured unique challenges, and become self-sufficient in our separate circumstances. Our seamless engagement of the new us was not dictated by marriage vows but by the fact we had been friends for years before we were wedded. Kim was five and had demanded to see her daddy. Robin did not want to share her time with me, so she told Kim the generals did not allow children in Hawaii. My daughter accepted her fate until she later noticed, after Robin's return, children in the newly developed R&R photos. An awkward discussion followed.

Robin had arrived a day early and attempted to register in the Hilton Rainbow Towers but there had been a clerical error. The hotel compensated by upgrading us to an elegant suite on the fifteenth floor. She then enjoyed our balcony and the hotel's pool and beach. Later that day, she visited the Honolulu WASAMA Chapter. An uncomfortable military bus then shepherded our psyched and recently de-planed group to Fort Derussy, an R&R facility on Waikiki beach, to check us in, inform us of local regulations, and provide the VD lecture. The army had also driven the wives to Fort Derussy. Robin looked great!

The suite itself was amazing but its best feature was privacy in a bathroom equipped with a flushing toilet! From our balcony, Diamond Head loomed a few miles away against a royal blue sky. The weather was perfect. The time was bittersweet because we had to separate again, but we enjoyed being together. The Rainbow Towers Hotel view was of Waikiki Beach with Diamond Head in the background. The sand was clean, deep, and welcoming. The water was warm, clear, and sea green (can't escape green).

There was also a pool located near the hotel directly below our fifteenth-story balcony. While relaxing at the poolside, I was experimenting with my telephoto lens and informed Robin that I could read the Kahlua label clearly on our balcony. After observing all the GIs with their cameras, she issued an embarrassed gasp for she had been on the balcony scantily clad the day before improving her tan. One day, we rented a white MG Midget and with the top-down drove east along the coast. As we progressed the topography became a lush green countryside. The highways we utilized have been altered over the years, but I remember climbing over the aged volcanic rock at the Halona Blowhole and having a delightful lunch at the Lion's Head Inn. There were fishermen along the coast skillfully throwing fine nets to trap their prey. We visited a surfing beach. The surf was not up, but we enjoyed walking on the damp sand.

We then diverted to the west and passed immense pineapple fields that extended to the horizon. Heading south and east, we returned past the Arizona Memorial to Honolulu and the Rainbow Towers, which is shown at the beginning of the Hawaii Five-O TV show. Another day, we traveled to the Polynesian Cultural Center, which defined the Hawaiian cultural and historical background.

We dined at a few fine restaurants within walking distance of the Hilton. Then there was the obligatory luau, huge crowds, drinks, hula dancing, comedian, and pig roast. To this day, I believe the MC on stage reflected the island's exhaustion of having GIs disrupting their lives, culture, and city in spite of all the dollars that were flowing into Oahu. He used the term "haole" incessantly to address his audience. The word refers to a white man or foreigner, but with a change in intonation, it becomes a most derogatory term. My turn to be referred to with disdain. The young kids and their wives and girlfriends had no understanding of the racist slur and laughed at his every word. I was pissed! We then departed paradise.

* "With the sun shining, the sky clear, and the heat rising, a perfect solution was a trip to the beach. Phu Bai was not far from the east coast and the South China Sea. On weekends, we boarded a CH-47 Chinook helicopter for the short trip over unsettled territory to Eagle Beach. There were steel plates on the deck of the chopper to deflect small arms fire. Up front, a crewman on the port-side manned an M60 machine gun.

Interest in volleyball and basketball subsided. Softball practices were beginning with Casey Blitt, our anesthesiologist, and Fred Brockschmidt, a Regular Army captain nurse anesthetist, organizing and coaching. After practice we would load up on Chinook (CH-47) and be taxied to Eagle Beach.

After walking up the C-46 ramp we sat along the fuselage in webbed jump seats with our towels, suntan lotion, and refreshments, a bit incongruous for a war zone. Upon liftoff, we could look out the rear of the chopper and watch the airport and its aircraft diminish in size.

That same transient feeling of doom one experiences today on a commercial flight in the United States passed through me, slightly magnified, every time I flew in choppers.

Eagle Beach was designated by the military as an in-country Rest & Relaxation (R&R) destination for the troops. At times, there were hundreds of GIs fresh from the boonies, both enlisted and officers. The new variable our arrival introduced were our feminine nurses. The ladies stayed close to us but were totally engaging when approached by an admiring trooper.

The water temperature was perfect and the waves moderate. We were cautioned about poisonous sea snakes, but no one was ever bitten. The sand was grayish white, deep, warm, and relaxing. With my eyes closed and the sun beaming down on me, I drifted back into my Hampton Bays, Long Island, New York, high school summer days.

*The typhoons in South-east Asia, where Vietnam is located, are equivalent to hurricanes we experience in the eastern United States. The loosely applied corrugated metal roofs of our plywood structures were easily lifted by the winds. Of most concern was the missing roof from our "O" Club; the sickly green plywood elevated shanty we frequented.

All buildings were on two foot stilts except the ED, OR's, and the Recovery Room/ICU. They were built on concrete slabs at ground level and were not ditched. All these areas predictably flooded and we worked in two to three inches of red- brown water. We dug aggressively to ditch the structures and avoid further damage. The brilliant Army Corps of Engineers should have thought to ditch the buildings when they were built. Eventually, as the flow of wounded ended, we used the typhoon as an excuse to resume drinking - even calling our activity a "Typhoon Party." This was "self-medicating" to *bury* the repetitive ugliness of war.

The Army was pulling away from I Corps, the most northern section of South Vietnam close to the DMZ, where my hospital was located. In doing so, troops of the 101st Airborne were being withdrawn. The powers that be predicted fewer wounded in our area of service since the pursuit of the enemy was becoming increasingly limited. But we were still relatively busy with wounded kids. Our number of surgeons was reduced from four to two. It was just me and a surgeon who was useless despite being advertised as fully trained. He was incapable of good judgement and operating effectively without me holding his hand. So, for two and a half months I was on 24/7. It was tiring. Our current causality volume required at least three competent trauma surgeons.

So what if more kids die due to the Army's position that the troops were expendable. To fill my new role, I had to be a more conservative drinker. I had some judgement remaining. *S*everal times a day we would applaud ourselves at being "Short." Doctors were not issued weapons. Although we all had M16s, Thompson Submachine Guns, .38 pistols, and .45 semi autos. We stole the guns from patients who arrived in the ED before the MP's could sequester them.

"A loaded .38 holstered revolver hung at the head of my bed, hopefully never to be used. There had been occasional attempted intrusions of the compound's perimeter by the Viet Cong (VC). It was reported to us that Vietnamese locals who had worked on the compound by day were killed at the wire at night. These sappers carried explosives hoping to slither through the encircling protective sharp-edged Concertina wire (improved barbed wire) to blow up personnel sleeping in their hooch's. One did not enter another's hooch without announcing your presence for you could be shot.

Robin, Kim, and I had a wonderful trip to Hong Kong and Bangkok. We flew into Hong Kong to spend a week in both countries. Robin and Kim arrived a day early from the US via Los Angeles, Honolulu, and Tokyo. As my aircraft negotiated its landing at the old Hong Kong

Airport, I was certain we would land in the harbor's waters. Robin and I had both arrived a day early.

*Upon my arrival home, Robin had planned to meet me at the airport with her hugs and Kim and Chris waving American flags. That was until my inauspicious departure from Vietnam.

She did call her medical contact in Washington and learned that I would be evacuated to Valley Forge Army Hospital. Leaving the children at home, she drove six hours alone to Pennsylvania worrying about me.

So there I was in the skies over the Pacific totally relaxed eating my juiced brownies. I do not remember landing in Japan but there was a Boy Scout World Jamboree taking place on that island country. An American boy scout's asthma became exacerbated, and he was given a ride home in our C-141. I'm not sure when but I was shaken awake by an Air Force flight nurse who advised me I needed to treat the boy scout for he was having problems. I have no idea what I utilized to treat him, but they did not bother me again. I awoke as we were about to land in Alaska. We deplaned, celebrated being on American soil, bought junk food, and selected Alaskan dolls for our children.

The C 141 next landed at an airport near the army post of Ft. Dix, New Jersey. We were transported to a nearby facility to stay overnight. A bus delivered a group of us to Valley Forge General Hospital where Robin was awaiting my arrival. She had planned the stereotypical welcome home.

I still had the same washed-out fatigues. I was sitting near admissions with the other patients when I spotted Robin heading to the window to ask where I was.

I stood, she came over, and we greeted in a reserved manner.

Well, they soon dressed me in the standard blue Army hospital PJs and I became one of hundreds wandering the halls. I was placed in a single room. Robin came with me, and as she was sitting at my bedside, a bossy nurse poked her head in and shouted, 'Don't close the door.' Sure I wanted to be with Robin, but in a bustling hospital?

My right arm was elevated with my elbow at a right angle. I was given physical therapy to increase the range of motion of my elbow. I was amazed at how difficult it was to regain adequate function. I called Ed Kayser, an orthopedist (my medical school roommate), and he advised me not to let Valley Forge's orthopedists surgically remove my radial head. They did suggest that procedure, and I refused. After bombarding me with multiple reasons why I would regret my decision, they finally left me alone.

My resulting disability was the inability to fully extend and flex my arm at the elbow by a few degrees. Thankfully, there was no impairment of my surgical skills. None of the previously predicted complications developed. But I could forget golf and tennis. I tried southpaw, but it did not work out.

My first official visitor at Valley Forge was a full bird colonel Army Catholic chaplain who, without requiring me to say a word, waved his hand over me making the sign of the cross absolving me of all wayward activity in Vietnam. I guess the typical soldier's laundry list of offenses was too long and repetitive to listen to over and over again.

I felt a sense of deprecation from the hospital physicians and nurses.. Robin suggested, and I agreed to wear my khakis with my major designation when in the hospital. What a difference a little golden leaf made.

Word of my arrival spread rapidly. A number of 85th Evac nurses and the patients I had operated on visited me. I easily recognized the nurses. The soldiers were another matter, for they had gained weight, grown their hair long, and sprouted facial hair. To identify the patients, I would ask them to lift up their shirt so that I could see their unique abdominal incisions, drain sites, and various other holes."

Excerpted from my memoir, *Welcome Home From Vietnam, Finally,* Chapter: *Inauspicious Departure*

Contradictory to my written orders to be stationed at Ft. Carson, Colorado, the commander at Valley Forge maneuvered to keep me there for the remainder of my active duty commitment. I successfully resisted.

I enjoyed a month's medical leave at Lake Panamoka on Long Island, NY in the house Robin had rented near her father. My family then set off for Colorado Springs, Colorado. We drove across the country to Ft. Carson. I was amazed that the United States was essentially flat from Rochester, NY to the Rockies. I was relieved to discover the lack of humidity once we left New York State.

In the Prologue you have read about my state of mind, and depth of PTSD when back in the United States. Robin's verbal intervention to immediately address my polluted mind-set was the game changer.

"Most of the docs at Ft. Carson's hospital had been in Vietnam. This post was a choice assignment and preference was given to those who had been in that combat zone. Our social life developed around our physician specialty groupings and former Vietnam friends. Excessive drinking and a fair amount of cannabis consumption were the norm for doctors newly returning from Vietnam. Robin and I hosted a party soon after arriving in Colorado. After everyone had returned home, hearing my voice, she searched the house for me. I could not be found until she entered the backyard to find me sitting on a tree limb, about fifteen feet up, screaming at the 'Fucking Vietnamese.' I had toxic levels of alcohol and Cannabis in my system.

The beauty of being with men who had the same experiences was that we were safe to express our feelings, nightmares, self-doubts, regrets, and cries for help in a receptive understanding environment. As time progressed, we learned to not depend on pot and drinking as an avenue of escape, but to begin to cope with our issues, to **(consciously** *not* **unconsciously** *as in Vietnam)* **compartmentalize** wartime traumatic events, and to begin to focus on our potentially fulfilling futures, leaving the past in the past."

Without stigmatization, while living and interacting with the other doctors at Ft. Carson, who had also served in Vietnam, I began to understand my predicament. In *trusting and sharing* with these Veterans, the stigma of PTSD was removed. I discovered *my descent into PTSD was predictable* as reflected in the commonality of our traumatic experiences. We were now better equipped to face our threatening demons.

Remember!

You are ***not alone.***

You are **not** ***unique.***

You are ***not weak.***

As for myself, ***you did not have a chance!***

The key for rehabilitation is to ***seek out others and share your stories.***

Last Thoughts...

To those who govern us:

Will elected officials ever read and abide by previously recorded failures, consider our warriors as equally human, and accept the fact that they must be returned home "whole.?" Shockingly. politicians continue to condone and perpetuate the attitudes of the humanity deficient

General Patton. Our brave men and women continue to be discharged to "sink or swim." I realize warriors die in combat but please do not treat them as totally expendable.

To the reader:

I've always believed that recording and studying history is of paramount educational importance.

For over half a century I have done so. All the information in *Letters* is factual.

I hope the reader has been enlightened concerning the evolution of PTSD, that *we are all susceptible*, and that PTSD may be dealt with by prevention or retroactive engagement. Gus has "Lived that and done that."

I'm eighty-six years old and still angry about the injustice I received from my country. However, I emphatically do not regret my service as a thirty year old Army trauma surgeon, I saved a lot of kids. I do regret what it cost me emotionally. I also regret the necessity of experiencing the weighty requirement of learning how to re-engage living in a peaceful society. However, that episode of my life spent in a Vietnam combat zone has made me a better Gus.

That time in Vietnam was the most formative of my life.

A Combat Surgeon in Vietnam
Wyatt S. Beazley, III, M.D.
General Surgeon

After graduating from the College of the University of Virginia, I attended medical school at the Virginia Commonwealth University Medical College of Virginia (VCU/MCV). I graduated in 1961 with a degree in medicine and completed my residency at MCV in 1966 as part of the Berry Plan. This plan allowed me to complete my five years of residency prior to entering the Army as a Captain in the Medical Corps.

My first duty station was at the Medical Field Service School for Doctors at Fort Sam Houston, Texas, for approximately six weeks. This school was geared to the treatment of traumatic wounds received in combat.

Thereafter, I reported to Fort Eustis in Newport News, Virginia, and was stationed there for nine months. After that, my orders were for Vietnam.

The 24th Evacuation Hospital was built in Long Binh, South Vietnam, in 1966 on what had been a rice paddy. I was a surgeon at the 24th Evac from July of 1967 to July of 1968. That time included the Tet Offensive which was in February of 1968. After med school and five years of surgical training, I thought I was ready for the world. But I can tell you, you learn a lot on the job in the OR at an Evac Hospital.

I'll never forget when I got off the plane and first arrived at the 24th. The sergeant major gave me a place to sleep. I asked, "how about tomorrow?" He said, "you're in the OR." I asked, "is anybody going to tell me what to do?" He said, "you'll know." And low and behold you learn on the job. We saw gunshot wounds, shrapnel wounds, and puncture wounds. You don't see wounds such as this in civilian life. I've said this over and over, and I mean it, it's a shame every surgeon can't spend some time in a combat zone. It's a real education.

The map of South Vietnam was divided militarily into I, II, III, and IV Corps from the Northern to the Southern Sectors. I Corps was primarily Marines, the others Army. The 24th was in III Corps. The IV Corps was in the Mekong Delta. For the enemy it was a short trip from North Vietnam to get men and supplies down to South Vietnam through Laos and Cambodia.

We were quite busy with casualties most of the time. However, during periods in between, we'd take the opportunity to visit the villages and countryside. We saw very heavy foliage. Imagine GIs fighting through this jungle. Right outside of a city would be rice paddies with people working in them. Water buffalo were the "John Deere" of Vietnam. They'd plow fields, pull carts, and provide food. There were rubber tree plantations. The French had been in Vietnam for about 200 years and they planted rubber trees throughout. They're quite beautiful and they tapped these just like we tapped the maple trees. You can see cuts on these trees from where the latex would drain into a bowl tied to the tree. Vietnam at that time was very primitive; roads with small bridges, lots of greenery, lots of sun. On the side of the road we'd see a small store on just a stand: their "7-Eleven." One could buy anything, cigarettes, marijuana. In the village markets the people would come in, take their places at their stands, sell their homemade goods, produce, and fowl. It would be bustling by noon. When venturing out of the hospital, we really had to be careful because you did not know who the enemy was. Some 15-year-old boy would all of a sudden throw a grenade at you. We never stopped at the stand because you couldn't trust anybody. This was a guerilla war. You're not very well protected.

There were almost no full-sized cars. We saw bicycles, lots of motorbikes and lambrettas, which was a wide motor bike for passengers. The city closest to our hospital was

Bien Hoa, about a 40-minute drive north from Saigon. Saigon is one of the prettiest cities I've ever seen. French, of course, beautiful houses, wide boulevards, tree-lined and well paved streets. Now it's called Ho Chi Minh City.

I was very taken that the women of South Vietnam appear to do all the hard work. They took all the goods to the market to sell; they carried things around; they took care of children. They would use a "carrying" or "shoulder pole" to carry heavy loads. Parents taught their children to carry produce in this way to be sold at the market. The men seemed to sit and take care of bicycles and doing a few things.

We saw a lot of filth and the dirt, especially in Bien Hoa. We saw houses on the side of the Saigon River. Their sewage is pumped right into the water. Very primitive, as you can imagine. It was said, on occasion, to catch on fire from the oil on top. We saw a man sitting. We called it the Vietnamese squat. His butt does not hit the ground. It's about 4 inches off the ground and he would sit like that for hours. All through Vietnam you'd see the local people sitting, squatting like that all day long. The children, urchins living in the city, asking for food, asking for clothes, asking for money, sleeping under tables. It's tragic. There were many homeless children. We saw a young lady with her baby. The baby actually looked quite healthy. The traditional wear of the ladies is the Ao Dai. The women were quite attractive, had beautiful skin and beautiful facial features. Some were a combination of French and Asian blood.

The following pages contain images of wounded men, women, and children that, for some, are very difficult to look at. They are meant to be this way. War is an horrific ordeal and the price that many soldiers, sailors, Marines, airmen, and civilians, paid is reflected in these photographs. Remember what you will see.

Photograph # 1 is a photo of a Vietnamese hearse. About ten days before Tet, it appeared that many people had died. The hearses were all up and down the roads. After Tet, we learned they weren't carrying bodies. They were carrying ammunition and weapons to get to the Viet Cong for the Tet Offensive.

I had a very good friend who was a helicopter pilot. I spent one night with him at his camp in the mountains and I saw our "8" guns. These shoot 20 miles with accuracy. Firing at night time looked like "the biggest July 4th," with a huge noise. The guys held their ears. I'm sure there were some ruptured eardrums.

The GIs were very innovative! For our shower there would be a can at the top which was a recycled 55-gallon oil drum. They filled it with water in the morning and the sun warmed it up. By the afternoon we would have a lukewarm shower. That's what we had at our hospital. We had five of them and they were built on stands of ammunition canisters. We'd take showers in the late afternoon, and needless to say, we didn't take a whole lot of them. We saw a GI-designed washing machine with operating instructions, likely made in the motor pool.

There was good medical care in South Vietnam. The 24th Evac had numerous medical facilities. Every one of those facilities was a medical unit. That was home. I was there for a year. We also slept there. We used a washer and hung our clothes to dry. We had cots. There were no beds. The latrine was about a block and a half away. So, if nature called at two o'clock in the morning, it was very convenient to just step outside. We'd come out in the morning, draw water, shave and brush our teeth. Very primitive. Under these circumstances, we all became very close friends.

In Vietnam winter was the dry season and spring and summer was the rainy season. During the rainy season, it rained every single day for about seven months. It would start about ten in the morning and continue on until about three or four in the afternoon. You could tell a new arrival because they tried to hop over the water and go around to where it was dry. But if somebody had been there six or eight months they just walked on through it. The rain didn't bother them at all. It was extremely hot, sometimes 110° in the shade. It was sometimes difficult to breathe the air was so heavy.

The military hired local people to come in to perform street maintenance and general cleaning services. They all wore conical hats. I think half of them were probably Viet Cong. They'd steal anything you had. So, you had to be very careful. They were always there up until Tet.

Photograph #2 was the dispensary which was open 24 hours a day. A doctor would be there from about seven o'clock until five in the afternoon. Medics were always there. This is where a soldier would go if he had a headache, sore throat, or the like. Diarrhea, unfortunately, was a common problem.

Photograph #3 (above) is our dispensary and shows what happened to it during Tet, when it took a direct hit from an enemy rocket. Fortunately, no one was hurt as no one was in there at the time. It's interesting that we still have the three cans there that didn't fall.

People ask, was the 24th Evac a MASH hospital? MASH stands for Mobile Army Surgical Hospital. MASH hospitals were used in the Korean War but not in Vietnam. A MASH hospital was set up as the front advances. MASH hospitals would advance with the Army to get hospital care as close as you can get to the front line. There was no front line in Vietnam. The fighting would be in a location for three weeks or four weeks, then it would shift to another area. It was much more practical for a helicopter to pick up the casualty and bring him to a fixed hospital than take the hospital to the casualty. The helicopter changed all of that.

This is a photograph of the Bell UH-1 "Huey." We called them "choppers, or slicks."

The 24th Evacuation Hospital was built by civilian contractors. There were a lot of these contractors over there. The military hired them. For protection from mortars there were sandbags around all of the Quonset huts. We had electricity about seventy-five percent of the time. We had four to six general surgeons and three neurosurgeons. The 24th was one of the hospitals with neurosurgeons. We were, therefore, very busy. Almost every belly wound had a head wound. So, we all had a lot of work. There were also three orthopedists, an ophthalmologist, a facial surgeon and four or five internists.

The 101st Infantry Division was nearby as the 25th Infantry Division, all in the III Corps area. The Huey was a lifesaver. Our tent was very close to the helipad. We didn't have any warning of incoming casualties. If you heard a Huey come in, you'd know there'd usually be one, two or three casualties. So, if you were on first call you just stayed where you were. There was also the Chinook, a much larger helicopter. If we heard one of these come in, you could have 15 to 20 wounded GI's. So, everybody got up and went immediately to the operating room. You knew you were going to be working for at least the next 24 hours.

This is photograph #4, and it shows two Army medics carrying a casualty on a stretcher, which is also called a litter. The significant thing is, those who are wounded get placed on a stretcher and they are never taken off that stretcher until they go to the operating room. It is very efficient. We didn't have to move a patient to a table then move him back onto something else. He stayed right on that stretcher until he went into surgery.

This is a photograph #5, and it was our triage area. It's the most effective place I've ever worked in my life. On either side there are six saw horses or stretcher stands. The casualty is brought in on a stretcher and it is placed on those stands. They are met by a host of nurses, doctors, medics, and sometimes chaplains. Clothes are cut off, airways established, chest tubes and IVs inserted. You try to pick a large vein, a femoral vein or subclavian vein. You are going to be pumping blood into this person so you always try to find the best vein you can. We used a lot of blood. Fortunately, we never ran out. They worked twelve hours straight and no one said it's time to go home. Everybody stayed there. They did their job and they did a great job at that. I never heard anybody complain. When the wounded arrive, the triage doctor comes right down the aisle and decides if you go to the operating room right away or you wait. Very quick decisions.

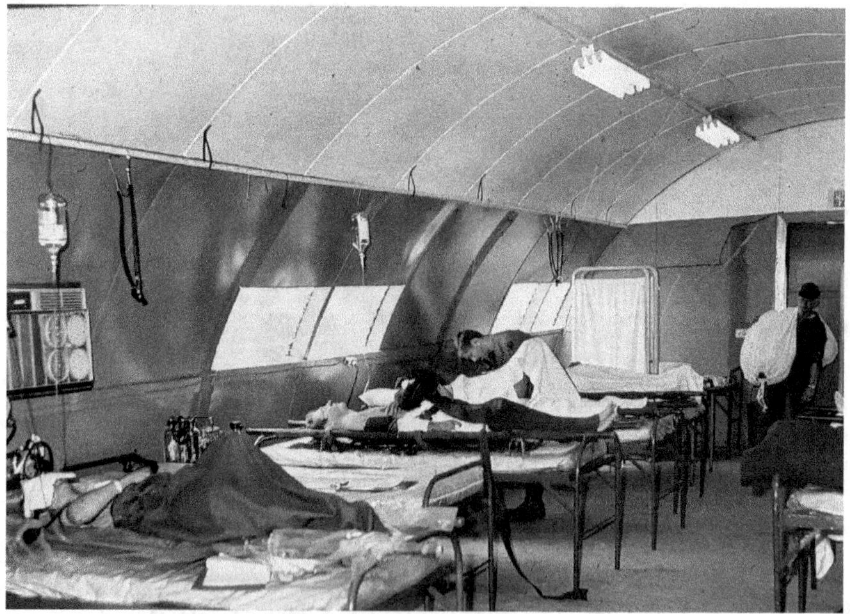

This photograph #6, and it shows the pre-op hootch. The wounded are on the stretchers, still on the same stretcher that picked them up in the field.

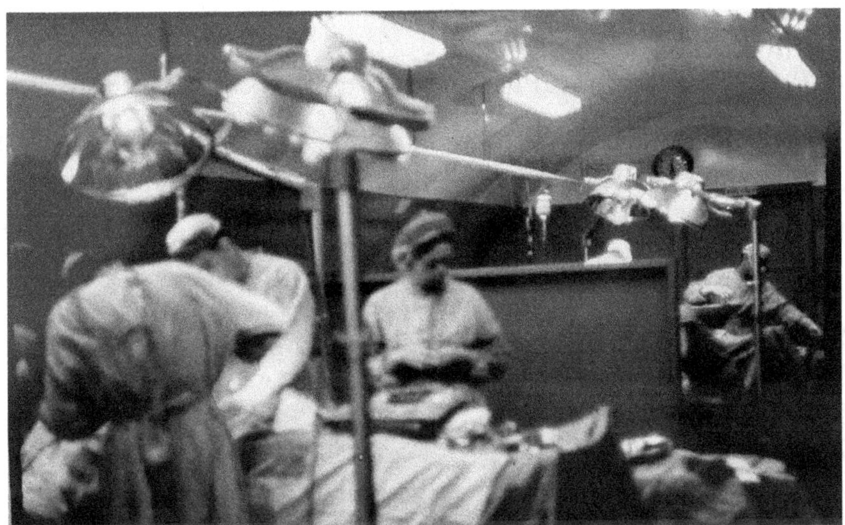

Photograph # 7 is one of our operating rooms: I don't think you'd call them operating suites. They were operating areas. There were two Quonset huts, three areas in each one for three operations. So, we could have six operations going on at one time. You can see back on the left is one. There's one in the back in the middle, and these two doctors are scrubbing to start a third case. The woman you see in the photo is a circulating nurse. Her job is in the three operating rooms. When surgeons needed something they called for it and she got it for them. The green dividers could be moved back and forth for whichever team needed more room. Buckets were filled with water on the top of the building each morning. By gravity water comes down. That's what we scrubbed with.

It was not unusual to have one doctor giving anesthesia to two patients at a time, sort of like a "V," he'd be at the head of the "V." It was also not unusual for three surgeons (neurosurgeon, orthopedist, and general surgeon) to operate on one person at one time. The only problem with this was we had to make a bigger space. You know surgeons are not very patient and so this poor circulating nurse had three Primadonna's all yelling at her at the same time. I can tell you she worked hard.

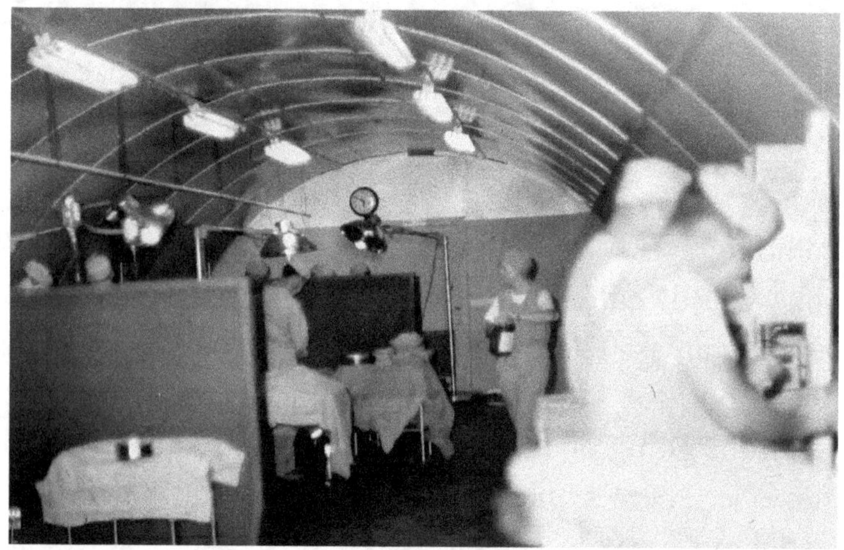

This is another view. It is a general surgery case. This is photograph # 8 and it shows a case in the back and one up close. One doctor, one medic, one technician and a circulating nurse. The Army medics were as busy as the surgeons. Great medics and they really did a fine job.

Photograph # 9 is a photo that shows a general surgery case in the recovery room.

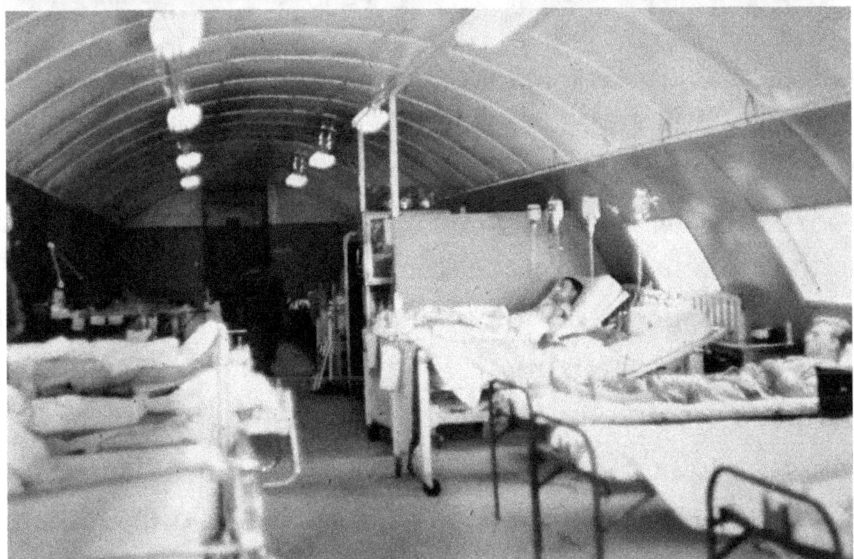

This is photograph # 10 and it shows a ward where we kept patients four to five days after surgery. Then they'd go to the Army hospital in Japan for about a week. That was the Camp Zama US Army Hospital in Honshu about twenty-five miles Southwest of Tokyo. There were no private rooms. The floor was often dirty and the beds were makeshift. The injured got well, though.

This photograph, #11, is a stretcher where anyone injured was picked up in the field and remained on it until he went to the operating room. You can see all the blood on the stretcher and on the sandbags beneath it.

Photograph # 12 is of a young man who had a piece of shrapnel go through his scalp, his skull and into his brain. He had a craniotomy. It may not be visible but written on his left shoulder is his blood pressure and pulse. We'd make up charts until we got to the operating room. Charts got lost. So, when you got to the OR notes were made on the patient which were then used.

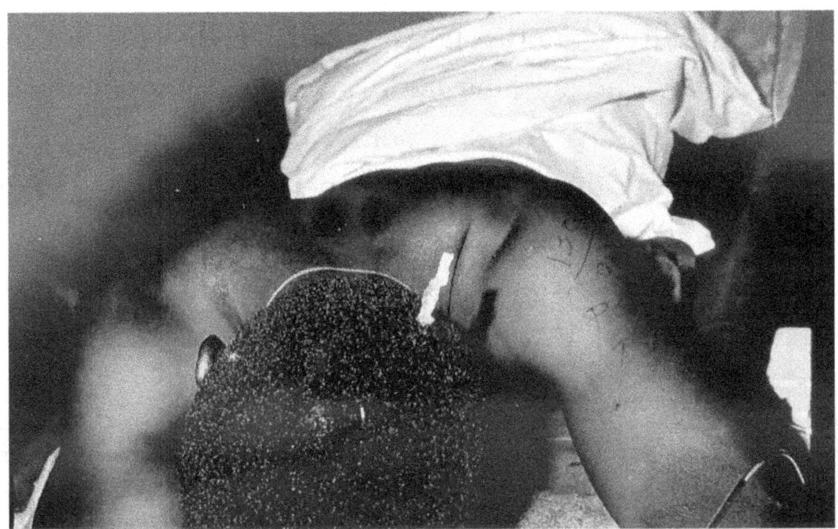

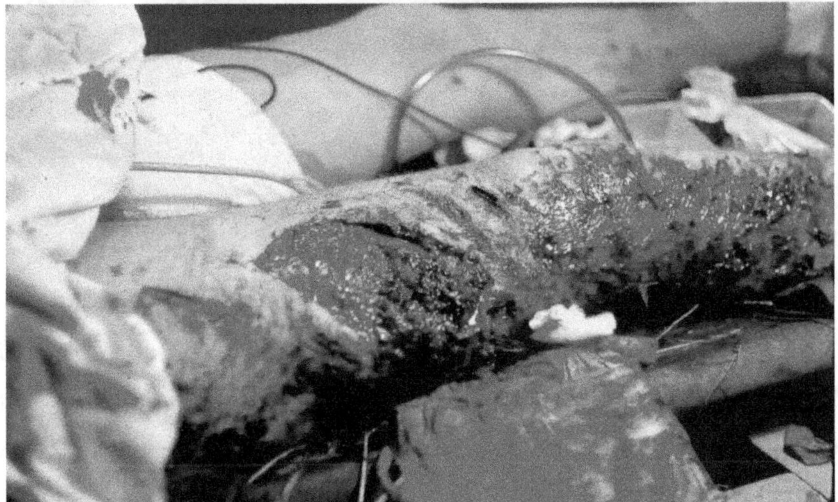

This is photograph # 13, and it is a typical soft tissue wound. We saw this often. This is from shrapnel. The photo shows what shrapnel does to the leg and to other extremities. You can see the yellow tube, and that's his oxygen. He's getting blood through his left femoral vein. So, he obviously had another injury because this leg injury would not require a transfusion. He probably had either a chest or a belly wound. These wounds took a lot of time for surgeons. The surgeon had to cut the damaged tissue out and clean it up. You don't close these wounds.

This photograph # 14, and it shows a typical wound, small hole going in, great big hole coming out. Bullets go in and they cause a great deal of damage coming out. I remember this photo well. You can see the entrance hole.

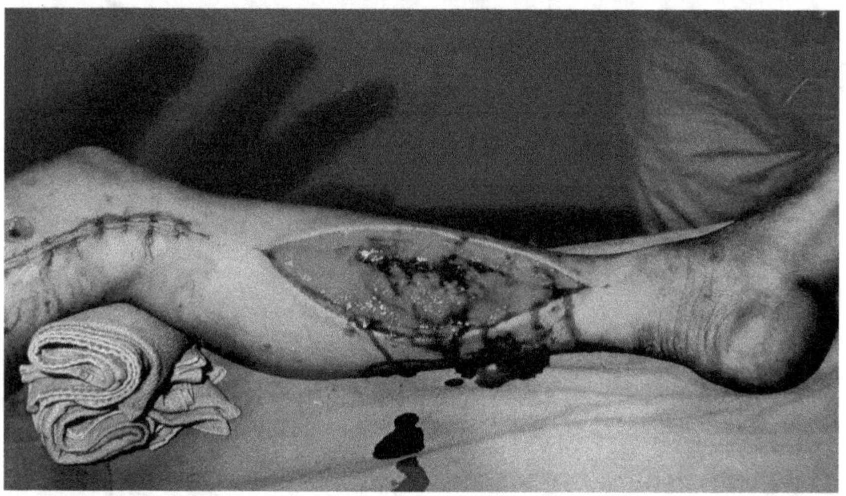

We made an incision under that because he had an injury to the artery. We repaired the artery. Then we went down to the exit wound, cleaned all of the material out and cut the dirt and dead tissue out. You leave this wound like this and the patient goes to Japan. There are two reasons: if you close that wound, it's going to get infected and swell, cutting off the circulation and the patient will then lose his leg. So, as it is now, this man has a repaired leg. He won't win any beauty prize. But he has a viable leg and he'll be able to walk and do most anything he wants.

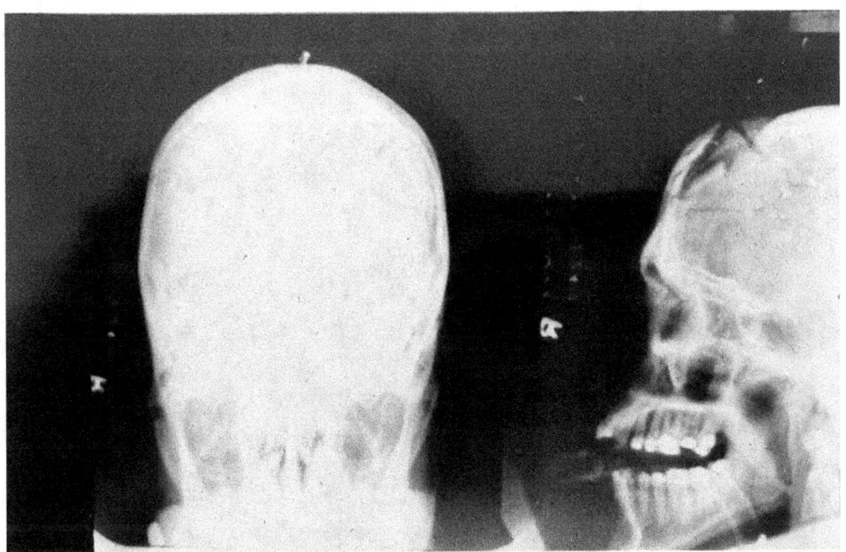

This photograph #15, shows the x-rays of a head injury. There were a lot of head fractures, from people being blown out of jeeps and around inside of tanks. Neurosurgeons were very busy. Surgeons made major strides in vascular surgery during those years. A flail chest, that's a tough one. A flail chest means multiple ribs are broken. Sometimes ribs are broken in more than one place. When you breathe, your ribs ought to expand. In flail chest your chest is collapsed so you can't breathe. The treatment is to put towel clips on those ribs and hook it up to weights so it pulls the chest up. But we didn't have weights. So, you'll get enough stones that you thought was about five pounds and put them in a bag. You improvise.

We took care of GIs first, American civilians next. The Americans civilians were usually construction workers. They didn't have war wounds but they had typical issues like appendicitis and hernias. I operated on three or four of them during my year. South Vietnamese soldiers were next.

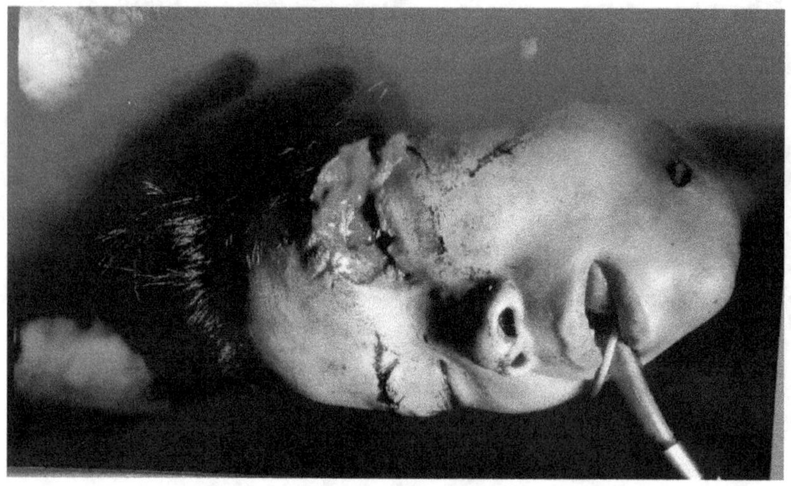

This photograph above, #16, shows an injured South Vietnamese woman. And last, I never saw any, but prisoners of war would be treated if they needed it.

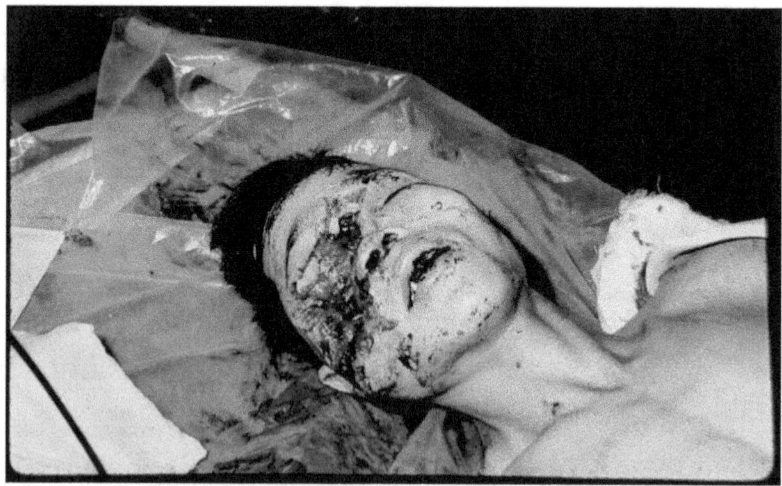

The photograph above. # 17, is that of a South Vietnamese ARVN (Army of Vietnam) soldier. Terrible head injuries. We would clean them up and make them as healthy as possible. Then they went to a South Vietnamese Army hospital. I wonder what kind of care they got after that. I have no idea.

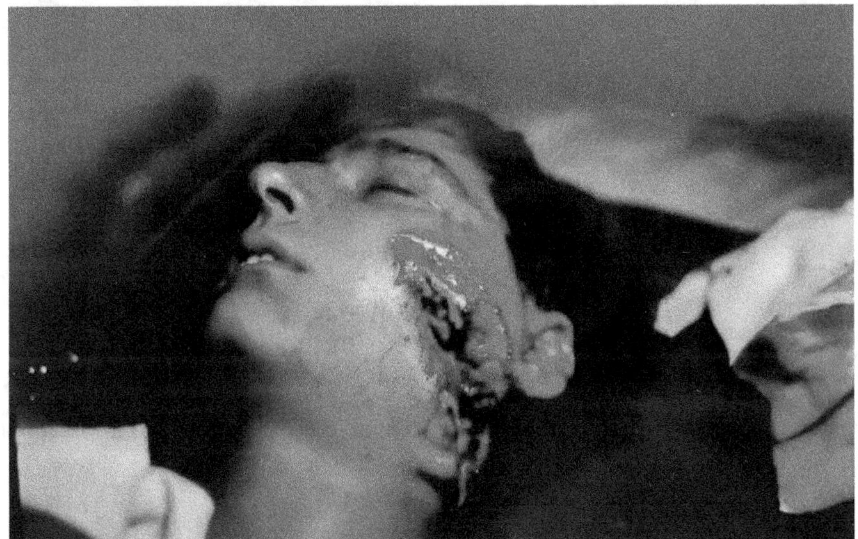

Here is photograph # 18, and it is a photograph of an American GI with a very bad facial injury. If you look down below you can see the flap of skin. We'd dig bone out, take out muscle and cut out dead tissue. We'd put it back as best we could and then we hoped he'd find a good plastic surgeon.

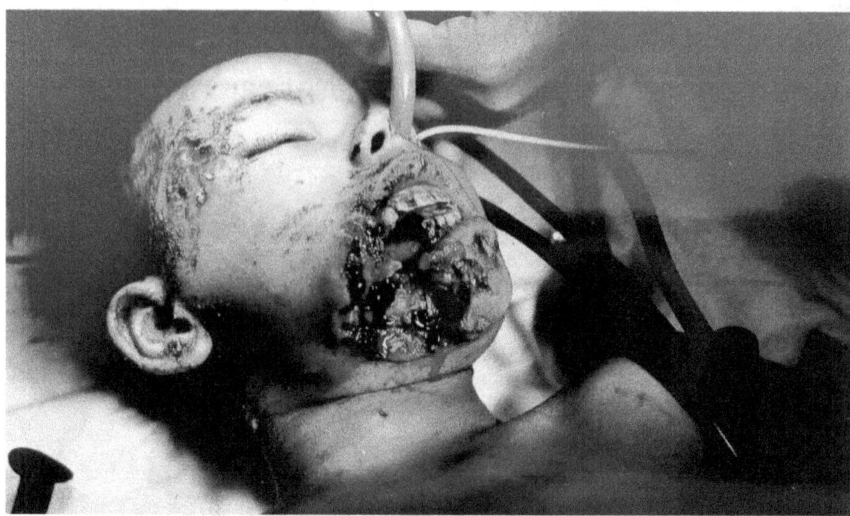

Photograph # 19 is a difficult to look at. It was horrible to see the poor children. Here's one with serious facial injuries. We didn't see many civilians, but they'd be brought in to us from time to time. I hate to think what happened to them afterwards.

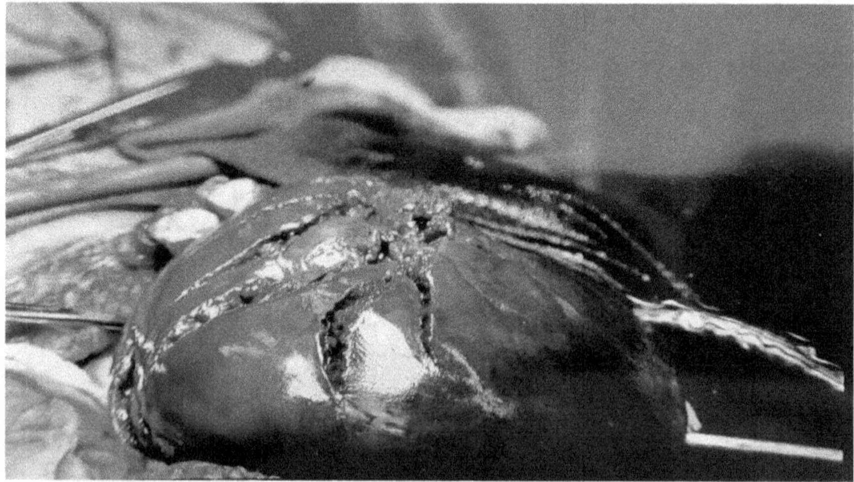

Photograph # 20 is a badly damaged liver. We saw a lot of these and they're very difficult for surgeons to handle. They bleed terribly and controlling the bleeding is really difficult. If you put stitches in, they tear through the liver. So, what I'd have to do is go down to each one of those bleeders, either coagulate it, tie it off or do something else to stop the bleeding. On some of these cases we cut the ribs so that we could get down to work on the liver. The liver is amazing, and it will regenerate. If you operate on this person six or eight years later the liver would almost look normal. The patient would have some scar tissue but if the surgeon could stop the bleeding, the patient would live. On occasion when we couldn't stop the bleeding, the surgeon would pack it with what we call a lap pad. We'd sew him back up and the next morning reoperate on him and take the lap pad out. By then the bleeding has pretty well stopped.

The Army had supplied us with some sort of glue that they thought would stop the bleeding. So, I tried it. I poured the glue on the wound but it didn't work well. The blood lifted the glue right off. About six or eight years ago, VCU, along with the military, developed something called "quick clot combat zone gauze." It was developed right here in Richmond, Virginia. You pack the wound with this combat gauze and it stops the bleeding. So, as a combat surgeon I give real credit to our school here.

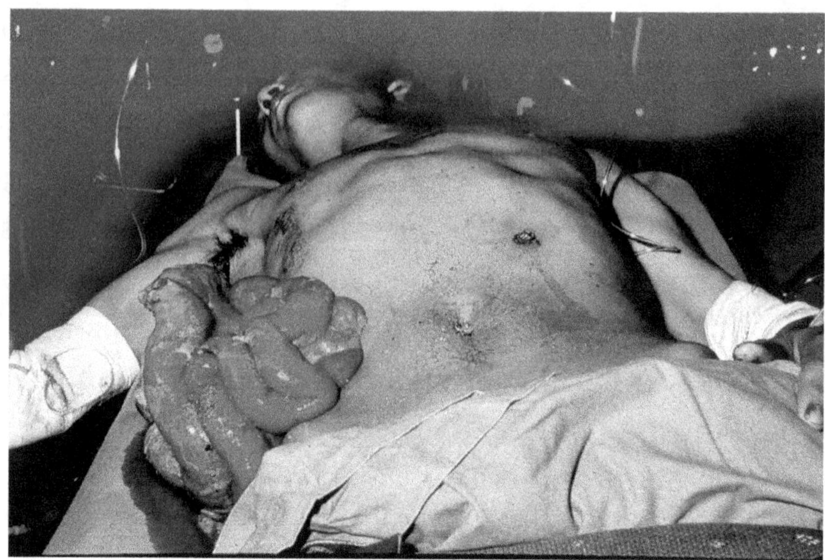

Photograph # 21 shows a GI with a small hole going in and a big hole coming out. The hole coming out is the size of a tennis ball with exposed small intestine. He had lain in the field for a good while. Yellow spots on the intestine are visible. The yellow spot are called exudate. Exudate is a mass of cells and fluid that has seeped out of blood vessels. It's really his body trying to heal itself. This is a real challenge for surgeons. We would have several big problems: One, we'd make a big midline incision starting at the sternum going way down over to the tubing. Secondly, we would pull all of the bowel back in after you cut out the part that is not healthy. Third, we'd sew it back together. Then we would have two more problems. We would have to close that hole because if we didn't, the bowel would herniate again. And then, we would have to close his belly. Intestines are all swollen in this photo.

Closing the belly is a challenge. The abdominal contents will swell, making the abdomen tight.

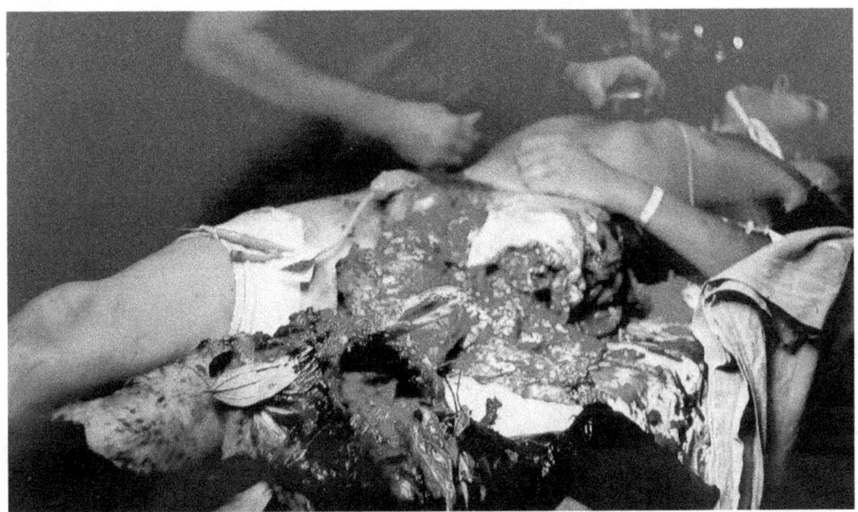

Photograph # 22 is another photo of a horrible wound. There's no way you can train a surgeon for combat wounds like this one. We had a lot of extremity wounds.

Look at that hand below, in photograph # 23. I give the orthopedists credit. They did not rush to amputate. They may do the best they can with this, then look at it the next morning and see if it's stable, okay, and fine. If not, then they'd amputate.

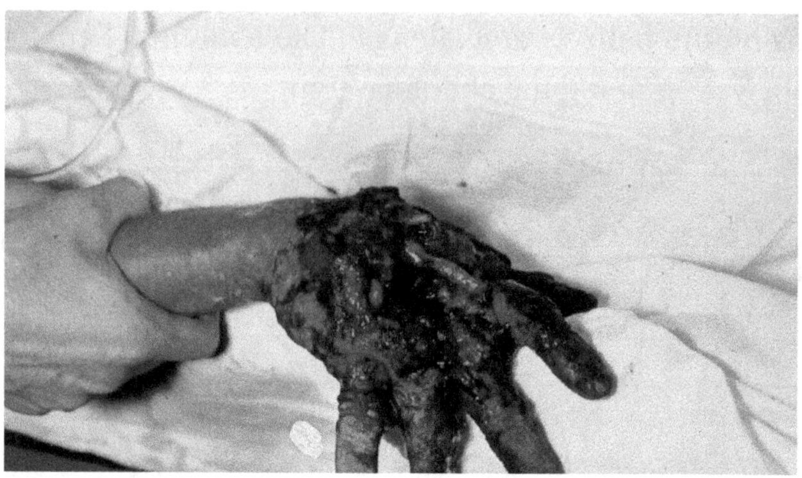

Photograph # 24. It is the same with the lower extremities. I credit them for being cautious. It was more work for them because if they had not amputated and it becomes necessary the next day they would be going back to the operating room. But they saved a lot of arms and legs this way.

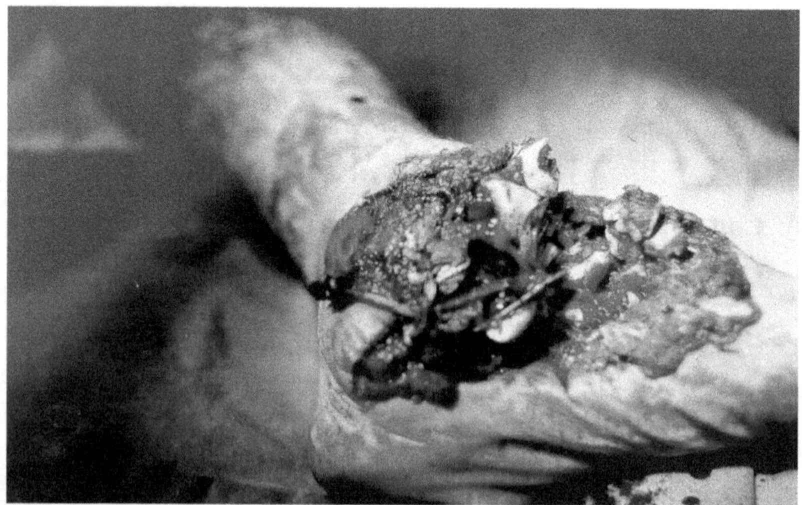

Photo 25. This is what an untreated burn looks like. This was a hand, with no treatment, and it's useless.

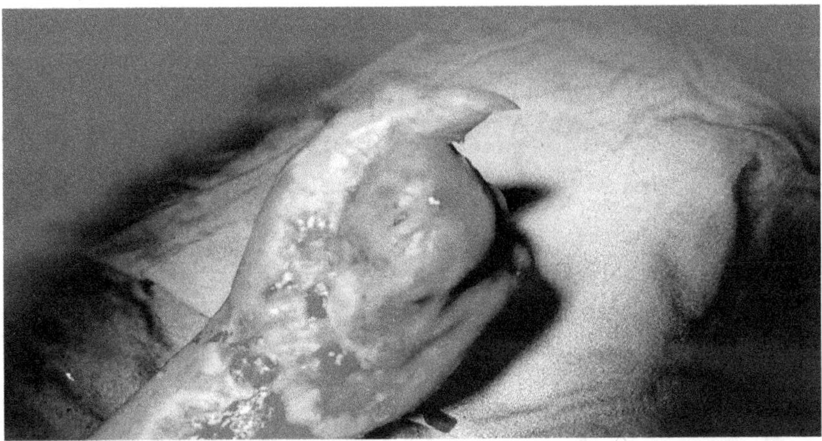

Photograph # 26 is a child's foot, or what's left it. The tragedy of war.

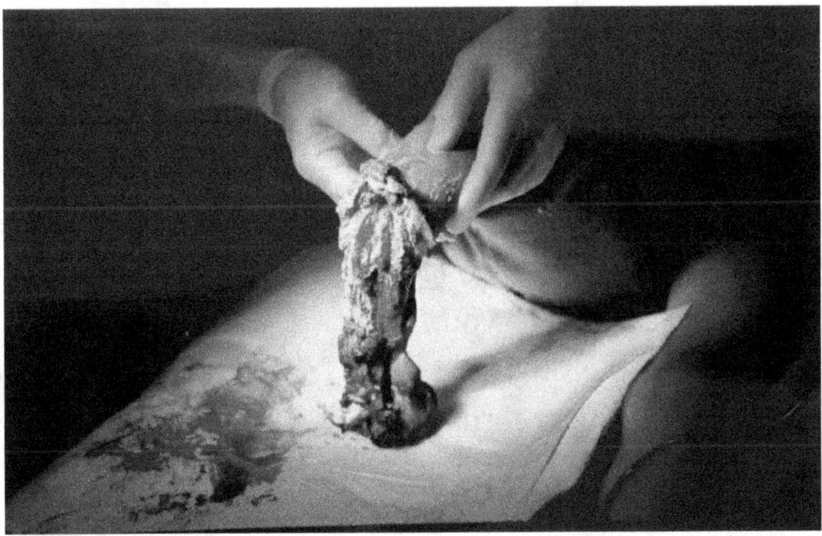

There was a prisoner of war camp about half a mile from where we were. I walked down there one day. This camp had been there about three years. There were weapons taken from the captives. Some were sophisticated and others very primitive.

The Army wanted to win the hearts and minds of the civilians. So, before Tet they would have us go out into the villages and provide medical care. We rode out in a jeep with a machine gun mounted on it which caused me a little concern. Anyway, we'd go out and treat the people. They'd have tonsillitis, ear ache, and skin infections. We pulled a lot of teeth. We gave a lot of penicillin and sulfur and took care of toenails. Most were very minor ailments. If they didn't get that care they didn't get any. The thing that was most impressive was if you gave children candy or chewing gum you won a lot more hearts and minds.

Before Tet, the Army would provide a surgical team to go into the civilian hospital in Saigon. There will be surgery, anesthesia, and a nurse. A full surgical team. We'd operate on people. We had never seen them before nor would see them after maybe a thyroid, breast cancer, or hernia. There was no good care in these hospitals, infection was wild. If your family did not provide care, food, or nursing, you didn't get it. You had to have strong family support to get through the system. Lots of wooden slats for beds, no sheets, just put some newspaper down and have the baby. The new mother will stay there six to eight hours and probably be working in the rice paddy in another 48 to 72 hours. During Christmas 1967 Bob Hope brought his show to our area. He was accompanied by Raquel Welch. I thought that it was great for him to do that. You have no idea what the morale booster this was. The soldiers walked miles to see this show. She'd get GIs to come on stage and dance with her. They thought they had gone to heaven.

Photograph # 27. Here's a photo of the luckiest GI in the world. He had just come out of the field, weary looking.

Photograph # 28. Look at his helmet and the liner, both with a bullet hole. He only had a laceration on his scalp. We repaired it, and he was back in the field the next day. The Army gave him a new helmet, of course. Lucky, lucky man. He was awarded a Purple Heart for it.

Photograph # 29. This photo below shows how we counted our casualties, by boots. This is only one day's worth of them. These weren't necessarily soldiers we lost at the hospital. But they were also those who had been out in the field and brought in to the mortuary to be identified and tagged.

What did we do when we weren't working? When it was not raining, we'd sit around, talk with each other, and cook on the grill. Some people would be in civilian clothes, others with their uniforms still on. You became close to those people.

There's one area that gets something out of war, and that's medicine and especially surgery. I learned priority when you operate. First, you go to what's really important. Second, you learn speed. Speed is so important for combat wounds. Third, I learned to defend my decisions with my colleagues. We'd meet about every 10 days and discuss the cases. It really was very useful for me in my following years as a surgeon in civilian life.

I learned something else very important. The military takes care of its own. We didn't have a burn unit in Vietnam and so any bad burns had to immediately go to the Army hospital in Japan. The patient had to be accompanied by a nurse and a doctor. So at four o'clock in the morning I got on the largest airplane I've ever seen in my life. You could play football in it. One nurse, one doctor, one patient, two pilots and an airman on a three and a half to four- hour flight to Japan. Think of what it cost the government to take care of one person. It was really reassuring to me and it should be to all of us.

Wars do change things. For patients to get back to good care in the States there'd be four days in our hospital and a week in Japan. In the Afghanistan War and Iraq War, surgery was the same, injuries were the same. But these casualties are back in Germany, Walter Reed, or the Brooke Army Hospital in San Antonio 48 to 72 hours after that injury. They get the care they need from the Critical Care Air Transport Team. So there was a lower fatality rate in these later conflicts.

I trained for my residency in a hospital where I thought that was the only way to do things. In Vietnam, I was with people who trained in other major places. There's a whole lot of ways to take out an appendix and you all end up with the same results.

About ten years after I got back from Vietnam I had an especially rewarding experience. I was at Costco with my wife pushing the cart when a guy came up and hugged me and said, "my Vietnam surgeon." He told me that I had operated on him in Vietnam. He was from Varina not far away from where I was living. So, we talked back and forth. I hadn't seen him since and I didn't recall his name. But I knew exactly the wound he had. Of the many, I remember that one.

One 4th of July in a local newspaper there was an article about the VA facility. There was a picture of one of the soldiers who lived there. I saw that name and it rang a bell to me. So I looked back through my operating book. I had indeed operated on him. So, I went out to the VA and spoke with him. He didn't remember me. I wanted to be certain, so I again looked at his chart and my handwritten notes. It was the same man. Another reward for my service in Vietnam.

Some things I think are very important to emphasize.

War is tragic. Money could be spent so well elsewhere. The loss of lives militarily, civilian, and property destroyed. Lives are totally changed, mentally and physically. However, medical advances are made and they benefit all of us in so many ways. After returning from Vietnam, I established and maintained a general surgery practice in Richmond, Virginia, for thirty-five years.

***NOTE FROM EDITOR: Dr. Beazley was awarded the Bronze Star Medal for Meritorious Service in the**

operating room of the 24th Evac Hospital under very difficult circumstances during the Tet Offensive in February of 1968.

*[THIS TRANSCRIPTION CAPTURES A PRESENTATION BY DR. WYATT BEAZLEY FROM HIS SERVICE AT THE 24TH EVACUATION HOSPITAL IN VIETNAM FROM JULY 1967 TO JULY 1968]

The General and the Baby
Dr. Rick Snider

Located in Saigon, the Third Field Hospital had a lot of dignitaries passing through in 1969, including a lot of high-ranking Army brass. The receiving area for wounded was in the paved lot next to the Emergency Room. Here were the familiar sawhorses ready to hold the stretchers. There were drains in the floor every few feet to receive the mud and blood washed from the wounded bodies. The area was covered with tin roofing and had fluorescent lights in rows overhead. At night, the lights, the insects, and the wounded GIs accounted for a surrealistic scene. The struggle to save those severely wounded soldiers under that tin roof proceeded in an intense and grave fashion that was strangely quiet at times. Doctors, nurses, and medics all knew what to do and their efforts were pursued in hushed desperation without shouting or even raising their voices. A quiet scene like that, it said a lot about the consideration and the efficiency of the workers. I worked on most of the wounded in this outside extension of the Emergency Room. Assisting in this outside area were two of the best medics I had ever seen. One was Perez, a Puerto Rican native whose first name I never knew. Everybody just called him "Perez!" He was nineteen, very good looking and he loved the ladies. While we were working, he would tell us all in great detail about his exploits with the women he had recently met. His prattle was never distracting and often helped ease the tenseness of the moment. His smile was infectious and his laugh comforting. He had a special way of helping the wounded GIs. He talked to each one like he knew them personally, and they responded as if speaking with an old friend. He had a heavy Spanish accent and was proud of his heritage. He loved to talk in Spanish with his fellow Puerto Ricans, and his gesticulations during those conversations there were something to behold. His sidekick and fellow medic, was a young man with the last name of Miller. I never knew his first name either, as Perez only called him "Meeler" so I, and everyone else, followed suit. "Meeler" was tall, prematurely balding, and very soft-spoken. He too had a way with the GIs and they responded well to him in kind. "Meeler" and Perez lent a certain lightness to this serious business. The nurses and doctors worked better when those two were on duty, and providentially, they usually were working when the "fertilizer hit the ventilator."

When a wounded GI was brought in, he was usually covered with thick jungle mud and blood, obscuring his wounds. Perez or Miller would begin to hose the covering dirt and gore off the soldiers to allow an accurate inspection. To facilitate finding the offending wound, Perez would ask, "where'd you get hit, soldier?" The reply was often, "Oh, about six clicks out of Trang Bang!" Perez would bristle and ask again in a harsher voice, "No, No! Where on your body? Dammit," his Puerto Rican accent being much more noticeable when he was irritated. The irony of that question with its answer as a map location, rather than an anatomical site of the injury, always evoked laughs from the medical personnel in attendance, often to the confusion to the unsuspecting wounded soldier. When they understood what Perez was asking, the GIs would point to their wound, and Perez would clean that area first.

Often Perez would visit the wounded men he took care of in the ER after they had been treated. The wounded were kept on a surgical ward until their transfer to Japan could be arranged. Those wards were dismal and sad places where despair and pain reigned. Perez's visits, unsolicited and out of the blue, were cherished by those he saw. He would make them laugh with his stories and antics. He would often tell them he really didn't come to see their sorry asses, but he was just checking out new nurses on duty. That Perez, he had a gift all right, and I learned a lot about interpersonal relations by watching him in action. He was remarkable. Everyone loved Perez. Nurses, doctors, high-ranking brass, and even the janitor had smiles for him as he passed by. He owned his world, and he loved his life. It was only natural that I became very fond of Perez, and I tried to coincide my work schedule with his so I could enjoy his charismatic company. Understanding each other as we did, surgeon and medic, we worked very smoothly together, and I liked that. A good assistant can make all the difference in the world to a surgeon and, knowing this, I always sought to work with Miller and Perez. Soon, Perez, Miller and I became an inseparable team, and their upbeat friendly outlooks rubbed off on me. The days flew by quickly and painlessly even with the war raging all around Saigon.

Often we would receive many wounded at one time. Calls would go out for help from the Emergency Room during those times of mass casualties. Doctors and nurses would rush en masse, adding to an already confusing scene. Paradoxically, it was during such a mass casualty situation, that an amusing moment occurred, and rumors of my being rude to a three-star general began.

In the outdoor treatment area I caught a glimpse of a struggling GI, cursing a blue streak as his stretcher was being positioned on the awaiting sawhorses. This type of wild behavior usually marked the wounded man as being very seriously injured and in shock. I singled him out as my first priority that day and he was indeed in shock. His ashen face held dark eyes filled with terror as he cursed the enemy that had done this to him. Assessing his wounds and generally poor condition, I opted for a shot of morphine. The shot would cause his low blood pressure to go even lower, but it would calm him enough to allow me to work. The morphine quickly gave him respite from the fear of the enemy that was frozen in his numbed brain, and he lay back on the stretcher, quiet now, but barely breathing. Not waiting for the corpsmen who began to cut away his clothes in order to find his wounds. I started a cut-down on one of his arm veins. To save his life, he needed blood rapidly and in large volumes. My first step was to locate a vein in his arm big enough to insert a large hose-like tube into it through which the lifesaving blood and fluids would easily flow.

Just as I made the cut over the upper forearm, the light with which I needed to see was repeatedly blocked. Shadows came over my surgical field at the most inopportune times, thwarting my efforts at performing the surgery this soldier so desperately needed. Glancing over my shoulder at my light source, I saw an overweight man in a khaki uniform positioned right in front of my surgical light. Irritated, I said, "Please get out of my damned light!" The man moved back slightly and then asked me what I was doing. More annoyed now, I answered curtly, "Trying to find a vein!" and added, "For God's sake, keep out of my light!" I heard Perez snickering in the background, and then I heard him explain to the person what I was doing.

The cut-down was completed, I proudly began pumping several units of blood into my patient through the new big IV line. Color was slowly coming back into his Ashen face and the wounded GI began to speak coherently! As he began responding to the infused blood, I examined the wounds. Grenade fragments had fractured the main bones, the femurs, in both of his thighs. There were no other injuries. He was very salvageable, and was coming around from his previous frantic presentation nicely. I called for an orthopedist to assess him, and I continued to administer blood. His blood pressure was stabilized. The orthopedist took my patient to the Operating Room for debridement of his wounds and fixation of fractures.

I was washing my hands at the small sink in the treatment area when Perez came over to where I was standing. He stood there by me, laughing and acting silly. "Do you know what you just did?" he asked. "You told off a three-star general! You told him to get the hell out of your light!" Not remembering exactly all that happened, I was somewhat confused, so I asked him what he meant. "You told that three-star general to get back and get out of your damned light, Doc. You should have seen him jump back! He turned pale and began to quiver a little. I'm telling you, it was something! A freaking three-star general, Wow!" Now I was getting the picture. Evidently, a visiting three-star general was looking over my shoulder, and I shouted to him to get out of my light. With a triumphant smile, I said to a nearly convulsing Perez, "Just goes to show you Perez, the real power in the Army belongs to the docs, man! Why I can push a big three-star general around with my little finger." Perez got such a big kick out of that incident, he would tell and retell the story to whomever would listen, laughing about my cursing out "three-stars" and ridiculing the Army's rigid system of rank. I, on the other hand, was more careful in the future. From then on I would try to look before yelling. I never told Perez that, because I enjoyed listening to him rattle on about mike. I guess it was flattering to hear the "No shit!" the story evoked from those who heard it. Perez would then point to me, and I would take a bow. Our mutual admiration was blossoming, and we became even more efficient working together.

In that same tin-roofed treatment area, something so horrible, and so unsettling happened to me that I will never be able to shake it from my consciousness. There is hardly a day when this specter doesn't haunt me, and hardly a night when I don't have the same terrible dream. Through the years I have found that a surgeon has a lot of nightmares, but this one beats all of mine.

I had been working the ten P.M. to eight A.M. shift for a week, and this night the work had been very light. At midnight, I had the luxury of falling sound asleep on a stretcher in the cool ER. About three A.M. Perez shook me awake. He was obviously very agitated. His face was pale, and he was sweating profusely. His Spanish accent was more noticeable, confirming his state o9f anxiety. "Come quick, Doc, there's a baby!" he said excitedly. His words dropped off with "baby." "Baby?" I asked, "What do you mean?" I rarely saw babies in the ER. "Come on Doc. Hurry! It's awful man, just awful. Hurry, the kid is dying!" We ran through the door to the outdoor treatment area. There, in the dark and hot tropical night, spotlighted by the bright surgical lamp, was a tiny baby! As white as the sheet it was lying on, the little one was obviously in extremis. The baby looked oriental, but more Chinese than Vietnamese. His right leg was nearly amputated at mid-thigh, but there wasn't any active bleeding any more. While looking at that poor little pale infant and trying to collect my thoughts, l the ambulance driver got another call and left. Cholon was the Chinese section of Saigon which explained why this child looked more Chinese than Vietnamese. I understood the Vietnamese had little love for the Chinese nationals who worked in Saigon, and ironically the NVA used Chinese Communist rockets to pelt Cholon. So here we were, with bugs flying into the lights, in the middle of the hot night, alone, in a struggle to save the life of the most innocent victim of war I had seen so far. I could not imagine anyone could be more innocent than a baby.

Perez snapped himself out of our momentary shared apoplexy by quickly opening a cut-down set, knowing that would jump-start me. During those few moments of gawking, I was trying to formulate my plan of action. To have any chance of survival at all, the baby would need blood right away! My guess was that the baby was about a year old and would have tiny veins, and a vein large enough to receive infused blood would be the key to this child's recovery. Chubby babies like this one are the bane of a surgeon's existence, and I remembered what Dr. Willis J. Potts, a famous pediatric surgeon, had said about operating on infants: it often took longer to find a vein than to do the operation. That was in my mind that night as I started to search for a vein. I knew this was going to be next to impossible.

The infant was groaning in agonal respirations, an indication that no more than a few moments of life remained. Only extreme youth allowed this child to survive this long! By this time, any older person with such a catastrophic injury would have died from blood loss!

Dr. Jim Guernsey was the surgeon on call for the ER that night, and I had asked

Perez to call him at the onset. Knowing a back-up surgeon was on the way helped me a little, and I began the cut-down at the elbow on one arm. Having no luck in locating a usable vein, I tried on the other arm in several locations and then on the remaining ankle. The baby was drained of most of his blood and there wasn't any left in the tiny vessels to help me find them. The veins were made invisible without the blue-red blood in them to contrast with the surrounding pale tissues.

By this time, I was frantic. The sweat was dripping off my face, and the insects had become intensely annoying. The futile cut-down procedures had taken only ten minutes, but, in those precious ten minutes, the baby's heart gave out . There were no more labored little breaths, no movement at all. The baby had died! The hot night now had a chill in it, and I shivered.

Jim Guernsey came down the lighted covered outdoor walkway and approached me, as Perez and I were standing in the light of the surgical lamp with the annoying bugs constantly circling around our heads. Jim looked at the dead baby, at Perez and then at me. I knew by his face that he already had accurately assessed what happened. The multiple extremity incisions displayed my frantic and unsuccessful efforts to find venous access. Jim studied the amputated thigh for a moment, and looking up at me, asked in a very kind voice if he could show me something. He said he was thinking of what to do as he walked over from his quarters, and he wanted to show me what he had decided. Since the baby was dead, his instructions wouldn't help in this case but maybe would in a similar situation in the future. Using a surgical pick-up he quickly and cleverly found the transected vessels at the amputation site. He demonstrated how I could have placed a large catheter vin this site and given blood through this severed vessel. Almost shaking, I told him that I had thought about that, but didn't choose to use this site because of the possibility of contaminating the IV line. Glaringly obvious to me now, at that point in the overall desperate situation, possible contamination of the IV site was a very small point!. Words began to stick in my mouth. If only there had been more time to think. Later, as a practicing surgeon, I would also think my treatment plans over as I walked into the ER to see a patient, just as Jim did that night. Perez had advised Jim the baby had an amputation in mid-thigh, so Jim was able to think over how to approach this problem on his walk from his quarters. Thinking things mover on the way to the ER is a luxury the ER doctors themselves don't get to enjoy, because they come face to face with disaster abruptly. Jim assured me he didn't mean any criticism at all. He just wanted to point out this possibility to me. Then he left to walk back to his quarters; I could feel my heart pounding in my chest. Perez and I never knew the baby's name, and I can't really remember whether it was a little boy or a girl. I don't recall having looked. What difference would that make?

There were no family members or anybody present at all, just Perez and me with our dead little pat5ient. The site of that baby with the alabaster skin, lying on the dark stretcher in the middle of the night under the glaring lights and circling bugs, has been indelibly etched into my brain. I still carry the mental picture with me. When I dream about that night, I awake thinking, "If only I had used that vein!" My emotions flare when I remember the Chinese baby died all alone. No mother, no father, just Perez and me. I imagine the eternal hour of horror that child endured as he bled to death that night. And for what? Death was delivered from an unseen and unknown enemy for no reason. What went wrong with the world that night? I think of the enemy soldier who fired that rocket that night. He should be told! He should be made to remember too! Words cannot accurately describe my confused state as I gazed upon that tiny corpse. I was terrified at the violence done to this completely innocent human being. I was severely disappointed in my surgical inability to save the child. Most of all, I was caught up in the recurring realization of the futility of war with its senseless loss of life. Perez and I baptized the tiny, mutilated body in hopes of possibly giving salvation. Despite the tenets of some religions, that child's soul had to be as pure as any soul could possibly be, and it should enjoy all of heaven's rewards by any standard. Just to be sure, though, we covered all bets with a little saline from the IV.

We left the baby in the cold morgue. The next morning, the body was gone. The disinterested clerk in the morgue told us a Vietnamese woman had come early in the morning and claimed the body and took it for burial. No forms had been filled out, and no more information was available. The baby was just another nameless soul. A victim of war, a victim of man, its life was over.

Unable to shake what had happened from my mind, I was pretty low for a week or two. Perez was the one who helped me out of my doldrums. When he was sure I was ready for it, he asked me if I had been able to start the IV, and given the blood, would the baby had survived? After all, over an hour had passed since the injury and breathing was already agonal. I had to agree there probably would have been brain damage even if we had been able to restore reasonable blood pressure, and the odds were certainly against meaningful survival. Talking it through with Perez helped lessen my anguish and disgust. The fact that the baby probably would not have survived wasn't the whole point. I think the whole incident reflected my feelings on the futility of war and the meaningless daily loss of life that I was witnessing.

To this day, when I pray in church on Sundays, I always ask God to care for that Chinese baby and my three men. Remembering is the only thing left for me to do.

A Snippet from Tay Ninh

Soldiers at the front fight for their buddies, and not for any political reasons. Being part of a team allows men to face the dangers of war and gives them the strength to persist. A man alone is more likely to surrender than if just one other buddy is left alive. Most GIs don't realize a bond of love develops between men in battle. Even if a GI realized this bond existed, male pride wouldn't allow him to admit to it.

This bond was a very powerful force. One night after a battle out in the field, our treatment area was once again filled with wounded men. One soldier had died on the way in, before anyone had seen him, and his body was placed along a side wall of the aid station, out of the way of rushing medics and doctors. As I was debriding a wound on a wounded soldier, I was positioned beside that corpse that night. A fully clothed and armed GI burst through the open front door. Our guardian clerk nicknamed Lurch (because of his size and deep voice like Lurch on the Addams Family) was up and right behind him in an instant. Lurch hesitated a second, then backed away a few steps. The sweating and out-of-breath soldier stood behind me along the flank of the dead man. Looking up, I could see tears streaming down his face. Kneeling alongside the body of his slain comrade, the soldier buried his forehead in his grimy hand and sobbed. After a minute, not having uttered a word, he grasped the arm of his dead friend and said in a low, composed voice, "See you on the other side." Standing up, he wiped his face, and looking dejectedly down at the floor, walked out of the aid station with heavy steps. I'm not sure, but I think I saw a tear in Lurch's eye. The soldier I was working on beginning to cry. "We lost a lot of good men out there tonight, why?" he asked. I tried to say something, but not finding my voice, I just kept on working. I had no right to speak anyway. Only these men had earned the right to question fate with "why?" There was no answer to that question. Later that night, Lurch and I discussed the profound faith that soldier expressed with his words, "See you on the other side." We agreed he must have ardently believed in a heaven for fallen soldiers, and by what he did and what he said, he had expressed faith better than any gifted preacher ever could have. After the last of the wounded had been cared for; we examined that dead body with new-found reverence. I found myself saying a prayer for him and for his buddy who had lived. The encounter I witnessed that night touched me deeply, and helped me to shore up the little war-shocked faith I had left.

Rick Snider is a retired vascular and general surgeon who resides in Cumberland, MD with his wife Margy. Doctor Snider served in Vietnam from 1967-1968. Since retirement, Dr. Snider and Margie have spent two or three months each year volunteering in Pago Pago, American Samoa, or on the Navajo Nation in Chinle, AZ. Together they raised four children and now enjoy the freedom retirement allows. With permission from Dr. Richard L. Snider's book; *DELTA SIX; SOLDIER, SURGEON.*

Patients
One patient's experience....
Lance Corporal Paul Keaveney, USMC, 3rd Force Recon Company

1970 at Phu Bai

2025 Paul Keaveney and "Doc" Norton

I can't say that my experience as a patient happened quickly because it certainly didn't. On the 7th of February 1970, I was a member of a six-man, 3rd Force Reconnaissance Company Team code named Snaky. Our mission, after being inserted by Huey helicopter, into the infamous A Shau Valley, was to locate elements the North Vietnamese Army, known to be staging there, and report back to our company, describing where the enemy was, how many of them there were, and what they were doing. But, sometimes our plans do not always go accordingly.

We had been on the ground for less than one hour, walking cautiously in the dense triple canopied jungle, when our point man made the costly mistake of walking up and onto a well-used trail. Before I could signal our team leader to stop this action, I was the target of an over-zealous North Vietnamese soldier, who decided to shoot me in my right leg just several inches above my knee, and springing their ambush.

Weighted down with 60 pounds of gear, and carrying my M-79 grenade launcher, I crumbled to the ground, not immediately sure of what had just happened. Within seconds, all hell broke loose as the hidden NVA opened up on the team with small arms and automatic weapons. Sergeant Arthur Garcia, our point man, was killed, as was our Team Leader Ted Bishop. The third man in our line of movement was LCpl James Furhman, and as he tried to retrieve the primary radio from Bishop's back, he too, was killed by a burst of machine gun fire.

With our combat effectiveness diminished by more than fifty per cent, we were in a very bad place. LCpl Guillermo Silva, who was carrying our secondary radio, crawled to me, and while LCpl Murray protected our precarious position, I was able to contact our helicopter support aircraft and alert them as to what was happening on the ground. Within a very short period of time, Huey's and Cobra gunships were circling overhead, but they, too, were receiving an extraordinary amount of enemy groundfire. The best they could do was to radio back to Camp Eagle and request a reactionary "Blue Team," to fly out to where we were and try to rescue us before we were overrun.

During that time, I was hit three more times by enemy fire. The second round hit my right arm in the bicep, which prevented me from using my right hand with any type of dexterity. The third round struck me in my left arm, a few inches below my shoulder, which rendered me as pretty useless as a grenadier. I was still able to load a fire my weapons, but with questionable accuracy. A short while later, I has struck again, and this time I was hit in my right side, and that was my last good effort at being an asset to the remaining two Marines in the team. To add insult to injury, I was hit a fifth time, but this bullet struck my holstered .45 pistol, and it caused two rounds inside the magazine well to explode without further injury to me.

While all of this excitement was happening, LCpl Murray took the initiative to talk with the gunships overhead and requested a Dustoff helicopter to come out to the A Shau valley and get me back to the 85th Evacuation Hospital at Phu Bai, about 30 miles south of our location. Now, it was a waiting game to see who would arrive first, the NVA or the 2nd &17th troopers of Delta Troop, from Camp Eagle.

I give a tremendous amount of credit to LCpl Wallace Murray, who, while waiting for the Delta Troop reactionary force to arrive, risked his own life by placing himself between me and the enemy fire, to help bandage my arms and leg and prevent me from going into shock from my loss of blood.

Within two hours after being wounded a Dustoff helicopter arrived overhead, but due to the thick canopy of the jungle, landing close by was not an option. The platoon from Delta Troop had landed some distance away, and had fought their way toward our location, first coming upon the bodies of Garcia, Bishop, and Fuhrman, before reaching Silva, Murray, and me. They requested the Dustoff's jungle penetrator be lowered down to the jungle floor so I could be tied in and hoisted up as part of their evacuation plan. Pfc. Thom Stoddert was a Delta trooper who helped tie me onto the penetrator, but I was in no physical condition to hold myself in place. As the winch began to raise me up, I was dangling about 10 feet off the ground, when I slid beneath the rope and fell in a heap onto the jungle floor. Without wasting any time, I was securely tied in, and with great success lifted up an into the hovering Dustoff helicopter.

The flight back to Phu Bai remains as a blurred event because of morphine that had been administered, but I do remember that once we had landed two familiar faces where on the pad; our company 1st Sergeant Lonnie Henderson, and HM-3 "Doc" Norton, our team Corpsman, helped to remove me from the Dustoff bird and walked beside me as we headed for the triage entrance at the hospital. Then, turned over to the medics, nurses, and doctors, things began to happen in rapid succession.

At first glance, one of the Army medics commented that he thought that I was the victim of having been badly burned. Doc Norton explained that what they were looking at was a face covered in camouflage paint, hardly the result of being burned. The medics then asked me where I had been wounded and could not believe that I had walked into the hospital after being shot in both arms, my right leg and in my back.

My utilities were cut away, as were my boots and socks, and I was given a detailed examination to discover the true extent of my wounds. My right leg had been hit close to the femoral artery, but miraculously, the bullet had not shattered my femur. To their collective amazement, neither the humorous, of either arm had been broken by the two AK-47 rounds that had hit me. Additionally, the round that had struck my right side had exited just short of my spine. As I was wheeled into surgery, numerous comments were made by the medical staff as to what a "lucky son-of-a-bitch" I was.

The day we were helicoptered out to begin our mission was a Saturday, and on the following Tuesday, the officers and men of 3rd Force Reconnaissance Company held a Memorial Service for seven Marines from 3rd Force Recon Company who had tragically been killed within 72 hours' time.

As I lay in my bed, at the 85th Evacuation Hospital, I was again greeted by 1st Sergeant Henderson and HM-3 "Doc" Norton, who had come to take me to the memorial service at the Phu Bai Chapel. Taken by jeep, I sat in the passenger seat up front, while Doc held two IV bottles over my head until we reached the Chapel and continued to do so during the entire memorial service. I was able to say good bye to some of the Marines in the company, before being driven back to the 85th Evacuation Hospital, as preparations were made for me to be medically evacuated to the U.S. Naval Hospital in Yokosuka, Japan.

From the 85th Evacuation Hospital, I was flown by helicopter to DaNang, where I was loaded aboard a C-141 Starlifter cargo jet, which was a Military Airlift Command aircraft, taking me, and a large number of other wounded Marines and soldiers to military hospitals on mainland Japan. Arriving by bus, comfortably sedated, and laying on a stretcher, I was taken to Ward B, a surgical ward for additional X-rays, additional examinations, and the debridement of my wounds. The tissue damage to my left arm was obvious, and a brief discussion was held by several doctors as to whether or not my left arm should be amputated. I voted against it, as did the primary surgeon, and they moved on to examine my back. Again, came numerous comments as to how fortunate I was to have not been killed.

The care provided by the Navy nurses and Corpsmen was nothing short of fantastic. Ward B held twenty-five patients, nearly all of them Marines, and several hospital Corpsmen, who had been wounded in combat in Vietnam. My days spent in bed where numbered, and soon enough I was ambulatory, and with the use of a cane, I was able to move around the ward quite well.

One incident, which occurred while I was still on Ward B, was the tremendous dressing down of a young Marine, by a LtCdr. doctor named Fragard, who came from Boston, Massachusetts. The doctor had become extremely tired of listening to one young Marine complaining about a small, nonserious wound to his hand, which was considered to be an extremely minor injury. Finally, and frustrated with this individual's constant whining and crying, the doctor had heard enough. He approached the young Marine and physically leaned into him. He stated that this Marine was in the presence of brave men who had been badly wounded in combat; some without arms, some without legs, and some without neither. None of them had ever uttered a word of complaint, nor asked for sympathy. He said that if he heard another word from this "whiny little bitch," he would have him physically removed from the hospital. You could have heard a pin drop after the doctor's outburst of criticism. This was far and away from a verbal reprimand – it was a classic, first class "ass-chewing" of the highest order and was richly deserved. Those patients with hands began to applaud the doctor's solution to the problem.

The patient care was exceptional, as was the food. The Navy spared no expense in the quality and quantity of fresh fruits and vegetables, and several well-cooked meat choices at every meal. I can only give great praise to what I experienced as the Yokosuka Naval Hospital. Within two weeks, I was again loaded onto another C-141 Starlifter, and this trip took me to the U.S. Naval Hospital located at Key West, Florida, which was finally closed in 1974. In the 1960's, it was the DOD's policy to bring wounded patients to the closest military hospital in their home state. While Key West Naval Facility was located four hundred south of New Smyrna Beach, it was very accessible for my parents to fly down to the tip of Florida for their visits.

Finally, after several weeks at the Key West Naval Hospital, I was discharged from the United States Marine Corps, as a Sergeant of Marines. Later, that year, I was invited to attend a reception for Florida's Governor, and former Marine, Claude R. Kirk, Jr., and was presented with the Silver Star by the governor.

A Bullet Through the Head: A Medical Aftermath

by Colonel John C. McKay, USMC (Ret)

Colonel John C. McKay, enlisted in the Marine Corps at the age of 17 and received an appointment to the U.S. Naval Academy in 1964. He served two tours in Vietnam where he was wounded twice, including losing an eye. An Olmsted scholar, he is fluent in Spanish and served in several diplomatic postings while on active duty. He currently is an adjunct professor at California State University, in Sacramento.

"Enemy small-arms fire is intense. Desperately, I was trying to make myself one with the earth, frantically, almost spastically, wiggling, scurrying, toward cover. As I turned my head to the right, looking for the holstered Colt .45 pistol on my hip, an AK-47 round travelling at 2,330 feet per second (710 meters/second), fired from about 15 meters out, entered my skull just above the left eye, enucleating it. Almost instantaneously the bullet exited forward of, but just below, my right ear lobe, and slammed into the right shoulder of my flak jacket. The upper left sinus was burrowed through and destroyed. Sight in my right eye vanishes, a black void enveloped all. The roof of my mouth was a gaping hole. A goodly portion of the lower right jaw was blasted outward in flakes of shattered bone, a multitude of fragments of upper and lower molars, flecks of shorn skin, and there was blood. Lots of blood.

A large flap of skin, torn on impact, hung loose from the right corner of my mouth over my chin. Flesh was shorn from my gums, bone and teeth were annihilated. I was completely serene knowing I was dead. Until my tossed body landed on its back, gunk and blood were choking off my breathing. I rose bodily on hands and knees, instinctively crawling toward cover. The second AK-47 round slammed into my left hand, flattening me face down.

Corporal Joe Hatton, USMC, the platoon Right Guide, killed the shooter, rushed out, and dragged me to cover. I remained conscious though blind. What's left of my mouth does not function. Instantaneously two thoughts flash through my mind: I will live; I will master braille.

The platoon Corpsman is new, being exposed to combat for the first time. In his highly charged emotional and psychological state of mind he administers morphine. But. Morphine must never be given if the wounded suffers a head or chest wound. I am befuddled as to why a field-expediency tracheotomy wasn't performed; blood and gunk continue to restrict my breathing. My former platoon sergeant, S/Sgt Napolean, USMC, a very large Samoan, recently moved up to be the company Gunnery Sergeant, disobeyed the company commander. He rushed forward through fifty meters of the heavy fire, grabbed me bodily, and half carried, half dragged me back to the company command post. He's crying. I was placed in an 8-inch artillery shell hole for protection from the pandemonium all around.

Two in-coming emergency medevac helicopters are shot down, one bursting into flames. I heard and felt the explosion and the intense heat. I was half-carried aboard the third helicopter by the company commander, Capt. William Fite, USMC. It's mid-afternoon, 13 April 1969. The same day, in different time zones, to be sure, my son Malcolm was born.

Above the cacophony of the medevac-helicopter's two loud engines and thumping rotor blades, a flight surgeon forcefully jerked down the lower lid of the right eye, and yells in my left ear, "You're going to be blind." He quickly moves on. Triage is chaotic. It was a bad day for Second Battalion, Fifth Marine regiment.

I was given Last Rites, though my dog tags read "N/P" (no preference) for religion. I worried mightily about being wheeled into a corner and left to die. The Catholic chaplain starts administering the final sacrament,

Viaticum, when I feel my boots being cut off. Then the removal of what's left of tattered, blood-caked clothing. Another Corpsman quickly makes a small incision in my throat. He forces a trach tube into the just-opened windpipe. I violently resist efforts to shave my mustache.

In extreme shock, but conscious, butt naked, covered by a thin sheet, I am wheeled into a freezing cold operating room. Surgery was performed to save my life, not to fix anything, lasts seven hours. A urethral catheter is inserted. The thin, dangling plastic tube and accompanying drainage bag are vexing. The catheter is replaced every four-to-five days to ward off infection. The exiting catheter is often blood speckled. Following surgery, liquified food – what's left of my jaw is wired – bed baths and bed pans.

In late fall 1969, the catheter goes away. After three weeks of "stabilization" at Naval Support Activity (NSA) hospital, Da Nang, Vietnam, I am evacuated to the 249th Army Field Hospital, Fort Drake, Asaka City, Japan. I spend thirty days warehousing on a ward of suffering, dying men. I was then medevacked through Travis Air Force F Base, California, to Balboa Naval Hospital, San Diego.

The one medical procedure carried out at Balboa NH was the painful removal of the packed gauze from the destroyed sinuses. Thirty days later I was transferred to Oak Knoll Naval Hospital, Oakland, California. A Navy screw-up. My parents lived in the San Francisco Bay area.

The abrupt transition from the twisted irony of intense combat, from being all but killed, to the relative sanctity of thinking I might survive - regardless how I survived – is jarring - in a, I am dead, to I am alive, sort of way.

At that time, there were over 800 Viet Nam wounded at Oak Knoll. I was initially bedded in the oral surgery department. Following a quaky ophthalmologist's failed attempt to inject a colored dye into my brain through the tear duct of my right eye, I was moved to the neurosurgery ward under the very capable department-head doctor, Captain Gale Clark, USN.

Early on a sunny Saturday morning in mid-June 1969, in the company of my parents, I met Capt. Clark for the first time. A severe, gruff, no-nonsense surgeon, he immediately informed me that I was to undergo a pneumoencephalogram, a procedure wherein ionized air is pressured into the cranium through a lower spinal tap. The patient's head is X-rayed to determine whether the bullet's impact caused a shifting of cerebral mass within the cranium. Not just perforating the skull, the bullet scarred the left frontal brain lobe. Trauma to the latter often cause seizures.

I was sitting to the right, my parents in front of his desk. Capt. Clark turned and leaned toward me. Very matter-of-factly, he said, "It hurts, it hurts like hell. I'm glad I don't have to go through it!" I looked over at my mother, a practicing RN. She was silently weeping. Capt. Clark was right. On that June morning, he ordered a regime of phenytoin (the anti-convulsant Dilantin), and a sulfur-based antibiotic to help mitigate brain infection. Recovery required, after the pneumoencephalogram procedure, four to five agonizingly painful days in a darkened room. The ionized air dissipated from my skull. The brain mass had not shifted. Capt. Clark sent me back to ENT for consultation on the damaged right eye, fused nostrils closing off an air passageway, and my destroyed sinuses.

The colored-dye-into-the-brain ophthalmologist was no longer on staff. (The pneumoencephalogram is no longer used as a diagnostic procedure.) I underwent three operations, under local anesthesia, for choroidal nevus on the remaining eye. The young Navy doctor performing all three choroidal nervus removal procedures was excellent. The operations were successful. The nose restoration was a bit trickier, and rather painful. Again, local anesthesia, a choice I was allowed to opt for, rather than general anesthesia. The cutting through and opening of the improperly healed nostrils could be felt as well as "heard." The re-positioning of shattered bone was crunchingly noticeable. The local anesthesia only dulled the pain partially and was disconcerting. The racking pain, black eyes, swollen nose and puffed face followed as the anesthesia wore off. The operation was short of successful. A second operation was contingent on recovery. A wait of at least three to four weeks. Then, repeated. The second operation, performed by the two Navy doctors, was successful.

I am a dirty-boot infantryman, not a medical doctor. What follows is an interpretation of what the doctors explained in the vernacular to the infantryman. The first major operation consisted of re-building the destroyed right jaw, or oromandibular reconstruction, in medical terms. The procedure was new in the fall of 1970. The lead oral surgeon was Cmdr. Hildebrand, USN, an excellent and caring physician. As explained to me, a titanium crib would be placed between the remaining mandible segments to restore mandible continuity. The crib would be filled with bone marrow extracted from the right, upper femur. A two-in-one operation. The surgery lasted three plus hours. Post-operative pain in the maxillofacial area was tolerable though there was swelling and discoloration. I remained on a liquid diet. What was less tolerable was the pain in the right hip, even with strong analgesics. After three days in bed I was semi-ambulatory.

The good news was that the trach was eventually removed. The small throat incision sutured. To this day, the titanium crib shows up brightly on dental X-rays. Perhaps the final operation, to patch the hole in my skull, a cranioplasty, was the most critical. After the jaw reconstruction sufficiently healed, for the first time in hospital, I gained a roommate. Chris, a young U. S. Navy Tug serving with the U. S. Navy riverine forces on the Mekong River, Vietnam, had had the left lobe of his brain ploughed through by an AK-47 round. Chris was not ambulatory. He was either bed or wheelchair bound. His bodily movements were more spastic than controlled and coordinated. His eyes were not lucid, but dull and lackluster. He only uttered loud, guttural, animal-like sounds. He seemed incapable of comprehending anything spoken to him. For the next three weeks, before my own scheduled surgery by Capt. Clark, I sat with and talked to Chris daily, usually holding his hand, rubbing his back. Nothing near or on his grotesquely disfigured head. The healing and soothing human touch is often ignored or discounted. I assisted the nurses and orderlies with routine hospital chores such as bed pans, bathing, grooming, and feeding Chris.

Early in the second week of being Chris' bunkie, he consented in his incoherent speech and jerky body language that I could shave him, a grooming he'd violently resisted in the past. And, yes, Chris could be very violent.

My own cranioplasty was a complete success. I remained in hospital for two more weeks all the while caring for Chris as best as I could. I remained on the patient rolls of Oak Knoll, often as an out-patient, until I returned to full duty as a USMC infantry officer in March 1972.

Following my final discharge from hospital, I'd stop by to see Chris on the frequent follow-on visits with Capt. Clark. Chris' first skull-reconstruction surgery did not go well. The second surgery fared much better. Over time Chris regained his ability to speak, he could feed himself and slowly regained the ability to walk about on his own.

His once dulled eyes showed life. Capt. Clark and his splendid staff deserve full credit for the latter. Well after my own return to full duty as an officer of infantry, Chris passed the bar examination and was practicing law in Arizona. As in my case, it is the indelible testimony to Navy medicine and to the indominable human spirit.

With the one exception, the doctors, nurses, and staff at Oak Knoll were exceptional. Dedicated, focused, committed professional men and women. One example was head nurse, LtCdr Jill Korbishly, USN. Jill had lost her fiancée, a Marine Captain, in the 1968 Tet offensive in Vietnam. She was the walking idol of compassion and caring. She was also tough. She later married a badly wounded USMC Vietnam veteran. Jill's husband retired as a Colonel. Another was Mrs. Beasley, Capt. Clark's personal secretary. Always pleasant, personable, yet professional, she put up with an irascible, yet superb, neurosurgeon while interacting with aplomb and courtesy with very damaged patients."

*Pneumoencephalogram

While posted as the Alliance's Crisis Management Officer at NATO Headquarters in Brussels, I had the occasion, in November 1993, to visit Fort Breendonk in northern Belgium, along the old Brussels-Antwerp Road, close to the border with the Netherlands. Constructed in 1906-13, it was part of the ill-fated defense line against German invasion. As in WW I, in WW II Germany smashed through Belgium. Fort Breendonk became a Nazi transshipment camp for internees of the Final Solution. Upon liberation in 1944, the restored Belgium government committed to maintain Fort Breendonk exactly as it was when liberated, including the torture room where all the accoutrements used by human beings to inflict severe pain, often death, on their follow humans continue to reside.

The 1993 visit did not cause a flashback, or anything of the sort. Rather it caused me to recall severe pain, experienced during a two-year ordeal of being put back together following a gunshot wound to the head in Vietnam. Specifically, I remember the diagnostic procedure, now considered obsolete, called a pneumoencephalogram. It has, thankfully, been superseded by the MRI and CAT scan. The lead neurosurgeon at Oak Knoll Naval Hospital, Capt. Gale Clark, USN, said the procedure would "hurt." He was wrong. The procedure was torturously painful; recovery was in a darkened room, over five days, as the ionized air dissipated from the skull. Any body movement generated excruciating pain throughout the entire head and upper shoulder area.

During the first couple of days of recovery I was subject to sporadic retching, dry heaves, and overpowering pain. Spastic convulsions and pain-induce blackouts occurred. Bodily functions were beyond control. Nourishment and fluids were administered via various intravenous (IV) catheters, which might be torn loose during spasmodic convulsions.

I am prepped the day before the scheduled procedure. No food or liquids are permitted. Early on a June 1969 morning, I am sedated, and wheeled into a scrupulously clean, cold, completely white-tiled room edging into an aura of sepulchral finality. In the center of the room there is a special devise chair. One of the attending corpsmen quips that it is the torture chair. To one side of the room is X-Ray equipment. In nothing other than a flimsy hospital gown, I lie on the cold, metal gurney in anticipatory dread. Dr. Clark said it hurts. The procedure's lead neurosurgeon is number two in the hospital's Neurosurgery Department. I am ashamed to say I do not recall his name, other than he is a U. S. Navy Commander. He's very good. He has an excellent bedside manner. He explains the procedure to me in detail, but as a complete medical naif, I comprehend little. I do understand that the purpose of the pneumoencephalogram is to determine whether the impact of the bullet, fired at close range – 15 meters - dislocated or shifted the brain mass within the skull. I am slid by four Navy corpsmen and the neurosurgeon from the gurney onto the torture chair. I am laid on my right side. The flap of the hospital gown is raised above the shoulder blades. On the area just above the crack of the buttock is a topical disinfectant and numbing solution is swabbed. It's cold. As the neurosurgeon prepares the injection needle, the four corpsmen hold me completely immobile. The needle is carefully inserted into the lower spinal lumbar.

As the ionized gas begins to enter the spine and slowly infuse into the cranium, I am violently shocked into a completely unknown realm of being. Instantaneously the entire body, not just the head, experiences searing, harrowing pain; colors of kaleidoscopic rapidity and intensity flash into and through the brain; the bowels and urinary tract are uncontrollably voided; projectile vomiting occurs. A slow, creeping sense of extreme coldness moves from body's midsection through the corporeal mass. The Corpsman holding down the upper body all but throws his entire body across the shoulders. I am in a completely altered state; the pungency of stench is overwhelming. It's nauseous. The injection of ionized air is not a one-shot affair. It is done in increments, each infusion seemingly intensifying the initial horrible physiological response. Time is meaningless. I have no idea or concept of how long the infusion of ionized gas lasts. I am told it went on for an hour.

Whenever it ceases, the purpose of the special-device chair on which I'm all but comatose becomes evident. I'm gingerly rolled over to the X-Ray equipment. Another round of extreme torment ensues. All the attending personnel are extremely courteous and caring. They continuously shift my body about to make the X-Ray machine happy. Moreover, I am beyond fathoming anything said to me. I am a limp, barely conscious ragdoll, aware of only continuous, relentless, piercing pain, crippling stomach cramps, and lose of all feeling, except the biting coldness. Personal dignity is absent. Of course, I am cleaned up – they may just as well hose me off. I wouldn't care. I am beyond caring. What I am experiencing in pain, disorientation, the complete absence of control, exceeds being shot through the head on that fateful day on April 13, 1969, the event that brought me to experience a pneumoencephalogram. Ireturned to the darkened hospital room before noon on long-ago June day, back in 1969. I am later informed the procedure took three hours.

Once the ionized air dissipates, and I am able to fend for myself, Capt. Clark and his number two, whose name I shamefully don't recall, visit me in the hospital room. The bullet's impact had not shifted the brain mass within the cranium.

Malaria

During the Vietnam War, there were 24,606 cases of malaria, an estimated 391,965 sick days because of malaria, and 46 deaths due to malaria. With the worldwide resurgence of malaria, the spread of drug-resistant strains of Plasmodium falciparum, the emergence of chloroquine-resistant P. vivax, and the increasing resistance of Anopheles mosquitoes to insecticides, malaria continues to be an enormous threat to U.S. Navy and Marine Corps personnel deployed to the tropics and subtropics.

1969 in the rice paddies. Midday in the hot March sun with the stifling humidity of central South Vietnam. For the past four days contact with enemy irregulars, undoubtedly Viet Cong, certainly not mainline NVA - parlance for the North Vietnamese Army - regulars, is sporadic but constant. An enemy sniper round finds its mark: a booby-trap severs the lower half of a Marine's leg, that sort of thing. More insidious, the area we're operating in replete with malarial mosquitoes. Getting the men to take the anti-malaria pill, always on Sundays – unless heavy engaged, which happened more than once – is a chore. The ritual is facilitated by no-nonsense Sgt Al Bresser, the platoon sergeant, and the platoon Corpsman, "Doc" Joe Sonderman. The anti-malarial prophylactic pill is mefloquine. The under-strength infantry platoon is down to thirty-two men versus the authorized forty-nine. Any loss hurts. In the past day, two men have been medevac'd with malaria. Rumor has it the company is down seven Marines due to malaria.

I am tired and strained. But, of course, officers don't get malaria. I'm running a fever, and starting to crap a loose, yellowish stool. Doc Sonderman tells me I probably have malaria and need to be medevac'd. My duty is to execute mission and take care of the Marines under my charge. I refuse. That night I can hardly get up to crap. I'm burning up. Early the next morning I'm medevac'd on a CH-46 Marine Corps helicopter to "Alpha" Med, short for

A – "alpha" – Company, 1st Medical Battalion, 1st Marine Division, Da Nang, Vietnam.

Triage at Alpha Med, in an open-side canvas tent, is swift. The quick diagnosis is suspected malaria, though blood test confirmation doesn't come until later. I am barely mobile; field boots are cut away with large surgical scissors, the camouflage field uniform is similarly shed. Barely covered in a flimsy hospital smock, I am roughly placed on a canvas stretcher. The "ward" is an unairconditioned Quonset hut. Almost all the utilitarian, certainly not hospital-issue, beds are occupied. The wounded, sick, and dying fill the "ward." The dead are unceremoniously removed, body bags are optional. The smell of death tinges the interior. I am quickly sponged down, the tepid water soothing on my burning body. I hadn't washed in over seven days. I'm put through the paces of "admission," blood pressure cuffs, thermometers – oral, rectal, and arm pit -, more blood is drawn. IVs are inserted. Then, inexplicably, suddenly, body shaking chills and freezing cold grab hold. I beg and beg for blankets, many blankets, despite a very high fever. I enter the distorted, delusional world of delirium.

In the morning, I am exhausted but wide awake. The body clammy, flimsy hospital gown and sheets soaked, but I am alert. I feel good. Doctors' rounds start around 6:30 AM. Like the attending nurses, the Doctors are professional, business focused, perhaps a bit curt here and there, but unquestionably dedicated. Daily, they toil for their stricken patients, ministering to the gravely wounded, trying to save the dying, in a dark realm of human existence. The U. S. Navy doctor bedside – I think he's a Lieutenant Commander - dryly notes to the attending nurse that I have no fever. He orders some other tests and moves on. The IVs remain in place. Bed pans are removed. I can use the bathroom on my own. I shave. I'm served breakfast on a cold, mess-hall metal tray.

I am hungry. Whatever is, it sure beats the C-rations I've existed on for over three months. Calculatingly, my mind starts working. I closely observe the ward's routine, observe the character traits and personalities of the attending nurses and Corpsman. By noon time, when a welcome metal-trayed- lunch is served, I decide I can escape the ward undetected. As the trays are being noisily collected, on the pretext of going to the bathroom, I slip into a small, semi-isolated room at one end of the Quonset hut where there is an assortment of discarded field uniforms and combat boots. I rapidly change into ill-fitting; some partially blood-stained, clothing and boots, and slip out the backdoor. The curious reader might well ask about ID. The only ID we carry in the field is the standard issue U. S. military ID card. These are often lost, chewed up, or destroyed during operations. With enough savoir-faire and proper demeanor, a lost ID card is easily gotten around. The helipad of the USMC 1st Force Reconnaissance Company is within easy walking distance from Alpha Med. I am back with my unit by mid-afternoon. The tactical situation is unchanged.

I am to lead a platoon-size combat patrol the following morning. I am briefed by the Company Commander, Capt. Bill Fite, USMC, who heartly welcomes me back. The malaria returns with a vengeance during the night. Abdominal cramps jump about my midsection. I soiled myself trying to get to the company's shitter. I alternate between bone-shivering cold and depth burning fever rake my body until, once again, I am delirious. I am back at Alpha Med by 11:00 AM that morning. No mention of court martials for being UA.

I had been seriously ill before, not frequently; but malaria is a whole different trip. After a cursory one-off few minutes in the open side triage, I am back in the Quonset hut ward. Intravenous tubes are reinserted. I am extremely cold, shivering uncontrollably, begging for blankets. The pathetic, sweat-soaked hospital gown is unceremoniously removed. The IVs are disconnected. Three Navy corpsmen lift me out of bed. I am half dragged, stumbling, floundering, a short distance. I am physically forced into a large, tin basin full of iced water. Instantly the body goes spastic. A complete dysfunction of all motor, sensory – except extreme coldness – and cognitive functions. I am screaming, yelling, violently trying to extract myself from a living hell. Now four Navy corpsmen hold me fast, the head just above water level. I am relentless in trying to fight, excoriating everyone around in the foulest language. For how long, I do not know. When finally extracted, roughly dried off, my temperature is taken rectally, the Navy corpsmen

holding me as still as possible. The nurse – yes - a female nurse, tells the doctor, "It's down to 101." I later learn the pre-ice bath temperature had been above 105° F. For three days I vacillate between being unbearably cold and burning up with fever. During that period, I receive two more ice-bath treatments. The IVs are removed and reconnected. Temperature is continually noted.

By day four I seem to stabilize. I become cognizant of my surroundings. Bed pans are taken away. For the first time I am allowed, escorted, to use the bathroom. IVs remain in place. I am told to shave. Under supervision, I am allowed to shower, IVs hanging on a pole outside the open shower stall. I am also allowed to take necessary medication orally. Food, again, draws my attention. Initially I eat sparingly, fearing a recurrence of the cramps, and yellowish diarrhea. By day five, I am ravenousness for food. The sickness, the sickly smell of human bodies in distress, and occasional deaths distract me not at all.

Daily, the doctors and accompanying nurses make their early morning rounds. They are always exceptionally professional, a few questions here, some tenuous responses there. Then on to the next patient. One of the young Navy doctors is a tad more forthcoming, willing to linger a bit, than the other physicians. I learn a lot about malaria. The requisite once a week anti-malaria pills are not effective against the strain of malaria, Plasmodium falciparum, that lays me low. That U. S. forces' deaths from malaria in Vietnam were usually caused by opportunistic infections such as pneumonia or meningitis. That I will likely be susceptible to reoccurring bouts of malaria relapses for at least the next twenty years.

On either day seven or eight, all but one of the IVs is discontinued. The one remaining is to ensure hydration. I am to remain one more day in hospital to regain some strength. On the day I am discharged, some fellow from the Division's Medical Battalion shows up with a new set of utilities – Marine Corps field uniform -, and a new pair of jungle boots that fit me. Discharge is as unceremonious as admittance. I say good-bye to the present nurses and thank the Navy corpsmen. I am driven -don't have to walk this time - to the same helipad from whence I "escaped" less than ten days previously.

I am heartedly welcomed back by the Company Commander, Capt. Bill Fite, of "Hotel" Company, 2nd Battalion, 5th Marine Regiment. I gladly rejoin my platoon, which has lost only one of our Marines, badly wounded. I am glad to be back.

A month later I am shot through the head. Six weeks later, Bill Fite, the Company Commander is seriously wounded in both lungs. During these days of March-May 1969, in the rice paddies of Vietnam, three other Marines contact malaria. The unit loses ten other Marines to enemy action.

The Defense Casualty Analysis System (DCAS) Vietnam Conflict Extract File record counts by CASUALTY CATEGORY (as of April 29, 2018)

This table contains record counts based on the codes recorded in the "CASUALTY CATEGORY" field of the **Vietnam Conflict Extract Data File**. In the case of the "PRESUMED DEAD (BODY REMAINS RECOVERED)" and "PRESUMED DEAD (BODY REMAINS NOT RECOVERED)" categories of the table, the record counts are based on the codes in both the "CASUALTY CATEGORY" and "REMAINS RECOVERED" fields.

Casualty Category	Number of Records
ACCIDENT	9,107
DECLARED DEAD	1,201
DIED OF WOUNDS	5,299
HOMICIDE	236
ILLNESS	938
KILLED IN ACTION	40,934

PRESUMED DEAD (BODY REMAINS RECOVERED)	32
PRESUMED DEAD (BODY REMAINS NOT RECOVERED)	91
SELF-INFLICTED	382
Total Records	**58,220**

THE END